Mr. Moussa Soomekh
325 N Oakhurst Dr.
Apt 300
Beverly Hills, CA 90210

INCREASING
YOUR
SALES
POTENTIAL

INCREASING YOUR SALES POTENTIAL

A PRACTICAL GUIDE TO SUCCESSFUL SELLING

Leslie J. Ades

HARPER & ROW, PUBLISHERS, New York

Cambridge, Hagerstown, Philadelphia, San Francisco,
London, Mexico City, São Paulo, Sydney

1817

To my angel wife Dorothy (my alter ego)
who always had faith in me

Sponsoring Editor: Earl E. Shepherd
Project Editor: Nora Helfgott
Designer: Robert Sugar
Senior Production Manager: Kewal K. Sharma
Compositor: American Book–Stratford Press, Inc.
Printer and Binder: The Maple Press Company
Cartoons: Steven Duquette
Charts: Danmark & Michaels

Increasing Your Sales Potential: A Practical Guide to Successful Selling

Copyright © 1981 by Leslie J. Ades

Library of Congress Cataloging in Publication Data

Ades, Leslie J.
  Increasing your sales potential.

  Includes index.
  1. Selling. I. Title.
HF438.25.A23   658.8′5   81-688
ISBN 0-06-040169-9   AACR2

Contents

Preface

Most contemporary business firms do an excellent job of indoctrinating their salespeople with product knowledge and company policies and procedures. These same firms, however, sometimes neglect the crucial areas of sales training and interpersonal communication. Aspiring sales executives are often obliged to move through a series of increasingly complex job assignments—from taking orders by telephone to field solicitation in a highly competitive market—without adequate preparation in selling techniques. A typical salesperson's day consists of anxiety, rejection, and frustration. Success in sales is inversely related to the individual's personal "FUD" factor (Fear, Uncertainty, and Doubt). Because selling will always be a problem if it is not learned as a procedure, legions of salespeople are sent out into the field each year to fail.

Therefore, if you earn your living by selling a product, service, or idea and would like to sharpen your sales skills, this timely book is a must! It is specifically designed for individuals who are considering a sales career, as well as current practitioners, because it fills a glaring gap between ivory-tower theory and grass roots application of corporate marketing strategy. I believe that salespeople are not only more important than they think, but are the very foundation and driving force of our economy.

In reality, you—the professional salesperson—are on the cutting edge of your company's future. You, more than anyone else, will determine the survival of your firm and the direction of the national economy. Our economic fate is in your hands. That is the underlying theme of this work.

The main approach of this book is to humanize the selling process by stressing the interpersonal aspects of buyer-seller interaction. We shall explore the psychology of why people behave the way they do and ways to shape that behavior. Persuasion, overcoming objections, and closing techniques are all covered within the context of needs fulfillment and customer satisfaction. Technical data of your product line is put into proper perspective in relation to interpersonal selling. Most importantly, the purpose of this book is to help you achieve a greater understanding of and capability in professional selling. I hope the resources contained in the following pages will enable you to increase your own sales potential. Good luck and good selling!

ACKNOWLEDGMENTS

This book could not have been written without the guidance, criticism, and encouragement of a number of fine people. Although space limitations do not permit an extensive list, a few prominent individuals should be singled out for their impact on the content of this volume.

Without the teaching opportunity afforded by the kindness of William D. Ash, Ph.D., former Chairman of the Marketing Department of California State University, Long Beach, this book could never have been written. The advice of Ms. Marion Sapiro, Curriculum Coordinator of the U.C.L.A. Extension, and the pragmatic direction given by Michael H. Reilly, Jr., Assistant Director of the U.C.L.A. Extension programs in management, labor, and business, helped to shape the format and content of the text material.

Thanks and appreciation are also due to my wife Dorothy and son Jon who patiently endured the preparation of the manuscript in deference to the usual family life. Particular gratitude (and perhaps the Purple Heart medal!) is acknowledged to Dorothy Ades for putting up with the project and its demanding author and for typing, proofreading, and editing the complete manuscript several times. I hope the reader's interest and approval will justify our joint efforts.

Leslie J. Ades

Part I
YOU, THE SELLER

Chapter 1
The New Breed

One last challenging frontier remains for the free spirit in our more and more regimented and computerized society—a career in sales. Like the hardy souls who forged our American frontier, the salesperson must be great just to survive. The challenge, though, of meeting new people, exchanging ideas, and getting orders makes selling a lifelong adventure. Although your performance is always on trial, and you are only as good as your last order, the financial rewards of a top salesperson can be enormous. For both tangible and intangible gains, the sky is the limit in sales.

SELLING: WHAT AND WHEN

What is selling? Many definitions have been suggested, most often by persons who have done little, if any, professional selling themselves. Charles Roth, an insurance consultant, is on the right track, though, when he says that selling is "getting prospects to act in the manner in which we want them to act." Let's expand his idea and say that *selling is persuading others to think as we think and feel as we feel so that they will act as we want them to act.*

No matter what we do, we sell. We exchange goods and services for other goods and services, and for money. The same fundamental psychology and methods are used whether the sales occur in industrial, wholesale, retail, door-to-door, or high technology areas.

We sell constantly outside of our jobs, too. To get a job or a mate, we sell ourselves. To campaign for political office, to convert others to our religion, or to secure funds for research or a good cause, we sell our ideas. As we rear and teach our children, we are selling traditions and social norms of behavior. Even in making the simplest agreements with others—whether to have fish or chicken for dinner, for instance—we are selling.

If you don't think we sell all the time, go to any cocktail lounge after 4:30 P.M. on a Friday. You will definitely find some men and women there trying to persuade other men and women to think as they think and feel as they feel so that the desired action may result!

THE BURDEN IS ON YOU

When you are the seller, you assume the driver's seat. You hold the initiative and the power; you control situations and exert influence on your clients. Obviously, this power carries with it a correlative responsibility. The burden of coping behavior is on you; you must adjust, without resentment or emotional involvement, to your client's apparent weaknesses or biases.

Customers may think slowly. Sometimes they seem not to think at all. They may communicate badly. They may have emotional problems or moral failings. As a professional, though, you hold the reins in the seller/buyer relationship. Your job as a salesperson is to cope with and overcome these interpersonal problems.

Elementary as it may sound, to sell successfully you have to know that your company has what your prospects want. You must understand their problems sufficiently to know how your firm's product or service can help solve those problems. Then you must learn how to distinguish the quick, intuitive decision makers from the crowd of prospects who require extremely detailed information. Many will waste your time, and some will buy from you, but the burden is always on you to know the difference. Selling is not easy; it requires a lot of hard work and persistence.

As you develop selling skills, you'll also develop the ability to analyze the needs and behavior of each person you aim to persuade. With practice you'll be able to read people as you do books.

Although men and women think about themselves almost constantly, they often are not consciously aware of their own needs. In the pages that follow, we will be looking at the inner desires, yearnings, and conflicts that motivate most people, both in their personal and in their professional lives. We shall analyze the irrational and confusing behavior of some prospects. We will work to see what fears and emotions lie behind the wall that many people erect to hide their real feelings. In time you'll learn to understand these feelings, to relate to them, and in so doing, to help your clients understand you, too.

Establishing this clear line of communication between you and your clients is your responsibility. And as you will see, this communication isn't just describing the features of your product or service. It means getting your customers to tell you what you need to hear in order to solve their problems. What do your customers need? When? What really motivates *this* buyer? When will this individual be ready to buy your product or service?

Establish a rapport with your clients and soon they will *show* you how to understand and communicate with them.

Two additional responsibilities, however, may be more difficult to accept. First, you must always do what is in the buyer's best interest, and second, you must stick to your own ethical standards. It may seem obvious that you should not sell buyers more than they need or samples of goods that they won't be able to reorder. You will know that you should keep in touch and follow through on promises, and that you shouldn't give in when clients make unethical demands.

For example, there will be times when you might have a pregnant spouse and a second mortgage, you have not written an order in months, and your boss wants you to unload a discontinued item on your best customer. Then you will comprehend the role conflicts and temptations of a typical salesperson. That is why you will have to be great just in order to survive! Selling is a career filled with opportunity and reward, but it is not an easy one. It may not be your cup of tea.

THE MAKING OF THE SALES PROFESSIONAL

If every human transaction is a selling transaction, then we are all selling all the time. Some of us are more successful at this than others. Are those successful ones just accidents of nature? Is the skilled and courageous sales professional about whom we have been talking born or made?

In a sense we are all born to succeed at selling. After all, we humans evolved as social animals. In order to interact successfully in this complicated society, we must initiate actions and then get the cooperation of our peers to help carry these actions to conclusion. Some people do seem to be "naturals" at selling, knowing from childhood the best ways to persuade others. Many more of the so-called born salespeople, though, learned their success by carefully cultivating these innate traits, and by acquiring and practicing certain other desirable skills.

Your success in selling will depend only on your ambition, willingness, and ability to learn—plus a healthy portion of persistence. You won't be held back by some arbitrary seniority scale. An exciting adventure lies before you, and through this book you will learn how to sell not just products and services, but yourself and your ideas. Your personal relationships and financial situation may well become stronger as you learn and practice these precepts.

In fact, if you sincerely desire to do so, you can become an entirely different person from the one who turns these first pages with curiosity. You'll be more likable, will command deeper respect from friends and co-workers, and most important of all—you'll learn to like yourself better.

Chapter 2
Setting and Achieving Goals

You possess within you the ability and the power to do whatever is necessary to guarantee success in life and selling. This power can be the catalyst to create a future you never dreamed possible. Yet, most people never exercise enough of their abilities to realize this potential.

How can you unlock this potential, unleash your own powers, and learn to succeed?

GOALS AND PRIORITIES

As the distinguished essayist E. B. White said, Columbus didn't just sail, he sailed west, and the world took shape from this simple design. If you want to create a new world of success for yourself, you must choose a definite direction or goal, otherwise your chances of success are small. Luckily, you do not have to rely merely on inspiration to do this. There is a simple method for setting goals, and your brain is already equipped to do so.

Self-Image and Psychocybernetics

Salespeople occupy a lonely territory. Their typical day consists of anxiety, frustration, and rejection. They may close one sale out of ten customer contacts. If so, they are rejected 10 times as often as they are accepted. After a dry spell of 40 or 50 calls without an order, they start to feel that clients are rejecting not the proposal, but themselves. It is easy to see how a salesperson's daily frustration can lead to a poor self-image.

Self-image is your mental and spiritual concept or picture of yourself. Your self-image sets the boundaries of your accomplishment in life and in selling. It defines what you can and cannot do. Most of us underrate ourselves; the picture we paint is too limited. We have mentioned the need to set goals. Actually, most of us already have goals toward which we are subconsciously drifting.

The human brain and nervous system operates purposefully according to the principles of cybernetics to accomplish our goals. (The word *cybernetics* comes from a Greek word meaning *steersman.*) The brain and nervous system are marvelous and complex goal-striving mechanisms that steer you toward success or failure, depending upon how you, the operator, set them up and what goals you establish. If your self-image is low or, worse, negative, you are setting "goals" of self-limitation or even failure. Then, the steersman in your head will automatically make your achievements small or nonexistent.

Dr. Maxwell Maltz[1] believed that self-image is the real key to personality and behavior. Thus, if you can change your self-image and set higher goals, you can break the limiting shell around your personality, behavior, and achievement. Your self-image is not changed by intellect alone, however, but by the experience of success. Here nature gives us a break, because experience, for this purpose, can be synthesized in the mind. In forming your self-image, your brain does not differentiate between a real experience and one that you have vividly imagined.

Visualize Success

You must escape from the hypnotic power of beliefs like "I can't," "I'm not worthy," and "I'm only a peddler." You will become a more effective person by dropping these self-limiting ideas, which contribute to a negative self-image. To replace old, negative goals with new, positive ones, all you have to produce is a simple visualization exercise. Place yourself in a relaxed environment without distractions, close your eyes, and form a picture of the person you would like to be and the things you would like to have in life. These goals should be realistic and clear-cut—things that could happen in the real world—and they should be things that *you* want, not things you think you should want or things that someone else wants for you. They must be described in enough detail so that you can see the end results clearly in your mind's eye. Arouse a deep desire for these things. Become enthusiastic about them. Dwell on them; keep going over them in your mind. Write them down, draw pictures of them, and constantly reinforce for yourself this image of what it will be like when your goals are achieved. Imagine it so clearly and vividly that you can feel the excitement of being there. You are experiencing your success in advance.

As you pursue this exercise, you actually are changing your self-image to that of a person who already has the new attributes or possessions you visualize. Now your mental steersman is free to commit your resources to achieving your new goals.

Power of the Right Brain

Recent studies indicate that the left hemisphere of the brain concerns itself with rational thought, the intellect, sequences, objectivity, realism, analysis, differentiation, deduction, and direction. The right hemisphere of the brain controls intuitive thought, multiples, subjectivity, impulses, holism (understanding and thinking of things as a whole rather than separate parts), integration, free thought, and imagination. Left hemisphere-dominant persons are much more aggressive, both verbally and physically. These "black-and-white" thinkers are logical and structured, and they focus sharply on what they are doing. They are task-oriented. Right hemisphere-dominant people tend to have a more diffused focus, are more artistic, and rely a great deal on gut feelings and intuition. They are more relationship-oriented.

This dichotomy in the brain permits us to work on problems quite unconsciously once they have been stated clearly. An easy way to gain access to these problem-solving activities is to state the problem—it can be any kind of problem—and then try to *visualize*, rather than verbalize, a solution. With complex problems, the "answer" may not appear for some time or may take several sessions to achieve, or it may never appear in the mind's eye, but simply pop up in one's behavior.

We have been using this technique to change our self-image as we vividly imagined a "solution" to the "problem" of "What should my self-image be?" You can apply it to other practical problems in your life as well, whether they sense immense (how to improve relations with a difficult boss or customer) or trivial (what is the most efficient route for your next sales trip). Successful salespersons can be both high achievers in terms of quotas (left-hemisphere-dominants) and most creative in their approach to unstructured situations and individual customer personalities (right-hemisphere-dominants). Thus to reach your maximum potential, you should strive to integrate the best elements of both mental hemispheres.

Some people have found it helpful to use this system of stating a problem and then visualizing a successful outcome while they do their regular jogging or walking, since repetitive physical exercise occupies the efforts of the left brain during this time and helps to prevent it from "interrupting" or overriding the right brain's work. Try this technique next time a problem or situation defies your analytical abilities. You may be surprised at the results—just don't expect them to be logical.

Will I Still Be Me?

Changing your self-image does not mean changing yourself, or improving yourself, but changing your own mental picture, estimation, and realization of that self. Most of us are better, wiser, stronger, and more competent right now than we realize. Creating a better self-image does not create new abilities; it releases them to be used. In our behavior, we are what we think, and to be a success, you must first see yourself as a success.

Working Toward Goals: Practical Matters

Let's go back to the mental picture you formed of the things, situations, and relationships you would like to have. After you've set your mental steersman in the right direction, there are still some practical, analytical, and verbal exercises you can do to help it along. The importance of planning and discipline in achieving goals of any kind is tremendous, and here is a method to use in making your plans.

First, write down a list of all those things, situations, and so on that you want. Next, put them in order from the most important down to the least. You are establishing priorities here, and because you must make decisions, and people always hesitate to make decisions, you may find this process rough going. Establishing your priorities may take several sessions, but persistence will pay off.

Your next step is to list these goals down the left side of a page. Now, in the next column, note what obstacles stand in the way of your reaching your goal. Some of these obstacles will be large, and you may quail at the thought of attacking them. The way to handle an obstacle is to break it into manageable pieces and deal with the pieces sequentially. Thus, in your third column you should list the first manageable piece of each large obstacle. Finally, in a fourth column, enter solutions to each third-column piece. Now you have a list of steps you can take immediately to start on your way to your goals (Figure 2.1). You should redo this exercise

Goals or Objectives	Obstacles	Subproblems	Solutions or Action Plan	Target Date	Risk	High Moderate Low
A goal that you are excited about achieving motivates you to positive action.	Problems to solve or obstacles to be overcome in order to reach your goal.	The most manageable pieces of each large obstacle.	The ways of overcoming each obstacle or subproblem.	When should each solution or action plan be finished?	If all of your solutions are too easy and the steps are low risk, you may have set your goals too low and they might not challenge or motivate you enough.	

Key Question: If this goal or objective is so important to me, why haven't I already achieved or attained it?
Then ask yourself: What has been standing in my way? What skills do I lack? What or whose help must I have? What must I do next and by when?

Figure 2.1   Goal-setting exercise.

Figure 2.2   Ben Feldman—a legend among insurance representatives. In 1975 he sold $83 million worth of life insurance. His annual earnings exceed $1 million. "I want to be the *best!*" is his motto. What is yours?

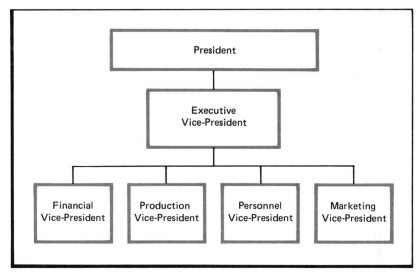

Figure 2.3   The organization chart of a typical company. Marketing is one of several functional areas that report on an equal basis either to the executive vice-president or directly to the company president.

every year to see where you are and set new tasks. Almost any problem can be analyzed in this way. Next time you are faced with one, remember: success by the yard is hard, but by the inch, it's a cinch.

REWARDS OF A SALES CAREER

Now that you have both sides of your brain in gear and working for you, what can you expect to achieve in the real world of selling? The talented and persistent professional can make a lot of money (Figure 2.2). Jobs in selling range from those in which you stand behind a counter and wrap what the customer chooses (which involves no real selling and pays very little) to those in which you take on the full burden of seeking out the customer, determining and filling his needs for him, and maintaining his satisfaction afterward. For the latter efforts, if you are conscientious and skilled, you will be paid very well. In both cases, your check is eventually paid by the customer, and he pays only for what he gets. Never forget that.

As a successful and disciplined salesperson, you can climb up the organization if you want to. Most companies have similar structures. A typical organization is seen in Figure 2.3. As a salesperson, you will be part of the marketing function, which is further diagramed in Figure 2.4. Many people are unclear about the relationship of marketing and sales, so we should define our terms.

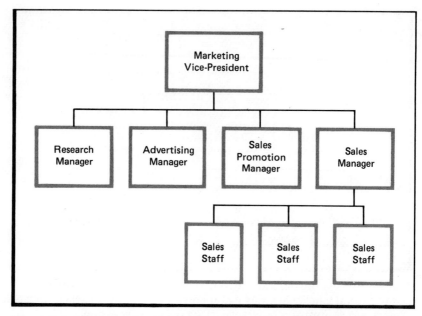

Figure 2.4   Organization chart of the marketing department.

A *market* is people with needs to satisfy, the money to spend, and the willingness to spend it.[2] A market is the people to whom we, as salespeople, want to talk. Marketing is the whole system of finding, reaching, and satisfying those people. More exactly, marketing is a total system of interacting business activities designed to plan, price, promote, and distribute want-satisfying products and services to present and potential customers.[3]

In Figure 2.4, you can see that the salespeople report to the sales manager, who in turn reports to the marketing director or vice-president. Each of the other managers within the marketing department has the same line authority as the sales manager. In other words, sales does not run the marketing department any more than advertising or sales promotion. They all work together with the research manager to achieve the overall goals of the marketing department, and all their plans must be integrated. The overall strategy or plan is developed by the marketing director or vice-president. Thus the sales tail does not wag the marketing dog, another fact to bear in mind. Marketing functions to make what people *want*, while sales tries to make people want what the firm has already made. Selling is to marketing as a component part is to a subassembly, while marketing is to a company what a subassembly is to a finished product. A business enterprise is to society as a star is to the entire universe. All are important elements in the business hemisphere and function to enhance overall welfare.

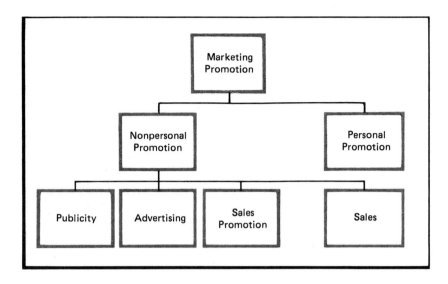

Figure 2.5   Marketing and promotional components.

A more realistic way to look at marketing is shown in Figure 2.5. Here marketing is viewed as a total sales promotional entity that can be divided into *personal* and *nonpersonal promotion.* Advertising and sales promotion are nonpersonal. Except in the case of mail order advertising, there are few opportunities to obtain customer orders here. These activities may soften up a market, making customers aware or even desirous of a company's products, but only the salesperson can complete the actual transaction (see Figure 2.6). He does so on a personal basis, so his part is that of personal promotion. The salesperson alone causes it all to happen: goods or services and title go to the customer, and cash flow to the company treasury. You are at the forefront of your company: without you, everything would grind to a halt. That is why we can define the salesperson as a *problem-solving, need-satisfying professional who links their company to the marketplace.*

Once you have established yourself as a successful salesperson, you can advance to the position of sales manager. The sales manager's job is quite different from yours: he meets sales quotas by hiring and training salespeople, assigning and supervising their work, and coordinating his activities with the other managers in the marketing department. To do his job, you will need to practice enforcing discipline on yourself, because discipline and organization are essential to his work. In some cases, he makes less money than you do; but if he does a good job, he has the opportunity to advance up the company ladder. Many salespeople would rather remain in sales, which they find more lucrative, varied, and challenging, than become sales managers.

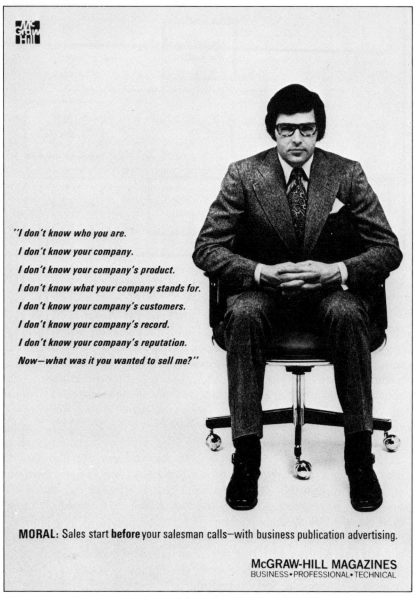

Figure 2.6   How advertising helps the selling function. (Reproduced with permission from McGraw-Hill Publications Co.)

There are rewards other than money and corporate advancement in a sales career. The more responsible a sales position you take on, the more you can be your own boss. Leave the clock punching and office routines to others. You can set your own schedule (as long as it is productive), travel and meet new people, and face constant new challenges. If you become a seasoned and disciplined sales professional, the step to entrepreneurship is very short, if you decide to take it. Many of the skills and attitudes required to succeed in your own business are the very ones you will develop over the years of your sales experience.

Notes

1. Maxwell Maltz, Psycho-cybernetics (Englewood Cliffs, New Jersey: Prentice-Hall, 1960), pp. vii and ix.
2. William J. Stanton, *Fundamentals of Marketing,* 6th ed. (New York: McGraw-Hill, 1981), p. 65.
3. Ibid., p. 4.

Chapter 3
Do You Have What It Takes?

The professional salesperson, as we have said, is more often made than born. Clothes do not make the person, however, and neither does a headful of new closing techniques make a sales professional. All the "clothing" of skills and product knowledge that your sales trainer can hang on you are worth nothing if they are not supported by a strong skeleton of personality traits.

Suppose for a moment that you and I have just formed our own company and are ready to hire salespeople. Most of our customers never will visit our home office; they will form their ideas of our company from our salespeople alone. Our salespeople must maintain and enhance our company's good name and image, so we are going to look carefully at each candidate to find the traits we want. Remember, that to *your* customers, you are the company. Therefore, what you *are* is more important than your words.

THE BASICS

The first traits we look for are simple but indispensable. Our salespeople must be *honest.* If they are not, they will hurt us, our customers, and in the end, themselves. They must be *presentable.* (Physical appearance, dress, and manner are discussed in Chapter 13.) Our salespeople must be *reliable.* We won't have time to be constantly checking up on them. We also look for people with *initiative.*

The traits we have described form the personal basis for a quality that the sales professional must have. They comprise *source credibility,* which is the ability to inspire faith, trust, and confidence in the prospective customer. If you do not possess this source credibility—are not honest, presentable in appearance, and reliable, and have no initiative—you are going to have trouble with the business of life. You will need help from other sources than this book.

THE SECOND TIER OF TRAITS

If our candidates have these traits—honesty, presentable appearance, reliability, and initiative—they can be taught to represent our product or service competently. However, we are looking for people who are going to be not merely competent, but great. What further traits should they have?

Our ideal candidates have a constellation of traits. Some of them are easy to see in an interview, while others will appear only as they start selling.

Intelligence

The ability to *learn* is of paramount importance. If people cannot learn well, they cannot be trained to give a respectable sales presentation. There is nothing more depressing than a salesperson who does not know the product, has only a vague idea of pricing, and is uninformed about competitive market conditions. Neither the industrial buyer nor the consumer will tolerate this. The creative salesperson must also have the ability to learn how to adapt to the many different personalities and situations that selling will present.

Positive Mental Attitude

An attitude, put simply, is a mental and emotional position. A *positive mental attitude*[1] is one of enthusiasm and optimism. A person who believes in his job, is convinced of the greatness of his company and products, and enjoys his work will be able to build up a good clientele. Sometimes limitations of education, poverty, and intelligence can be overcome through this perseverance and enthusiasm.

A positive mental attitude (PMA) has the power to attract wealth, success, happiness, and health; but a negative mental attitude (NMA) repels these things and prevents you from obtaining all that makes life worth living.[2] PMA lets you climb to the top; NMA keeps you at the bottom. Great thinkers and popular sages alike have always recognized this truth: you have heard that a glass containing water to its midline will be seen by the pessimist (NMA) as half-empty, while the optimist (PMA) sees it as half-full. Emerson wrote that to different minds, the same world is a hell, or a heaven. An *optimist* thinks that this is the best of all possible worlds. The *pessimist* is afraid that it is true. What is your viewpoint?

If our applicants are down on selling, on our company, or on our customers, they will never make it. No matter how many selling techniques we teach them or how well they know their product's features, their negative attitudes will ooze out between the lines of their presentation and alienate customers. They will have no source credibility. They could not even sell gold at half-price.

The people we are looking for are so optimistic that if we ask them to project sales figures for the year, each one probably will take his or her best day ever, double it, and then multiply it by 365! Their enthusiasm is infectious. As Frank Bettger put it. "If you want to see people, they want to see you."[3]

How does one develop or encourage this positive quality? First, you should represent a company, product, or service that you do believe in. It helps to be well prepared: know all about your product, know the techniques of selling, know the marketplace. Most important, continue to use all your mental resources: visualize yourself as a success. Visualize successful outcomes to your sales calls, and your inner steersman will guide you toward them. Bettger suggests behaving in an enthusiastic manner even if you do not feel enthusiastic. Strangely enough, our minds are built so that the feedback from these enthusiastic actions causes us to feel enthusiastic as well.

The power of a positive attitude cannot be overemphasized. Our future salesperson must have it, because success in selling often seems to be 5 percent ability and 95 percent attitude.

Trainability

Trainability is not exactly the same as intelligence. Trainability is not just the ability to learn, it is the willingness to learn. If our future salespeople are the kind who resist new ideas, we had better pass over them in favor of others. They also should respond well to constructive criticism, taking criticism as an opportunity to find out how they can improve themselves. They should be flexible rather than rigid. They should be achievers who thrive on new data and welcome a new challenge. Not all intelligent people have these qualities. The ones we are looking for combine intelligence with drive and inquisitiveness.

Personal Motivation

We probably won't be able to tell if our candidates are personally motivated until after we have trained them and sent these rookies out into the field. Will they succeed? Only if they have this elusive quality, this inner urge that incites them to action. An idea, emotion, desire, or impulse, it is the force that starts an action to obtain personal objectives.

Motivation encompasses the commitment a salesperson must have to the work. We have all at some time run across that supercilious shoe salesclerk who is obviously "too good" for the job, doing this lowly work until something more worthy comes along. With this attitude, our clerk friend will wait forever. In addition, he never will be good at his present job because he has failed to make a commitment to it. Were we to revisit him after 10 years (unlikely, in view of his treatment of us), he still would be haughtily selling the same shoes and hating every minute of it. Still "temporary" and looking to move on, he never will know why he is a loser. A negative mental attitude coupled with this lack of commitment can rob us of our power to succeed and fulfill our great potential.

To examine your own personal motivation, ask yourself several questions. Do you *want* to sell? What do you want out of selling? What is your personal payoff: ego, status, pride, or money? Do you have a personal need for expression through role playing? A need to excel and succeed? Do you want to achieve adventure, freedom, or independence? Most successful salespeople have these driving desires. Motivated from within, they are self-starters. Highly motivated people have a disciplined goal orientation toward life. They have programmed themselves for success in their careers.

Maturity and Self-Discipline

A mature person has completed natural growth and development and has made good personal adjustment to people and circumstances. Oriented to tasks and objectives and not to self, such a person usually has clear goals and efficient work habits.

Salespeople show maturity in their ability to control personal feelings. Not all tasks and customers are pleasant, and the burden to make the encounters successful in these cases falls on the salesperson. Mature salespeople tolerate these stresses well: they are said to show a high threshold of tension binding. Remember that just because an unruly customer casts doubt upon the legitimacy of your birth, you do not have to act as if he is correct.

Objectivity is another characteristic of mature salespeople. They obtain the facts, evaluate alternatives on their merits, and tend to disassociate themselves from personal feelings or biases that might prejudice them in their decisions.

Finally, they are intelligent planners who carry through their plans. Their planning and organizational abilities are administrative qualities that put them in line for sales management positions.

Leadership

Related to motivation is the desire or willingness to take control of situations or of other people and to assume power. We shall see as we go on that the assumption of control starts at the beginning of the selling process and must not be relinquished even after the sale is complete. In a sense, the salesperson must be like the champion racehorse who, without knowing exactly why, has a strong desire to be out in front.

Personal Magnetism

Easy to recognize but hard to analyze or even to describe, personal magnetism is a trait that strongly attracts others to those who have it. Various attempts have been made to explain this quality that is present in the most effective salespeople. Robert McMurry[4] calls this person a "habitual wooer" who needs to win and hold the affection of others, and he adds that this quality cannot be taught. Either you have it before you start training, or you do not and cannot have it.

Napoleon Hill goes even further, maintaining that the factor of personality commonly called magnetism or charisma is nothing more than an expression of sexual energy. He details his theories, based on hundreds of interviews with successful men and women, explaining how people channel libido to help them accomplish objectives.[5]

> The experience of Gene, a young encyclopedia representative selling door to door, illustrates the points made by McMurry and Hill. Gene recently was married to a young lady whom he met when he called on her to sell her encyclopedias. He did not succeed in closing on the first call; and when he started to set up a call-back appointment by asking whether he should return on Tuesday or on Wednesday, she replied, "Forget the books—just come back!"

The *You* Factor

As we choose our fictitious salespeople, there is one more requirement that both we and they must keep in mind. Learning to be a good salesperson is much the same as learning to be a good human being. It is forgetting oneself and being considerate of other people. Successful salespeople are fine, sensitive human beings who think of other people's needs. They respect customers' attitudes and feelings, yet are convinced that their products and services are things their customers should have.

This dropping of the "I" and striving to think in terms of the other person's situation we shall call the "You" factor. This vital perspective enables you to develop long-term mutually beneficial relationships.

Notes

1. Napoleon Hill and W. Clement Stone, *Success Through a Positive Mental Attitude* (Englewood Cliffs, N.J.: Prentice-Hall, 1960), pp. 3–14.
2. Ibid., p. 14.
3. Frank Bettger, *How I Raised Myself from Failure to Success in Selling* (Englewood Cliffs, N.J.: Prentice-Hall, 1972).
4. Robert N. McMurry, "The Mystique of Super-Salesmanship," *Harvard Business Review*, March–April 1961, pp. 117–118.
5. Napoleon Hill, *Think and Grow Rich* (New York: Hawthorn Books, 1967), pp. 200–225.

Chapter 4
Your Abilities: How To Cope

Throughout our fictional interviews with prospective salespeople, you undoubtedly have cast yourself in the role of candidate and examined yourself for the necessary traits. Once through this ordeal and having accepted yourself as a trainee, you now must turn your attention to the practical side and look at your abilities.

Abilities differ from traits in that traits are inborn or learned very early and are hard to change. Abilities, however, can be developed. It is no longer a question of what you are, but of what you can do. The abilities we are about to discuss mainly concern communication, and you can acquire them through practice.

EMPATHY AND SYMPATHY

In selling, as in every other human transaction, the ability to empathize with your prospect is a basic necessity. *Empathy* is placing yourself in other people's positions, walking in their shoes. It is seeing what they see, hearing what they hear, and thinking what they think. To do so, you must try to forget your own background, prejudices, and attitudes, and attempt to assume the other position.

This can be quite a trick and takes considerable practice, but once you have been in other people's positions, you will understand how they want you to behave, what they want to hear, and what will appeal to them. Empathy is the essense of source credibility.

Empathy is not the same as sympathy. When you feel sympathy you feel sorry for a person, as a mother feels sorry for her hurt or frightened child. You do not necessarily feel *as* that person feels. To illustrate, when your neighbor becomes unemployed, it's a *recession.* But when you lose your job, it's a *depression!*

Feeling empathy with the buyer will help you to sell to that person, but there is another, more sophisticated use of empathy. During the psychological process leading up to the sale, you want to make the buyer empathize with *you.* After all, you feel that this product or service is top quality, you know your company offers the best deal around, and you own and use the product yourself. If you can get the buyer to *think as you think and feel as you feel,* won't he then tend to *act as you want him to act?* What else is this on his part but strong empathy? That is what the selling process tries to develop.

THE FINE ART OF LISTENING

The Bible tells us that Samson once slew 10,000 Philistines with the jawbone of an ass. Since that bygone day, many salespeople have killed far more sales with their own jawbones. They didn't know when to stop talking. You can never learn anything while you are talking. You need to *listen* to pick up buying clues. Avoid the Samson syndrome and learn to listen.

Listening is the other half of talking, the art of interpreting both the literal meaning and the intention of the speaker. If a friend calls you a character, the word may be insulting, but the tone probably is affectionate, and you take it as an expression of friendship.

Most of us are not very good listeners; we tend to talk much more than we listen. Many of us, while ostensibly listening, are inwardly preparing our own responses. When the other speaker takes a breath, we interrupt to continue our own line of chatter. This is called *stepping on sentences,* and it tends to destroy our source credibility.

Detouring occurs when the speaker uses a word or phrase that starts a chain of associations, causing us to lose track of what is being said. Finally, our own private planning for later, unrelated situations often intervenes.

Faking attention is another poor listener habit. Faked attention is a by-product of lack of interest. A common faker is the nodder, one who nods continuously as the customer talks, regardless of the point being made.

Interrupting your prospect's sentences is immature behavior that doesn't let him finish his thought and deprives you of information. When you interrupt, all you are really doing (besides infuriating him) is talking things over with yourself.

Let the customer talk. Sometimes he even will talk himself right into your proposal.

> The owner of a women's boutique once asked her top saleslady how she made such a high percentage of sales. "It's easy," she replied. "I just shut up. As long as they're talking themselves *toward* buying, I don't say a thing. Now, if they start talking themselves *away* from buying, that's when *I* talk."

Tactful *interjection* is different from interruption. It is an occasional comment that shows your prospect that you are following his train of thought. Keep these remarks short and appropriate. You can bet that our top saleslady wasn't completely silent as her customers sold dresses to themselves—she probably had an arsenal of small positive comments that she wasn't even aware of.

Here are some suggestions for improving your listening ability:

Interest

Discipline yourself to concentrate fully on your customers and what they have to say. This takes practice and perseverance, because we sometimes daydream or mentally debate the speaker and lose the train of thought.

Eye Contact

The best way to sustain your own attention is by keeping eye contact with the customer. Research has shown that in a conversation, the person who is speaking tends to let his or her eyes move away from the listener and back again repeatedly, but the listener's eyes remain on those of the speaker. To break this steady regard is a nonverbal signal to the speaker that you are not interested and have stopped paying attention. It is an insult and damages your source credibility.

Don't be afraid to look the customer squarely in the eye. If you find doing so very difficult at first, or if you are with a belligerent customer, concentrate on the spot where his eyebrows meet above his nose. It will appear to him that you actually are gazing into his eyes. If this trick does not work and you still are intimidated, try looking at the person's mouth as he talks. This is a form of lip reading, and it helps you to understand him.

Note Taking

Take notes as the customer talks. To translate what he is saying into notes, you are forced to pass the material through your brain, which helps you to maintain attention. Note taking also enhances the speaker's own sense of importance. Therefore, he will tend to like you better. That is why some teachers insist on note taking in class.

Peculiarities

If the customer has distracting mannerisms or physical peculiarities, do not allow yourself to become so preoccupied with them that you eventually lose the gist of the conversation. You already know that it is rude to stare at a blemish or deformity, don't let your mind stare at it while your eyes are carefully focused elsewhere.

Speed

Salespeople learn to think on their feet and adapt quickly to situations as they occur, and they often become more articulate than their customers. You may become impatient or distracted because you already have received the message your prospect is sending long before he finishes talking. Slow down and relax. Remember that a slow pace is less threatening, and appearing to think over what your prospect is saying is flattering to him and can only increase your source credibility.

The Big Picture

While you are listening to every word, do not forget to synthesize those words into the general idea that the customer wants to get across. Listen for ideas and concepts—some of which the customer may not be very clear about himself.

Anatomical Hint

The necessity of avoiding the Samson syndrome cannot be too strongly emphasized. Remember that you have one mouth and two ears. You are meant to do twice as much listening as talking.

PSYCHOLOGICAL CONCEPTS RELATED TO COMMUNICATION

Communication is the passing of information and understanding from one person to another.[1] The English word is derived from the Latin *communis,* which means *common.* Thus communication attempts to share a "commonness" with someone, it is a sharing of meaning. In his *Rhetoric*, Aristotle noted that communication was composed of three elements: the speaker, the speech, and the audience. He added that the purpose of communication is to persuade, and that we must adjust our thoughts to the audience.

Communication is vital to selling, and not all communication is verbal. Less than 10 percent of meaning comes from words, 40 percent comes from the way you say the words (conviction, vocal implication), and 50 percent comes from body language. In fact, there are six types of language systems: verbal, nonverbal (sign), action, object,[2] space, and time languages.

Verbal Language

Verbal language is composed of words written or spoken according to logic based on a set of rules accepted by both the speaker and the audience. Obviously, English and Chinese are based on different rules, and you would not try to speak English to a Chinese; but consider the subtle differences in the rules accepted in different parts of your own country. What is quite clear in New England may be misleading in the South; and words like "cool" or "bad" may have opposite meanings to people from the same city. Be sure you understand your customer's rules. It is not always safe to assume that he understands yours.

Your enunciation, voice tone, volume, and inflection also vary the meaning and emphasis of your spoken words. By raising your pitch at the end of a sentence, instead of letting it fade, you can change a statement of fact to a question. You can convey meaning by speaking loudly or softly. You can alienate your listener by choosing too complex a vocabulary level.

You also can frighten a prospect off by speaking too quickly. Nervousness, coupled with the fact that you already know your material far better than the prospect does, can cause you to speed up. You must slow down and allow his thought processes time to catch up. *You can never speak too slowly.* The prospect must never feel that he is being subjected to a verbal barrage and cannot get a word in himself. A slow pace, on the other hand, conveys your confidence to the listener; you appear neither belligerent nor defensive. If you are enthusiastic about your product or proposal and speak with authority and conviction and vary your tone and tempo, you need not fear interruptions. The human voice can be a beautiful and persuasive instrument, learn to use it well.

Nonverbal (Sign) Language

Nonverbal language varies from the gesture of the hitchhiker to complete systems for the deaf. People communicate nonverbally all the time, and these signals are ancient, going back to our prehistoric forebears and predating verbal language. Many people are not aware of what their own bodies are communicating, but you can still "read" their unconscious signals. Several interesting studies have been done of this form of communication.[3]

FACIAL EXPRESSIONS
Sometimes you can read the response of a silent prospect in his expression: tense and impatient; or pleasant, smiling, and relaxed. Some expressions can be misleading. For example, some people scowl when emotionally touched, so as not to show their "weakness."

BODY POSTURE
Tense or relaxed, menacing or inviting—body language is an area of nonverbal communication that recently has been studied and publicized heavily. Certain postures on the part of your prospects indicate certain feelings and attitudes. It is worth your time to look into these findings.[4] You might recognize some of your own behavior as well as that of some of your customers.

GESTURES
It is easy to think of examples of gesture language, not all of them printable. If you travel abroad to sell or sell often to foreigners, be careful about using any gestures, they do not mean the same things in every country.

OTHER FORMS
Silences can be ominous, pregnant, or pensive. As we shall see when we discuss closing techniques, silence can be powerful. Touch can be helpful or damaging. It ranges from welcoming (a warm handshake) to condescending (as when a man places his arm around a woman peer's shoulders), and, of course, it can threaten as well. We have mentioned eye movements of speakers and listeners; we are also familiar with the signals of rolling the eyes or of downcast eyes.

Action Language

What people do is often more important than what they say. Action language includes all movements that are not used exclusively as signals. They make statements to those who see them. During a sales call, if your prospect is busy answering the telephone, dictating, or signing letters, he obviously is communicating something to you. Sometimes actions do speak louder than words.

Object Language

Object language includes all intentional and unintentional display of material things, as the human body and how it is dressed. Art objects, awards, trophies, mementos, collections of objects or books, and even plants are talking to you. In addition to observing your customers, look around their offices or homes when you first come in and see what adorns desks and tables or hangs from walls. These things usually are reliable indicators of personal interests and hobbies or recognition and status needs. In fact, if you want to know the true personality of an individual, you can tell what he cherishes most by examining the items in his bedroom, particularly around his dresser and mirror. (Obviously, most clients don't make this opportunity available.) Recognizing and getting your prospect to talk about a prominently displayed object can have a strong positive influence on his attitude toward you.

> Ted, a salesman for a restaurant equipment dealer, was sent by his boss to see a hospital administrator who was in charge of the hospital's kitchen expansion. The dealer had successfully bid on the job of supplying new equipment, but he wanted Ted to get the administrator to substitute a different brand of gas range from the one specified by the food service consultant involved.
>
> The hospital administrator, an irascible old gentleman, preferred the original brand, and the discussion started off badly and got worse until Ted suddenly noticed an unusual obsidian letter opener on the prospect's desk and commented on it. The letter opener turned out to be a cherished memento of a particularly happy Mexican vacation. Immediately the tone of the encounter changed. The two men became friends; and eventually the desired change of equipment was made. A small but significant object had turned an encounter from confrontation to cooperation.

Space Language

The physical distance between people during communication means something to each one. In our culture, the meaning varies with lessening degrees of confidentiality, from distances of 3 to 20 inches for personal discussions to distances of 20 inches to 5 feet for normal speaking distances of 5½ to 20 feet for group speaking. Prospects vary in their perception of the most suitable distance between yourself and them. Be alert to their signals in this respect. If the prospect barricades himself behind a desk or uses chairs, counters, or store racks to keep you at what he considers a safe distance, relax, back off, and let him relax too. If, on the other hand, he allows you to sit next to him at his desk or on a sofa or to join him for a meal away from the office, you can see that you have penetrated his defenses.

The normal speaking distance for business matters, where impersonality is involved at the beginning of the conversation, is 5½ to 8 feet.

Time Language

People manipulate time quite unconsciously, but they get their messages across very well. Times of the day have different meanings. If a buyer telephones you at home very early in the morning or after 10:00 at night, the timing of the call signals a matter of the greatest urgency. A call during sleeping hours is taken as a matter of life and death. In the social world, a person invited on a date at the last minute by someone not very well known is likely to feel insulted, and someone extending a dinner party invitation only a few days in advance feels the need to apologize.

Your being prompt or tardy can elicit strong favorable or unfavorable responses in the buyer, since many people think of promptness as a virtue. How do you think your purchasing agent feels when he sets aside some of his limited time for you and you are half an hour late, or when you turn up suddenly without giving him the courtesy of advance notice?

In every transactional situation, you must be the cushion, the buffer, always flexible and adaptive, ever adjusting in the communication process, but never putting the burden of the communication process on your customer. It is never that he was too stupid to understand you, but perhaps that you did not express yourself clearly enough.

By listening effectively, you can allow an upset customer to get things off his chest. After he has relaxed and calmed down, you can go on to solve his particular problem. Many times, he will thank you for listening to him!

When we discussed the role of the salesperson in marketing, we referred to the role as that of personal promotion, as opposed to the nonpersonal promotion of advertising and other efforts. Personal promotion involves communication, and effective communication involves not only a message from the sender, but also feedback from the receiver. Your persuasive ability will be enhanced if you follow these guidelines:

The message—your sales talk—must be as clear and precise as possible.
There should be provision for feedback.
The recipient must *want* to understand and accept the message.

In Chapter 16 we shall discuss the questions you should ask if mere listening has failed to make clear your customer's problem.

THE CONCEPT OF ROLE

Role is a customary function or part. You perform different roles on different occasions. This concept is expressed in slang as wearing different hats. It has nothing to do with faking or play-acting for effect.

In selling, you perform several roles. These activities may vary from passive information-giving to counseling, closing, and expediting orders. The dual functions of Health Maintenance Organization (HMO) sales representatives illustrate the idea of roles. HMO representatives spend more time with their clients after enrollment than they do during the actual sale of the health plan. Hence, they are called Enrollment Counselors* to describe their roles accurately.

TRANSACTIONAL ANALYSIS: BASIC CONCEPTS

Transactional analysis is a tool that we shall borrow from clinical psychology to help us understand human and business behavior. Dr. Eric Berne, the originator of transactional analysis, defined a *transaction* as the unit of social intercourse.[5] An exchange of *strokes*, a stimulus and a response between two people, establishes a transaction. We are most interested, of course, in those cases where a buyer and a vendor are involved.

Parent, Adult, and Child

To analyze and categorize a transaction, we must look at the personality traits that the participants are exercising at the time. Dr. Berne found that each human being has three ego states, the Parent, the Adult, and the Child, which influence his behavior.

THE PARENT

The Parent ego state is copied by a child during the first few years from the parents and other older people. In the Parent, as on a cassette tape, are recorded all the admonitions, rules, and laws that the child heard and observed, and nothing requires these rules to be rational or consistent. This permanent recording is available for instant replay throughout life. It is the carrier of customs, traditions, and manners from one generation to the next.

The most significant inputs to these recordings happen during the first five years of life. That is why many educational psychologists believe that the first five years of a child's life are more important than the four or five years later spent in college. During this crucial period, habits are formed and permanent impressions are made.

* This term was originated by the author in 1972.

The Parent within us has two phases: it is critical and admonishing, but it is also supportive and nurturing. Some Parent characteristics are shown in Figure 4.1, which also details those of the Adult and the Child.

THE CHILD

Within each of us is the same little person that we were at three years old. The Child ego state is an expression of our emotions, basic tissue needs, and need for the approval of our peers. It is creative, playful, irresponsible, and spontaneous, but compliant under pressure.

THE ADULT

This ego state is unrelated to age. We are all able to process data objectively and respond intelligently to people and problem situations. The Adult, the cranial computer, unemotionally analyzes situations and predicts results based on facts and relevant experience. It examines and tests what the Parent and the Child are telling it, gathers its own data, and grinds out decisions.

The mature individual has all three ego states in balance. Each person differs slightly, however, in the proportions of the three states. We all know people who seem to live unthinkingly by rigid rules. This kind of person is said to have a very large Parent, a very small Child, and a rather weak Adult that has not been able to examine and sort out the strictures of the Parent. Conversely, there is a type of person in whom the Child dominates. This person may be very creative but cannot be relied upon. Those in whom the Adult predominates are perhaps the least interesting people. Strongly oriented toward facts, logic, and decision making, they may be amoral for lack of a strong code (Parent) and do not know how to have a good time (Child).

It is amusing, though perhaps not entirely kind or accurate, to caricature three familiar types in Parent-Adult-Child terms. In the "snowman" drawings in Figure 4.2, the size of each snowball indicates the relative size of that component in the individual's personality.[6]

In the salesperson, the Parent can cause trouble by preventing necessary actions. If your Parent is saying "Never speak to strangers!" and "Don't ask for money!", it can inhibit your selling ability. The Parent, however, also contains that code of ethics that will stand you in good stead when you are confronted with pressures and temptations.

The typical salesperson, however, has a much larger Child than Parent, as we have seen. The salesperson's Child helps him sell through spontaneity, enthusiasm, and creativity, but it also can hurt him. Can you imagine a salesperson who, at 4:30 on Friday afternoon during a long road trip, would suggest going back to the hotel room to work on call reports? The Child in the salesperson is much more likely to assert itself and go out and play.

EGO STATE RESPONSES

VERBAL & NONVERBAL INDICATORS	PARENT		ADULT	CHILD	
	Critical	Nurturing		Adaptive	Free/Natural
Tone of Voice	Exasperated, hypercritical, accusing.	Warm and reassuring.	Modulated . . . never harsh.	Highly emotional.	Light . . . joyful.
Verbal Indicators	"No, I mean no!" "Stop it . . . immediately."	"Let me help you." "Thank you."	"That's very interesting; can you tell me more?" "You're probably right. . . ."	"I'll do as I please." "I hate you!"	"This is fun . . . just you and me."
Attitudes	Exaggerated sense of paternal importance.	Friendly—helpful, interested.	Very attentive and courteous. Matter of fact.	Self-conscious but anxious to be noticed. Smiling.	Warm and unassuming.
Facial Indicators	Frowning . . . annoyance. Grimace.	Smiling, pleasant. Patronizing.	Confident, eyes alight, alert. Expressionless. Intense.	Demands attention. Excitable . . . quick to cry. Pouting.	Self-assured and quick to laugh.
Gestures	Authoritative stance. Finger pointing.	Reaching out to help.	Completely relaxed . . . yet closely attentive to everything said or done.	Boisterous—nervous and ill-at-ease.	Uninhibited and friendly.

Figure 4.1   Characteristics of the Parent, the Adult, and the Child. (Adapted from *Games People Play* by Eric Berne, New York: Grove Press, 1967.)

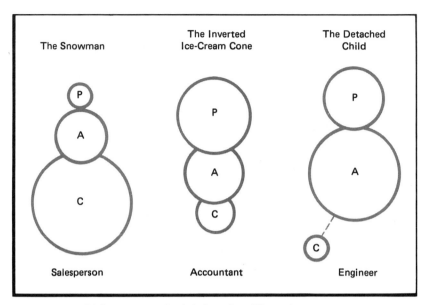

Figure 4.2 PAC ego state by job function. The salesperson snowman shows the dominance of the Child state. The accountant actually looks more like an inverted ice-cream cone—mostly cold; and the engineer, in whom logic dominates, has a vestigial Child that is best shown as detached and noninfluential. Have you met these people?

The salesperson's Child can ruin him if his Adult does not step in and maintain control. The Child is always telling the story of the Big One That Got Away. It is prone to chasing the nonproductive account; the secretary, waiter/waitress, or receptionist; the very small account; and even the nonprospect. The Child thinks, "I'm going to get that order if it's the last thing I do!"—and usually it is, because he gets fired.

When you see a new car in a dealer's display room, a typical dialogue between your three ego states is as follows:

CHILD: Wow! Look at that super car! I want it! I want it!
PARENT: You can't have it! You don't deserve it. Your old car still runs well enough.
ADULT: How much does it cost? What is the mileage? What's the deal?

The Buyer and the Transaction

Of course, the three ego states appear in the buyer as well as in the salesperson, and transactional analysis can help you to understand your buyer's behavior. We shall discuss the buyer's ego states in Chapter 7 and continue our study of the transaction itself in Chapter 16.

KEEP AT IT

We have examined several important abilities that you must develop to succeed in selling. A final point: none of this wonderful knowledge will do you a bit of good if you do not also have *patience* and *persistence.* It takes much time and preparation and many sales calls and presentations to make you a good salesperson, and even more to make you a great one. Your first few attempts will not be professional or even good, and there will be times when you will do very badly, question yourself and your choice of career, and be tempted to give up. Remember that you learn to know yourself through these experiences. You have to fail first before you can succeed.

> A visitor to New York City, having taken a wrong turn on the way to a concert, pulled up near a ragged old man who was sitting on a stoop, playing a violin.
> "How do I get to Carnegie Hall?" the stranger called.
> The old man smiled sadly. "Practice, practice!"

Notes

1. Keith Davis, *Human Relations in Business* (New York: McGraw-Hill, 1957), p. 228.
2. Jurgen Ruesch and Weldon Kees, *Nonverbal Communication* (Berkeley: University of California Press, 1956), p. 189.
3. Edward T. Hall, *The Silent Language* (Garden City, N.Y.: Anchor Books/Doubleday, 1973), pp. 180–184.
4. Gerard I. Nierenberg and Henry H. Calero, *How to Read a Person Like A Book* (New York: Pocket Books, 1973).
5. Eric Berne, *Games People Play* (New York: Grove Press, 1967), p. 15.
6. Ibid., p. 29.

Chapter 5
Nothing Can Stop You

We all could name, among our many acquaintances, a few lost souls, those wonderfully talented, intelligent, creative, tragic individuals who somehow never got going. They could have done anything—or perhaps one particular thing very well—but they never got off the ground, never rose above mediocrity. Eventually those unfortunate men and women died with talents unsung, having lived lives of little lasting value to the world or to themselves.

Why? Those lives were wasted for one or both of two reasons. Deep inside themselves they were afraid to try and never overcame that fear, or they were ambivalent about their career selection and development.

FEAR

Fear causes more waste of human abilities than any other emotion. According to Webster, fear is the anticipation of danger or pain, not the reality of it. Fear keeps us from being productive because we try to prevent painful experiences. Thus, pushed to the extreme, we become immobile, incapable of making any decision or move. The subtle influence of fear impairs our ability to sell ourselves, to establish customer rapport, to close sales, or to prospect effectively. It keeps us from establishing productive day-to-day methods for achieving our goals. Fear provides us with the three P's for failure:

1. perfection
2. procrastination
3. paralysis

What are we afraid of? The root of the problem is that, inwardly, most of us suspect that we are not really worthwhile, "not OK" as Dr. Thomas A. Harris, author of *I'm OK—You're OK*, put it in his well-known work on this subject.[1]

Most of us are basically insecure. This suspicion that we are not "good" comes out as fears; we are afraid that any action or decision will prove that we are not good, so every encounter or attempt at achievement on our part is a test of this hypothesis. We constantly question ourselves, "Am I living up to my personal and professional standards?" Each time we feel we do not, we face the possibility, to ourselves, that we aren't OK.

On the other hand, each success or achievement opens up the possibility that we really *are* pretty good after all, and helps to defeat the specter of worthlessness.

None of us consciously wants to believe that we are bad, and there are two ways around this belief. We can persist in every way possible to succeed and hold up these successes to ourselves as evidence of our basic goodness, or we can avoid the issue, never confront the question and never have to know the answer. Clearly, these two paths are those of the optimist and the pessimist, of the person with Positive Mental Attitude and the one with Negative Mental Attitude.

The most basic fears of salespeople, as of all people, are personal fears. We fear rejection or loss of love. We fear humiliation and disapproval. (Remember that the typical salesperson has a large Child, and the Child needs the approval of others.) Fears of expression (shyness) and of criticism are other aspects of these personal doubts.

In practical terms, these fears directly inhibit your performance as a salesperson. They can make you a weak closer. If you are motivated as much by your desire to avoid disapproval (NMA) as by your desire to gain approval (PMA), you may make your appointed calls (to avoid displeasing your sales manager), yet never close a sale (to avoid displeasing your prospect). Why do so many salespeople "forget" to close? Simply because they do not want to be rejected! If a purchasing agent calls one of these fearful souls a wonderful salesman, do you think the representative will risk changing that opinion by asking the potential customer to buy? Certainly not! He will avoid the possibility of disapproval by simply doing nothing.

Salespeople who cannot shake this fear-caused inhibition ultimately lose out. They insulate themselves from the pain of disapproval by adhering to the three golden rules for avoiding criticism of their behavior: (1) say nothing, (2) do nothing, and (3) be nothing!

They are destined to become the most successful failures who ever carried sales kits. Unfortunately, we encounter them every day.

Fear of humiliation causes call reluctance and telephone avoidance. A rookie sales representative on his first day out in the field is so nervous that he usually cannot give you his own name when asked. This kind of behavior may be acceptable in a raw recruit, but it is not in a veteran representative. A productive salesperson values self-responsibility and achievement above the absence of pain. He has learned to discount his disappointments and remember his successes.

On a less personal and more professional level, we confront the fears of failure and of competition. Fear of failure to achieve personal goals such as the next purchase order or a sales target result in lack of commitment to the job. We already have met that supercilious shoe clerk who is too good to be like his peers and get down to work. Not only does he refuse to get down on his knees to serve his customers; he has never really committed himself to the job. He is too good to be a salesperson because he is afraid of failing. He is just like the credit manager who reports no bad debts; he is afraid to take a chance on his own judgment or ability. He thinks that if he does not try, he cannot fail; but he can never succeed either, and in the achievement-oriented field of sales, lack of success is the same as failure.

In a related mode, some salespeople fear competition from other companies, the salespeople working for other companies, and even their own past performance. Will they make quota this year? Will they get the order tomorrow or next week? These paranoid individuals feel that they are only as good as their last orders and that their jobs are always on the line.

> John, a high technology salesperson, used a competitor's fear of competition to his advantage when negotiating an important contract. He merely asked the customer's project director or other influential person to be sure to "say hello" to his rival. When informed by the customer that John was his competitor on the project, this particular salesperson would become so unnerved that he would usually drop out of the bidding. John said that he "got the order over this rival, *every* time."

Harry Truman once said, "If you can't stand the heat, get out of the kitchen." Some people do not have the strength to stand up to the pressures of sales competition, and they should get out of the business.

Often, however, a positive attitude can overcome initial fear. Don't give up without trying.

Everyone has fears—buyers have them, too, and we shall look at them carefully in Chapter 8. It is comforting to know that other people have been through the same struggles with fear that you face yourself and have learned how to overcome them.

Your first step is to identify these fears. A nameless threat is far more intimidating than one you can name. Once you know what these fears are, you can work to overcome them. Franklin D. Roosevelt said, "The only thing that we have to fear is fear itself." He knew that fear is nothing more than a state of mind and that with determination, we can control and direct the states of our minds. In Chapter 2 we discussed psychocybernetics and the use of visualization techniques to establish goals. The same techniques can be used to establish a positive mental attitude and conquer fears. Treat the situation that you fear as a problem for your right brain to work on. Visualize various outcomes and your responses to them. It also helps to divide a problem into small, manageable pieces if you can.

Reading books and attending courses and seminars can help you, but in the end it is your own determination and perseverance that will enable you to win out over fear. In the words of Franklin D. Roosevelt, "The only limit to our realization of tomorrow will be our doubts of today. Let us move forward with strong and active faith."

MOTIVATIONAL MURKINESS

Is selling a good thing to do? You must believe that it is, or you cannot do it well. Your source credibility is based upon your own beliefs. In some quarters, there is a bias against selling and the salesperson. The questioning of salesmanship goes back a long way, and generations of economists, philosophers, novelists, and others have written negatively about selling. Although fascinated by the salesperson's art, Americans—and American writers from Mark Twain to Arthur Miller—have been uncertain about whether to bestow upon the salesperson contempt, derision, or sympathy.

Where there is a public bias against salespeople and selling, it is based on outmoded business practices that are no longer used or on unsatisfactory experiences with inept retail clerks or overly aggressive door-to-door peddlers, who are the most visible salespeople. These public types, however, are only the tip of the sales iceberg, which includes many professionals whose activities do not touch most people's daily lives.

Selling is not only worthwhile, but vital: it is the lifeblood of our economy. In our system, every other activity depends on the sale; nothing can go on without it, whether in planning, production, or advertising. Sales create jobs, jobs create income, and income supports life for the members of our society.

Ironically, our society's cultural conditioning causes us to be overly suspicious of the motives and ethics of salespeople in exchange situations. Since the seller obtains money from the buyer, we somehow feel that the buyer is being exploited. Rather than taking such a narrow view of selling, society should focus on the ethics of exchange relationships. The seller is not inherently wrong. An exchange of values—cash for needed products or services—has occurred, and both parties profit. According to economic theory, the party who receives the goods or services is the one who benefits most.

The seller is in the wrong only if he misrepresents what he is selling or coerces or threatens the buyer. Otherwise, it is not possible for a salesperson to make a customer buy what she does not want to buy. Even under hypnotism, people cannot be induced to do something that they do not want to do. Selling does not have hypnotic powers, especially in our society where persuasion and counterpersuasion exist side by side.

In Chapter 2 we defined the salesperson as a problem-solving, need-satisfying professional who links the company to the marketplace. At best, the salesperson does what is called *consultative selling,* performing a function that raises customers' satisfactions above what they could have achieved themselves. The key to consultative selling is to enter before customers are aware of the problem, help them identify the problem, and then help them solve it. The consultative salesperson works together with the client to elucidate needs that the client may not have identified clearly and to determine which product or service is best suited to satisfy those needs. The key to success in this process is to identify a need or problem before the customer does and then raise the customer's awareness level.

The purchasing pyramid[2] in Figure 5.1 diagrams the same idea in another way. The higher up the pyramid you are when you enter the decision process, the more consultative is your function.

Is selling a good and worthwhile occupation? Can you be proud to be a salesperson? You certainly can. Ever since the days of the better mousetrap came to an end, you have made our economy function by beating a path to the buyer's door.

THE GRID FOR SALES EXCELLENCE

You can believe in yourself as a salesperson if you have the right attitude toward selling. The Sales Grid® concept of Blake and Mouton[3] is a set of theories about the relationships between vendors and customers. You have two considerations while selling: one is concern for making the sale,

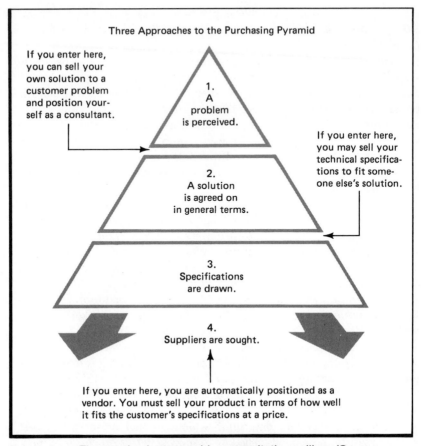

Three Approaches to the Purchasing Pyramid

If you enter here, you can sell your own solution to a customer problem and position yourself as a consultant.

1.
A problem is perceived.

If you enter here, you may sell your technical specifications to fit someone else's solution.

2.
A solution is agreed on in general terms.

3.
Specifications are drawn.

4.
Suppliers are sought.

If you enter here, you are automatically positioned as a vendor. You must sell your product in terms of how well it fits the customer's specifications at a price.

Figure 5.1   The purchasing pyramid—consultative selling. (Source: Mack Hanan, ''Three Approaches to the Purchasing Pyramid,'' *Sales & Marketing Management,* July 12, 1976. Reprinted by permission.)

and the other is concern for the customer. The way you resolve these considerations determines your selling strategy.

The Sales Grid diagrams these two scales and their relative values (Figure 5.2). The horizontal axis indicates concern for making a sale, while the vertical axis indicates concern for the customer. Each is expressed as a 9-point scale, where 1 represents minimum concern, 5 represents an intermediate degree, and 9 represents maximum concern.

In the lower right corner is the point 9,1. Here, high concern for making a sale is coupled with little or no concern for the customer. Prospects are perceived as mere means to an end—the purchase order. Such 9,1 assumptions result in insensitive, hard-sell behavior that may alienate clients. A typical 9,1 salesperson views selling as a win or lose occupation

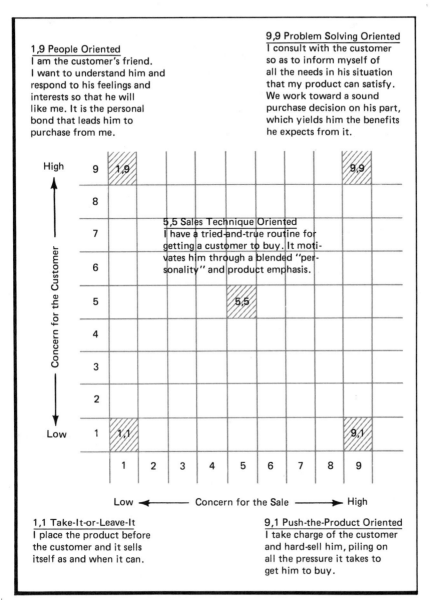

1,9 People Oriented
I am the customer's friend.
I want to understand him and
respond to his feelings and
interests so that he will
like me. It is the personal
bond that leads him to
purchase from me.

9,9 Problem Solving Oriented
I consult with the customer
so as to inform myself of
all the needs in his situation
that my product can satisfy.
We work toward a sound
purchase decision on his part,
which yields him the benefits
he expects from it.

5,5 Sales Technique Oriented
I have a tried-and-true routine for
getting a customer to buy. It motivates him through a blended "personality" and product emphasis.

Concern for the Customer
High / Low

Low ← Concern for the Sale → High

1,1 Take-It-or-Leave-It
I place the product before
the customer and it sells
itself as and when it can.

9,1 Push-the-Product Oriented
I take charge of the customer
and hard-sell him, piling on
all the pressure it takes to
get him to buy.

Figure 5.2   The Sales Grid.® Concern for the sale is shown on the horizontal axis; concern for the customer, on the vertical axis. (Source: Robert R. Blake and Jane Srygley Mouton, *The Grid for Sales Excellence,*
New York: McGraw-Hill Publishing Co., copyright © 1970, p. 4. Reproduced by permission.)

and has very strong needs for esteem and independence. Thus every order becomes a "victory" over his customer and feeds his salesperson's shaky self-esteem. This individual is usually an excellent "closer"—he captures a lot of business quickly—but his high pressure tactics do not wear well with customers during long-term relationships. Almost every buyer has experienced the 9,1 salesperson so bent on pushing his product that he is blind to the customer's needs or possible benefits. This is the salesperson who causes prejudice against salespeople in the general public. He is one of those notorious graduates of the old "foot-in-the-door" and "knee-in-the-groin" school of high pressure selling.

In the upper left corner of the grid is the 1,9 strategy. Here a minimum concern for making a sale is joined with a maximum concern for the customer. Under this selling style, little direct persuasion is used to get the customer to buy. The salesperson is so concerned about the customer's feelings—and needs the customer's friendship or approval so much—that he spends most of his time just being nice. He views the hoped-for sale as a by-product of friendliness rather than as a consequence of the selling initiative. We became acquainted with this salesperson before when we discussed fears. He would rather lose a sale than a friend; but these "friends" may also be frustrated by his lack of help with their mission, which is to buy. Do not depend on personality alone. This was Willie Loman's mistake in *Death of a Salesman.* He thought that the key to success selling was "not to be liked by your customers, but to be *well* liked!"

At the lower left corner of the grid is the 1,1 strategy. Here the salesperson's concern for making a sale and his concern for customers are both at a low ebb. This salesperson is passive: he neither pushes to establish a better relationship with the prospect nor does he try to build acceptance for his product. Selling is merely a job to which he has no commitment. He makes the minimum number of calls and writes the minimum amount of business in order to stay employed. This is the salesperson who fills out call reports for the next week on Sunday and then goes out and plays golf instead of making those sales calls.

In the center is the 5,5 strategy, which contains equal intermediate amounts of both types of concern. This salesperson avoids a 9,1 hard sell. His selling pressure is best described as sustained nudging. He shows a concern for the customer by trying to add a pleasant social taste to the proceedings. Under this pseudosweetness is a methodical, conservative attitude that relies on tried and true selling techniques. His pat presentation comes across as mechanical and monotonous. We call these salespeople *mechanical men and women.* Just wind them up and place them in front of any customer, and they will always say and do the very same thing! Every time!

Finally in the upper right corner is the 9,9 strategy, in which a high concern for making the sale and high concern for the customer are integrated. This grid position is, of course, the ideal. Here, the salesperson expresses concern for the customer by asking:

Can my product be really useful to the customer?
What need does it satisfy?
What benefits is the customer likely to gain?
Will the customer cut costs or improve productivity by using my product or service?
Does my product have any drawbacks from the customer's point of view?
Why should the customer buy from me?

Unlike the superficial friendliness of 1,9 this concern for the customer's benefit is deep and real. The 9,9 salesperson does not push a bill of goods in the 9,1 way, but his concern for the sale is evident as he tries to relate what he offers to the customer's needs.

Clearly, the Blake and Mouton 9,9 is that same consultative salesperson—the problem-solving, need-satisfying professional who links the company to the marketplace. Emulate that salesperson, and indeed nothing can stop you on the road to success.

Notes

1. Thomas A. Harris, *I'm OK—You're OK* (New York: Harper & Row, 1969).
2. Mack Hanan, "Three Approaches to the Purchasing Pyramid," *Sales & Marketing Management*, July 12, 1976.
3. Robert R. Blake and Jane Srygley Mouton, *The Grid for Sales Excellence* (New York: McGraw-Hill, 1970), p. 4.

Part II
WHY YOUR CUSTOMER BUYS

Chapter 6
Buyer Needs and Motives

One of the most distressing problems of our fragmented society, and the one problem that sends many perfectly normal people to psychologists, is that many of us have no one to talk to, no one who really cares about our fears and ambitions. Few nuclear families now include elderly grandparents, those traditional wise counselors of the past. Divorce splits husband from wife, and neither then has a built-in sounding board off which to bounce ideas and plans. Young people "doing their own thing" pull themselves away from the family circle at an age when most still need and crave guidance. As a result, many of us now live on the surface—no roots, no commitments, and no depth.

All this has created a society which longs for emotionally satisfying interaction with other human beings. We respond eagerly to the person who offers us friendship, affection, and love—the person who really seems to care that we exist.

Understand this common need and you understand the importance of empathy with the buyer, a need which we discussed in Chapter 4. Most people will react favorably to the salesperson who shows genuine interest in their well-being. The key here is that the interest must be *genuine,* not fabricated just to play upon a buyer's particular weakness or need.

As a salesperson you must have the capacity to get out of your own head and into your customer's head. Like our other skills, this one takes practice. When you find yourself slipping back into your own concerns, just remind yourself that in the end it is your buyers who pay your check. They deserve your genuine interest.

WHY DO PEOPLE BUY?

Unfortunately, most customers buy *despite* what most salespeople say, not because of it. To avoid joining the ranks of the ineffective, you must understand that people buy for one of two reasons, either to gain an end benefit or to avoid a loss. Most people will see no reason to buy from you when they do not foresee gaining a benefit they do not already have, or avoiding the loss of something they presently have.

Whether we speak in terms of our buyers' benefits or of ways to avoid losses, we are speaking our customers' language. *Loss avoidance,* however, is a stronger motivation than *benefit gain.* Most people will take action more quickly to save something they already have earned and possessed than to take chances on potential but untried benefits.

You must learn which are the appropriate times to use these different motivational factors. For example, you will find that an engineering, production, or purchasing executive moves much more quickly to a decision when faced with an interruption of a production line's activities than when presented with a product idea that provides only some vague future potential benefit.

NEEDS, WANTS, MOTIVES, AND PRIORITIES

Most people buy to fill their needs and solve their problems, not yours. A *need* is the lack of anything that is required, desired, or useful. People have unlimited needs and wants, but they have limited means. Thus they must establish priorities, placing needs ahead of wants.

Your success in selling depends upon your sensitivity to people and their interests, needs, and desires. Both professional and personal needs are important. We shall take up personal needs here and discuss professional ones later in this chapter. What are the basic personal needs and desires of human beings? No two individuals are exactly alike, but their basic needs are similar.

Maslow's Hierarchy of Needs

When asked what the labor unions wanted, Samuel Gompers, the father of the American labor movement, responded, "More." Today, most of us probably would say "Much more." Our needs and wants are unlimited, although our resources are not. Therefore, we must establish priorities.

According to the noted psychologist Abraham H. Maslow,[1] human beings are perpetually wanting animals, and our needs are physiological and social. Needs have a certain priority. As the more basic needs are satisfied, people turn their attention to higher needs. If the basic needs are not met, they claim priority, and efforts to satisfy the higher needs must be postponed.

Maslow's hierarchy of needs (Figure 6.1)[2] shows the succession order in which humans seek to satisfy needs. As a need of lower order is being satisfied, it becomes less and less important, and the need of next higher rank becomes more important. Maslow puts economic and physiological wants, or "tissue needs," at the bottom and the need for self-fulfillment at the top.

Peter Drucker[3] believes that the order of wants is not of first importance. What matters most is the insight that wants are not absolute: the more one's want is being satisfied, the less its satisfaction matters.

We want to be able to identify those needs that are currently most important to our customers, because these will influence their buying behavior. Current needs are action motivators (see Figure 6.2).

People at the subsistence level are not interested in luxuries or self-actualization; they want to survive. A person whose head has been underwater too long wants not a mink coat or a new car, but air. This need is purely physiological. Only after it is satisfied is the individual free to focus on the next level of need. Leo Tolstoy once said that it is difficult for an empty sack to stand up straight. Starving people do not attend concerts or art exhibits. The same is true of a marginal customer who is being asked to consider the purchase of a luxury item. That is why some of your customers are not buying what you are selling. They buy only because of their needs, and often despite what you say.

Learn where your customers' current needs are within their own personal needs hierarchies so that you can make the appropriate selling appeals. If you aim too high or too low, you will miss the mark completely.

A person's need structure is not static. Once a lower need has been satisfied, it cannot necessarily be permanently forgotten. A person moves up and down the need scale depending on circumstances, and one small incident can cause a rapid downscale shift.

Dorothy, the self-actualized Santa Barbara sculptress, has everything: a beautiful home with an ocean view, a Rolls Royce, every possible charge account, membership in the best country club, and a large studio employing several people. She is happy and financially successful doing the work for which she is best suited. She is satisfying needs at the top of her scale.

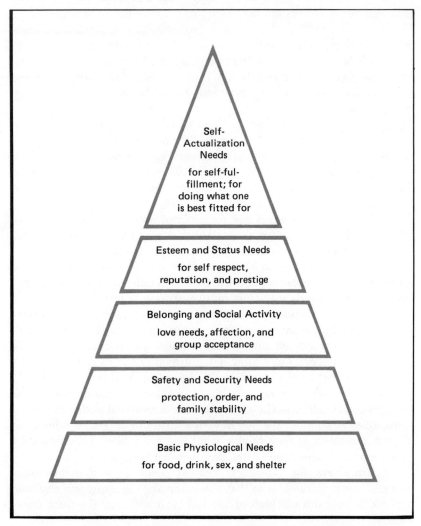

Figure 6.1   Maslow's hierarchy of needs. (Source: Abraham H. Maslow, "A Theory of Human Motivation," *Psychological Review*, vol. 50, 1943. © 1943 American Psychological Association. Reprinted by permission.)

One day, however, a letter arrives from Dorothy's bank, saying that there is a $25,000 debit in her account. All the checks she wrote last week surely will bounce. All at once she is concerned not about self-actualization, but about esteem and status needs. What will her suppliers and employees think of her? If she cannot pay them, she could be forced out of business.

If that happens, she might lose her club membership and charge

Figure 6.2 A direct appeal to social needs. (Courtesy Marina City Club, California.)

accounts. All her friends might desert her. Now she is worried about belonging and social activities.

Suppose she cannot straighten out the bank problem, and her home and cars are repossessed? How will she live? She is at the level of safety and security needs. By the time she arrives at the bank to discuss the matter, Dorothy is angry and ready to punch her friendly banker in the nose. In only a few moments, a fully self-actualized human being has dropped all the way down her need structure to the primary physiological level.

Because human need levels constantly fluctuate, it is part of our job to find out where our customer is at the moment on the scale. Only then can we make our sales approach acceptable and timely.

Maslow's hierarchy of needs theory has contributed much to psychology, but it does not tell us much about the process of need satisfaction through buyer-vendor interaction, problem solving, and decision making. Since these are the crucial areas where salespeople operate, a knowledge of how human needs are translated into buying actions (i.e., purchase orders) is vital to the entire selling process.

THE SIX BUYING MOTIVES

Customers, as we have seen, buy to fill needs, to acquire benefits, and to avoid losses. More immediately, however, most people buy products, services, or ideas because a salesperson has appealed to one or more *buying motives,* which can be summarized in six categories: profit, utility or essential need, pride, emulation, fear, and love.

Profit

Stocks, bonds, artworks, and capital goods are purchased because an individual or corporation hopes to make a profit through appreciation of value at a subsequent resale. In industrial selling, this is the purchasing agent's *prime* buying motive. The agent is interested in machinery or equipment that will increase efficiency, improve productivity, and thereby lower costs. Assuming no change in sales levels, a decrease in costs means a corresponding increase in *profits.*

People can also profit in a nonmaterialistic manner by attending a lecture or an opera, or by investing their time and money in other types of self-actualizing activities. Therefore, in order to appeal to the profit buying motive, you must prove to your customers that they will make money, save money, or be happier as a result of purchasing your product. If your product can indeed produce these results, your chances of selling it are quite good.

Utility or Essential Need

Utility or generic need is the attribute of a product or service that makes it capable of want-satisfaction. It has several significant dimensions. We speak of *place utility* as the value added to a product by having it in the right place. For example, a color television set sitting in a Bakersfield warehouse has less value to your Portland customer than does a similar set sitting in your retail store. It is in the wrong place. If you are out of stock and cannot switch the customer to another model, this buyer will leave your store and shop elsewhere. Transporting that television set from Bakersfield to Portland creates place utility and adds to the value of the product in your customer's eyes.

Should you persuade your customer to accept shipment of the color television set that is in the Bakersfield warehouse, you both hope that it arrives undamaged. This is called *form utility*. Many orders are also lost because the wrong size, shape, or assortment of products were shipped.

A related value added is through *time utility*. Here is where efficient order processing, warehousing, and shipping creates value by avoiding delays. Many orders have been canceled because of this time factor. Christmas merchandise ordered in September and delivered in Janurary has no value to the customer whatsoever.

Finally, *possession utility* has great emotional value to customers. They cannot wait to wear that new garment or show off that new automobile to their friends and associates. Besides deriving tremendous satisfaction from their new purchases, they are influencing future purchases by their peer group through this positive form of word-of-mouth advertising.

Both customers and industrial accounts are willing to pay handsomely for the basic utility value of a need-satisfying product and its other important dimensions. From these examples, it is clear that all of the activities of a firm's marketing department impact the effectiveness of its sales force. Your company's physical distribution system can enhance your customer goodwill by assuring delivery of the right amount of the right products to the right place at the right time and in the desired form.

Industrial firms are constantly searching for new equipment, processes, or methods that will improve productivity and efficiency. Next to *profit, utility* is the strongest buying motive that purchasing agents have. Evaluation of job performance by management focuses upon the profit and utility value of the agents' buying decisions. They usually emphasize product quality, vendor service, and evaluated price in their selection of suppliers.

To appeal to the utility buying motive, get your client to visualize how your product or service will solve an immediate and basic need.

Pride

We should not be too quick to condemn the motive of pride. If it were not for our natural desire to have better things for ourselves, our country would not enjoy the high standard of living that it does. A family bread-winner deserves to feel pride of accomplishment.

Pride in one's appearance, possessions, or accomplishments has prompted people to buy all sorts of things, from hats to airplanes. Some people take pride to an extreme: they must live in the biggest houses, have the oldest antiques or the most expensive automobiles, and send their children to the most fashionable schools. Some of your buyers want only the "best," and others opt to travel "first cabin."

To succeed with proud customers, you should appeal to their ego-tism by praise, make reference to their important opinions, ask their ad-vice, call them by name, and ask them questions about themselves.

Emulation

Closely allied to the motive of pride is that of emulation. People's cul-tural surroundings and the groups to which they belong strongly influ-ence their perceptions. Your customers' buying behavior is partly deter-mined by the social groups to which they belong or wish they belonged. In selling, we sometimes refer to emulation as "keeping up with the Joneses," and it often is a strong buying motive. The emulation-prone in-dividual may be completely immune to all logical and psychological selling appeals until that Jones neighbor or colleague is mentioned as being interested in or owning your product or service.

Your customer feels every bit as worthy as the proud Mr. or Ms. Jones, who has everything and is the peer group leader. When this leader chooses or does something, the emulator must have or do the same thing too, and very often without due regard for price. The industrial buyer as well as the consumer is often an emulator. In one case, a reluctant plant owner suddenly reversed a three-year stand against plant renovation when told that his competitor had bought the plan. This owner did not want to be left out.

A person does not have to belong to a group to be influenced by it. Many residents of Los Angeles are not involved in the motion picture in-dustry, but they frequently pattern their dress and other behavior on that of movie stars.

When you are trying to sell to an emulator, try to refer to the expe-riences and opinions of other respected customers. You can use testimo-nials and reference leads effectively here, but be careful to do so in a subtle and indirect manner, and do not confuse the proud buyer with the emulator!

Fear or Caution

Fear or anxiety-inducing appeals, although often overused by salespeople, can be quite effective. The technique is to warn your customers of the undesirable results of not buying your product or service. This is a direct appeal to the "fear-of-loss" syndrome, which was mentioned previously. Things as diverse as deodorants and real estate are sold on the basis of fear. For example, if you do not own life insurance, your family may be in a difficult position when you die.

When using the fear appeal, you should get your customer to visualize vividly the bad results of not buying. In effect, you are inducing a headache before offering aspirin. Just be sure that the problem is a real one and that your product is indeed the solution to it—or you will wind up with a problem yourself!

Love

Love, whether of self, family, or sweetheart, is one of the most powerful buying motives. Figure 6.3, 6.4, and 6.5 illustrate effective appeals to the "love" buying motive. People buy things to express love or to obtain it. Research proved people love to travel in New York State and love Broadway shows. *Love* became the operating word. The simplicity of the "I Love New York" graphics and musical variants became marketing history in 1979 and 1980. Department stores have never lost money at Christmas time by betting that people love their children more than their money. Some people will do anything for love. Witness the story of the late Duke of Windsor. He gave up an empire for the woman he loved. H. L. Mencken called it "the greatest story since the resurrection!" Some people commit crimes of passion because they cannot get love. When utilizing the love motive, you should prove how the object of your customer's affection will gain health, wealth, and/or happiness through the purchase of your product. However, be careful that you do not oversell love: it could turn into customer wrath!

Identifying Motives

As you might expect, the burden of identifying those motives most susceptible to appeal in the individual customer is up to you. Actually, you must not expect to identify only one motive per customer; most people are motivated by more than one force at a time. Customers have certain individual motivational power switches that, when flipped, make them buyers. It is part of your job to find them. That is why you must learn how to read people like you read a book. There is infinite variety and motivation on every page.

Figure 6.3 "Because You Love Them®." (Courtesy Life of Georgia®, Life Insurance Company of Georgia. Reprinted by permission.)

Figure 6.4   (Courtesy Wells Rich Green.)

FROM NEEDS TO PURCHASE ORDER:
A PSYCHOLOGICAL CHAIN

How can you be sure that you are appealing to your customers' buying motives? This is a critical question. A particular need and a particular behavior are not necessarily consistently related. In customers' minds, needs may or may not be consciously recognized. If your clients do not recognize needs, and if it is appropriate to do so, you should raise their levels of consciousness so that they become aware of the needs.

A recognized need alone, however, will not of itself lead to a purchase order. The prospect must have not only a need, but also a motive, which is the force that propels a buyer from need to purchase action. In selling, we can appeal to a motive directly.

Thus our method is to proceed through three steps: (1) determine the customer's needs, (2) know what motives usually can be used to translate these needs into action, and (3) use appeals that are known to address those motives.

Motives Related to Needs

In general, your customers will not state clearly that they currently need safety and security or esteem and status. They are much more likely to say that they need coats, computer programs, or good dinners. Your first job, then, is to figure out which personal needs are hidden between the lines of the requests. The coat may represent a basic physiological need to maintain body temperature, or it may be related to esteem and status needs: mink or cashmere symbols of having "arrived." Similarly, the good dinner may range from basic proteins, fats, and carbohydrates for a starving refugee to a refined exercise in gastronomy when two self-actualized chefs get together to share ideas. And what personal need is hidden behind the problem-solving computer program? It could be something as obscure as the esteem and status that your customer wants with the boss.

Suppose that we have identified a need for esteem and status behind

Figure 6.5 An effective appeal to the ''love'' buying motive. (Courtesy Somerset Importers, Ltd. Reprinted with permission.)

our customer's overt statements. Should we immediately identify this need to the customer and say that we have just the thing to fill it? Probably not. How would you react if, when you asked for an umbrella, the clerk said, "Here, this designer-autographed style should satisfy your obvious craving for the esteem of your betters!"? No, we must proceed to ascertain the motives to which we should appeal: profit? utility? pride? To what is our customer likely to respond? What are the motivational power switches?

To do this kind of thinking, we need to know how the six motives of profit, utility, pride, emulation, fear, and love match up with the Maslow needs. An overview of these relationships is given in Figure 6.6. As you can see, the profit, utility, fear, and love motives apply to all the needs, but there are subtle differences between need categories. Utility, for example, changes in meaning as the individual moves up from the physiological need level to that of social needs. A Cadillac and a Volkswagen both transport riders from one location to another. Although each has a motor and four wheels, their values are perceived differently by people at different need levels.

Profit fits very neatly into each need category, as it is indispensable to self-improvement and enables people to advance to their next higher level of aspiration. Even a fully self-actualized person requires a profitable financial position to have those things that make a fulfilled situation possible. Profit, in this case, also can be viewed as increase in knowledge, wisdom, or spiritual depth.

We may think of pride as a motivation related only to the wealthy, but it also appears strongly among others. The need for esteem does not only result in the purchase by the rich of expensive houses and cars. It also prompts the lower-income family to send a child to a school it cannot afford, just to prove that it can. Even at the lowest level of existence we encounter pride of place, or territorial rights. Everyone has played King of the Hill at least once. We cannot tamper with pride, but we certainly can appeal to it.

The emulation motive is related to love needs, group acceptance, and other forms of social intercourse. The "keeping-up-with-the-Joneses" syndrome enables some people not only to survive, but also in many cases to improve their stations in life. Their aspirations may be expanded through contact with people whom they admire and emulate. An elite reference group can spur the less favorably endowed person on to greater accomplishment.

Imitators model their behavior patterns so as to resemble that which is genuine, original, or superior. Even fully self-actualized individuals once were influenced by other fulfilled people or heroes. The great Albert Schweitzer's life continues to inspire and motivate people throughout the world.

NEEDS

MOTIVES	Basic Physiological	Safety Security	Belonging Social Activity	Esteem Status	Self- Actualization
Profit	Material or non-material Survival Physical gain	Protect material and nonmaterial possessions	Enhance personal and professional status	Material possessions Cultural symbols	Nonmaterialistic Psychic income Professional achievement
Utility	Basic needs Survival	Basics; style un-important	Higher style	As symbols	As means to end
Pride	Pride of place	"I'm stronger or safer than you!" (I have a higher wall around my home.)	I'm in the best club, school, com-pany, etc.	I am the best.	Pride of accom-plishment

Emerson: "Hitch your wagon to a star!"

Emulation	Ride on the coat-tails of a survivor to rise above the survival level	Initiate success in order to avoid failure	Of group activities Envy Imitate success patterns of others "keeping up with the Jones'"	Of successful individuals	Of hero
Fear	Of illness, death	Of attack	Of loss	Of loss	Of loss
Love	Of self (Of others)	Of Self (Of others)	Of Self and others	Of Self and others	Of Self Of others Of mankind Altruism

Figure 6.6 How the six buying motives are related to the Maslow needs.

Fear and love are motivators at every level. Fear moves from the most basic anxieties about illness, death, and attack at lower need levels to the fear of loss of what one has achieved at higher levels. Love follows an interesting pattern in which love of self is paramount at the survival level, love of others enters the picture at intermediate levels, and love of self returns strongly at the level of self-actualization, although it may be mixed with love of mankind.

Making Your Appeal

Once you have identified the customer's personal needs and the motives connected with them, you can appeal through those motives. Always make your appeal tactfully. You do not want to antagonize your customer by appearing to play amateur psychologist with statements like "I see that you're an emulator." Instead, use the more subtle approach: "John Jones has one of these, and he told me you'd probably be needing one. . . ."

THE INDUSTRIAL BUYER: SPECIAL NEED/MOTIVE FACTORS

The industrial purchasing agent, like the consumer, buys when an aroused need is motivated to action. The buyer acts to satisfy that need. Unlike the ultimate consumer, however, the industrial buyer is motivated by both personal and professional needs.

The Firm's Needs

Industrial buyers must consider such parameters as profit goals, utility values, and cost-benefit guidelines. They must justify purchases on the basis of measurable performance. Consequently, these buyers tend to base their choices of one supplier over another on differences in quality, service, and price, in that order. With respect to the firm's basic functional needs, the buyer seeks profit and utility, and the salesperson must appeal to these motivations.

The Buyer's Psychological Needs

These same industrial buyers also are people with personal needs such as those we have been discussing. They want to improve their positions in their firms. They also have a stake in improving their companies' public images, since they are publicly associated with these images.

THE PARALLEL TECHNIQUE OF SELLING

The industrial buyer thus has two parallel need structures and attempts to satisfy both of them in buying. This customer, in buying a product,

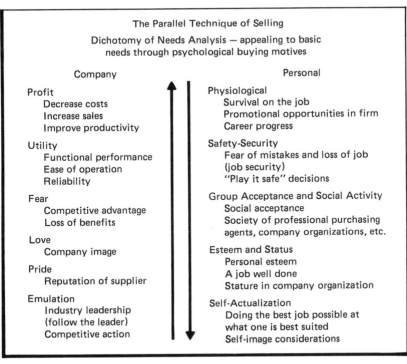

The Parallel Technique of Selling

Dichotomy of Needs Analysis — appealing to basic
needs through psychological buying motives

Company	Personal
Profit	Physiological
Decrease costs	Survival on the job
Increase sales	Promotional opportunities in firm
Improve productivity	Career progress
Utility	Safety-Security
Functional performance	Fear of mistakes and loss of job
Ease of operation	(job security)
Reliability	"Play it safe" decisions
Fear	Group Acceptance and Social Activity
Competitive advantage	Social acceptance
Loss of benefits	Society of professional purchasing
Love	agents, company organizations, etc.
Company image	Esteem and Status
Pride	Personal esteem
Reputation of supplier	A job well done
Emulation	Stature in company organization
Industry leadership	Self-Actualization
(follow the leader)	Doing the best job possible at
Competitive action	what one is best suited
	Self-image considerations

Figure 6.7   People buy the expectation of benefits, not the generic products themselves. In addition to obtaining the want-satisfying qualities of a product or service, purchasing agents buy for various personal reasons. These combined benefits *are* the product. The Parallel Technique of Selling takes into consideration the dichotomy of buyer's needs in a purchasing situation.

seeks to satisfy both personal and operational requirements. The *personal* requirements are those factors in his inherent psychology that influence his personal and individual actions. The *operational* or company requirements are his business needs for a product that performs a particular job function. The parallel technique of selling takes this dichotomy of needs into consideration (see Figure 6.7).

To use this parallel technique, the salesperson identifies both the buyer's professional need (for example, price, which affects the firm's profitability) and personal need (for example, the safety-security need of keeping a job, which again hinges on the firm's profitability). The salesperson then knows that an appeal to profitability will address both needs.

Each buying motive appeals to a parallel structure of complementary needs of the purchasing agent within the firm's environment.

As another example, a customer might be motivated to buy your product because of your firm's reputation (a pride motivation). This motivation is related not only to the firm's quality needs but also to the buyer's self-esteem and status needs within the organization. Such "reputation buyers" buy only the best from the most prestigious firms so as to enhance their own stature within their organizations. Their personal self-esteem rises when their bosses commend their choices.

> Mike, a computer sales engineer, applied this powerful technique during a big-ticket negotiation with an indecisive purchasing agent. Detecting that the buyer's concern for service was partly based on personal needs, Mike pointed out that regardless of what salespeople said, the buyer's own professional standing and livelihood would be on the line once the contract was awarded and the salespeople were gone. "That means that you must make an objective decision," he said.

Thus you are involved on the one hand with the problem-solving and decision-making mechanisms of your buyers and on the other hand with their emotional needs on the job. Buying action is the result of motivation, and you must direct your appeals to motives that are related to both need structures. Your detective work in figuring out the relative strengths of these needs will enable you to solve your buyers' problems more effectively. You can understand why your customers buy and help them to do so in a manner that is mutually profitable.

Because most buying behavior is multimotivated, your main selling task is to focus on the most urgent need or want which is susceptible to arousal by your sales presentation. Your creative strategy should arouse or identify that need and then clearly present your product or service as a desirable means of satisfying the need. Maslow's hierarchy of basic needs helps us to focus on goals of behavior—on ends rather than means. Therefore, your appeal should be the *central idea* of your sales message. Your customer must be sold, and the selling is done by appealing to the customer's most active needs.

Notes

1. Abraham H. Maslow, "A Theory of Human Motivation," *Psychological Review*, vol. 50, 1943, pp. 370–396.
2. Ibid.
3. Peter H. Drucker, *Management: Tasks, Responsibilities, Practices* (New York: Harper & Row, 1974), p. 195.

Chapter 7
Buyer Behavior

We have been examining our buyers' needs and motives for buying, but of course their behavior is much more diverse than that. Let us move on to look at some of the psychological interpretations of human behavior and how they apply to buyers. Why do they do what they do?

PERCEPTION AND SET

Perception is a psychological process whereby stimuli are received and interpreted by an individual and translated into a response. It is a delicate filtering mechanism made up of a complex system of interacting screens: attitudes, traits, needs, feelings, and thinking or cognition processes.[1] How your clients perceive you and your sales proposition is conditioned by their entire life experiences in relation to their environments.

This point was driven home most unpleasantly to a consultant who lost a large contract because of the shirt he wore. After he had made his final presentation, a member of the corporate buying committee objected, stating that several years before, another person had made them a similar proposal that ended up costing the company around $19 million.

"He sat in the very same chair you're sitting in now, and he also wore a flashy shirt like yours. Whenever I see a shirt like that, I associate it with a $19 million loss. No, sir, we're not going through that again. . . ."

Such is the power of perception and association.

Perception refers to the act of perceiving or awareness, whereas *set* affects what will be perceived and how it will be perceived. Set is in general the preparedness of the individual to make a particular response.[2]

Sets are closely related to attitudes. "An *attitude* is an organization of concepts, motives, traits, habits, and knowledge put together in an evaluative way toward an individual, group, happening, or event."[3] How likely is a buyer to make a buying response to the stimulus of a salesperson's presentation or personality? The buyer's set will partly determine the answer.

Some people have positive or negative sets toward salespeople in general. Thus, they tend to behave in predetermined ways when salespeople appear. A positive set, of course, produces no problems for you, but a negative set on your customer's part can cause difficulties.

To deal well with a negative set, you must have as much advance knowledge as possible about your customer's needs, attitudes, and prejudices. Then, through adroit questioning and careful listening, you can adapt your sales presentation to harmonize with the client's particular situation.

In some cases you can change a client's negative set to a positive one, although to do so is no small order. You will be more likely to succeed in this effort if you use a strong stimulus pattern rather than a weak one. Be well prepared in advance, project empathy, and present yourself with authority, conviction, and sensitivity to your prospect's needs.

TRANSACTIONAL ANALYSIS: BUYER BEHAVIOR

Buyer Ego States

In Chapter 4 we discussed the basic concepts of transaction and ego states developed by Dr. Eric Berne. You will remember that there are three basic ego states: the Parent, the mental recording of rules, traditions, and customs; the Child, the spontaneous, creative, irresponsible, and compliant state; and the Adult, the evaluating and decision-making cranial computer.

As a salesperson, you will find it very helpful to be able to understand and recognize the size and relationship of these ego states in your customer. Once you know which ego state is dominating the buyer's behavior, you can respond appropriately to it.

Buyers, like any other humans, give off clues that help you to identify this dominant ego state. These clues are both verbal and nonverbal. Thus, gesture, facial expressions, body posture, and tone of voice all contribute meaning to verbal statements. Clues to the three roles are summarized in Figure 7.1.

In the Parent role, the buyer is oriented toward values and concerned with right and wrong. This ego state could be described as judgmental, moralistic, prejudiced, critical, directive, and demanding, but also as nurturing, comforting, and approving. Confronted with a problem, the buyer might say, "Can't you idiots *ever* get those specifications right?"

With the Adult state dominant, the buyer is oriented toward facts and copes with current reality. This state is logical, rational, objective, organized, reasoning, problem solving, autonomous, unemotional, and evaluating. This buyer, facing the same problem, might say, "Why is there a difference between this set of specifications and your former specs?"

If the Child state dominates, the buyer is oriented toward emotions. This state is fun-loving, expressive, creative, intuitive, impulsive, stubborn, rebellious, sulking, selfish, affectionate, manipulative, adaptive, compliant, and procrastinating. This person might respond to criticism either with "I'm sorry, sir! We won't do it again!" or, in a different mood, with a rebellious obscenity.

It is not hard to guess which buyer state leads quickly to a productive working relationship. One of the benefits of recognizing buyer ego states is that it helps you to allocate your time and persuasive talents where they will be most needed, a subject we shall discuss in more detail in Chapter 16.

Buyer Games

Dr. Berne extended his theory of transactional analysis by defining a *game* as an ongoing series of complementary ulterior transactions that progress to a well-defined, predictable outcome. They are a recurring set of transactions, often repetitious, superficially plausible, with a concealed motivation: a series of moves with a snare, a "gimmick." Every game is basically dishonest, and the outcome has a dramatic, as distinct from a merely exciting, quality.[4]

An insecure purchasing agent may play a *Space Game* with you by constructing an artificial barrier between the two of you to control the interview. Office furniture may be placed so that you are obliged to face a silhouette against the glare of an office window. The buyer's chair is

TRANSACTIONAL ANALYSIS CLUES TO VARIOUS ROLES			
Gesture Cluster	Parent	Adult	Child
Voice Tones	Approving Caring Condescend-ing Criticizing Demanding Judging Questioning	Direct Evaluating Matter-of-fact	Bright Crying Eager Emotional Excited Full of feeling Whimpering
Words Used	"Everyone knows that." "Every time this . . ." "You are al-ways doing . . ." "You ought to do . . ." "You should never . . ."	How? What? When? Have you tried this? Why? Who?	"I'm mad at you!" "I can't, I'll try, I've just got to . . ." "If you say so . . ." "Hey! Great!" *Words that have a high emotional or feeling value*

Figure 7.1   Verbal and nonverbal clues to the buyer's ego state. Gesture clusters are groups of nonverbal communications which are associated with different ego states and attitudes. In negotiating situations, you must be aware of the meaning behind both the verbal and nonverbal clues. (Adapted from *I'm O.K.—You're O.K.* by Thomas A. Harris, M.D., Copyright © 1967, 1968, 1969 by Thomas A. Harris, M.D. Reprinted by permission of Harper & Row Publishers, Inc.)

higher than yours, so that you are placed in the position of a suppliant or vanquished foe. Physical obstructions such as file cabinets, typewriters, and stacks of papers are designed to make you feel uncomfortable and hence more compliant with the buyer's demands. He or she may offer you a cigarette when there are no ashtrays in the room, and then watch you squirm. Sometimes this is called a *stress interview.*

The *Time Game* is a very effective tool used by buyers to keep salespeople waiting in order to dominate the relationship and extract the best possible terms for themselves. The *Lobby Game* may be played when a salesperson arrives and is kept waiting for an hour by the buyer.

Gesture Cluster	Parent	Adult	Child
Postures	Rigid, uptight Very proper Welcoming Puffed up	Attentive, alert Good eye contact Active listening	Slouching Playful Self-conscious Overburdened
Facial Expressions	Smiles Worries Frowns Disapproving Chin thrust forward Lips pursed	Alert eyes Open, objective Relaxed Faint smile	Excitement, surprise Downcast, sullen Moist bright eyes Quivering lip or chin Smiling with glee
Body Movements	Hands on hips Pointing a finger Arms folded across chest Clenched fist Open arms Open hands	Leaning forward Moving closer to see or hear better Attentive	Spontaneous activity Wringing hands, anxious Clenched fist Withdrawing Laughter Raising hand for permission

Figure 7.1   (Continued)

If the salesperson has arrived late, the buyer's game plan is to make the salesperson pay for the crime of tardiness. The client wants to take advantage of the salesperson's guilt feelings and thereby control the interview. Here is an opportunity to push for all kinds of concessions, from price to delivery. Unless this delay really is beyond control, the buyer is being childish and manipulative. (Of course, there are some cases in which the salesperson is intentionally late to show self-importance or indifference to the need for a sale. In this situation, the salesperson is the game player.)

Your best recourse if you become caught in this game is tactfully to remind the buyer (through a receptionist or secretary) that you are still here but you have another appointment coming up; if today is not convenient, perhaps the appointment should be reset. If this approach does not stop the game, then you should courteously depart within 15 minutes.

If the salesperson has arrived on time and is kept waiting, the punitive element of this Lobby Game has been removed, and it becomes an exercise in pure intimidation. The same game-breaking tactics should be used.

What about the case in which the salesperson who drops in without an appointment is kept waiting? Here we have a reverse situation: the salesperson is being childish. Here, gratification comes from controlling the behavior of others. A busy purchasing agent cannot be interrupted to pass the time of day with a drop-in salesperson. What the salesperson is implying by just dropping in is, "I have no respect for you or your time." There will be times when cold calling is appropriate, but that will be covered in Chapter 10.

THE CUSTOMER GRID

In Chapter 5 we introduced the Sales Grid® of Blake and Mouton, which describes various sales strategies in terms of the salesperson's concern for the buyer and for the sale. The other half of the buyer-seller equation shows that the customer also has two concerns: one for the purchase and one for the vendor. In Figure 7.2, the vertical axis indicates concern for the salesperson, while the horizontal axis shows concern for the purchase. As on the Sales Grid, the combination of various strengths of concern produces various customer attitudes. There are five basic grid styles with associated assumptions, strategies, and ways of interacting with salespeople.

In the lower right corner is the 9,1 customer, whose great concern for making a purchase is coupled with little concern for you, the salesperson. These individuals feel that you need them more than they need you, and they try to control the sales interview. These defensive purchasers fear that you will take advantage of them, so they try to dominate the transaction through criticism, price haggling, and other manipulative techniques designed to extract every possible concession from you.

A purchasing agent who acts under 1,9 assumptions is found in the upper left grid corner, where minimum concern for making a sound purchase is joined with maximum concern for the salesperson. These buyers have an extreme need to be liked and appreciated by everyone, including the salesperson. This type of buyer parallels Willie Loman in Arthur Miller's *Death of a Salesman*.

> Buyer Jones is constantly harassed by his boss for making poor buying decisions. His wife calls him a knucklehead for not earning enough money for the family. When he returns home from work, his children are too absorbed watching television to acknowledge his greetings.

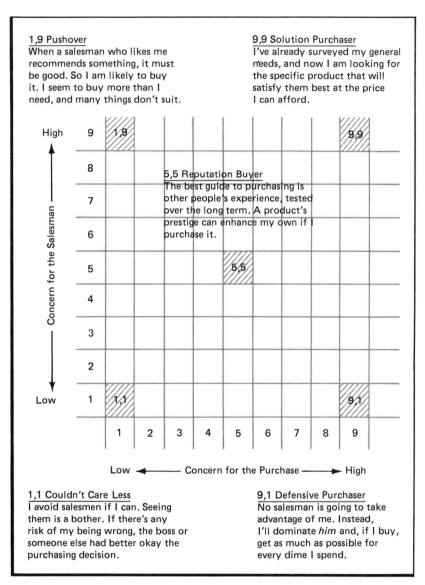

1,9 Pushover
When a salesman who likes me recommends something, it must be good. So I am likely to buy it. I seem to buy more than I need, and many things don't suit.

9,9 Solution Purchaser
I've already surveyed my general needs, and now I am looking for the specific product that will satisfy them best at the price I can afford.

5,5 Reputation Buyer
The best guide to purchasing is other people's experience, tested over the long term. A product's prestige can enhance my own if I purchase it.

1,1 Couldn't Care Less
I avoid salesmen if I can. Seeing them is a bother. If there's any risk of my being wrong, the boss or someone else had better okay the purchasing decision.

9,1 Defensive Purchaser
No salesman is going to take advantage of me. Instead, I'll dominate *him* and, if I buy, get as much as possible for every dime I spend.

Figure 7.2   The Customer Grid.® Concern for the salesperson appears on the vertical axis; concern for the purchaser, on the horizontal axis. (Source: Robert R. Blake and Jane Srygley Mouton, *The Grid for Sales Excellence*, New York: McGraw-Hill Publishing Co., copyright © 1970, p. 10. Reproduced by permission.)

> When Jones goes out into the back yard to call his dog, even the ani-
> mal does not respond. Poor Jones—nobody loves him! No one, that
> is, until an alert salesperson appears in his office. This vendor actually
> sits there and listens to Jones! For the first time in his life, someone
> appreciates him and gratifies his ego and esteem needs. He buys the
> salesperson's friendship with a purchase order.

Although it is an effective short-run strategy, taking advantage of
such a friendship-oriented personality entails a long-run risk. These
buyers seek approval from all their vendors, so they maintain these
"friendships" by dividing up what would be one substantial order into
many insignificant pieces of business, which are then distributed among
their courting salespeople. Under this arrangement, the 1,9 buyer reasons, everyone wins because no one is rejected. However, if a purchasing
agent actually buys more than is needed and many things that do not suit
from you, you may both have short careers.

The attitude of 1,1 buyers is that they couldn't care less, one way or
the other. These people buy in a perfunctory manner because they want
the products, but not the pressure. They seek the path of least resistance
with salespeople, while at the same time trying to keep out of trouble
with their bosses. Like the 1,1 salespeople, these buyers merely go
through the motions of their jobs. The 1,1 buyer is like a 500-pound
marshmallow. You can pound all you want on it, and all it does is give in.
It never moves.

In the middle of the grid are the customers who act out of 5,5 assumptions. Except in the most routine situations, these people are tenta-
tive and uncertain. They are not as weak as 1,1; they are challenged by
short-term tasks. They want to purchase something, but like the 9,1
buyers, they are afraid of being taken. As soon as one product or service
in a category starts to appeal to them, they worry that another might actually be better. Their purchasing decisions are likely to be based more
on the status of others who have bought than on the quality and suitabil-
ity of the product. The motivational power switch here is emulation, and
testimonials from other, admired buyers will help you. The company
name and reputation also are important to these buyers, who place their
confidence in the tried and true.

In the upper right corner of the grid are the 9,9 customers. Before
the sales interview, these ideal buyers know what they want in general, if
not in specific, terms. These rare, mature individuals respond favorably
to you when you consult with them in an open, problem-solving manner
on how your product or service fits their requirements. They are prepared to be sold on the basis of facts, data, logic, and reason. They have a
high concern for your welfare as well as for solving their own business
problems. Therefore, a genuine buyer-seller empathy can be developed
with these individuals over the long run.

PSYCHOLOGICAL PROFILING OF YOUR CUSTOMER

"As he thinketh in his heart, so is he." This Biblical proverb tells us that our own personalities are merely outward expressions of our attitudes toward life. The sum of our experience causes us to assume specific, predictable roles. The habits formed in early childhood tend to stay with us throughout our lives. Application of this sensitivity to the human condition shall enable you to make dramatic progress as a professional salesperson.

To use the role behavior concept in improving our sales skills and awareness, let us divide human personality characteristics into five groups.[5]

1. Avoiders/Abdicators. These individuals do not like conflict or trouble. They are indecisive and insecure, they rarely take chances, and they are afraid to fail. They bring their lunch to work in a brown paper bag and then close their door and worry. Avoiders/Abdicators require a lot of data and take the longest time (of the five types) to make a decision. Sometimes they will never make a decision. Avoiders/Abdicators when in charge, ponder; when in trouble, delegate; when in doubt, mumble. Then they refer the whole problem to a committee!

2. Affiliators/Pleasers. They need people. They are joiners, team players, followers, and compromisers. They are dependent and

are compelled to satisfy the people with whom they work. They take a relatively short time to make a decision, and that decision is usually based on personal chemistry. The quality of their decision making is only average. Their motto is: "If you can't say anything nice, don't say anything at all." They know everything that's going on in their company, industry, and boardroom. They are great sources for gossip and information.

3. Power Boss/Commander. Aggressive, intolerant, and insensitive leaders, these people must win in negotiation and will not share credit with anyone else. They make decisions quickly with little or no data. They want a predictable path, not a risky one. Their motto is: "Do things right, or not at all!" Quality of decisions is fair to poor.

4. Achiever/Craftsman. They are confident, analytical, independent, and task oriented. They are directed toward short-term goals and like to have a lot of information to help solve problems. They require data and statistics before making a decision. Quality of decision making is quite good, but the process can be quite

POWER BOSS/COMMANDER
9,1

lengthy. Their motto is: "We'll do the best possible job." They would also rather be right (based on statistics) than president.

5. Manipulator/Gamesman. These persuasive opportunists use other people in pursuit of long-range goals. As long-term strategists, they are perceptive and sensitive to people, but they tend to play corporate games. They also require a data base that often exceeds your own. Quality of decision making is superior, but the process varies in length depending on the needs and objectives of this decision making; Outstanding quality—flexibility (chameleon-like).

Each of us is made up of various proportions of each of these behavior types. You probably will see some of each personality in your own role behavior at different times. Most people, however, have one dominant style of role behavior. If you can understand your various customers' styles or personality roles, you can plan your sales strategy accordingly.

ACHIEVER/CRAFTSMAN
5,5

INTERCONNECTIONS: THE GRID, PSYCHOLOGICAL PROFILING OF CUSTOMERS, AND MASLOW NEEDS

By integrating some of the theories we have discussed, we can identify some important methods of handling each buyer type. An Affiliator/Pleaser may be a 1,9 buyer with needs for belonging and social activity. There is a need here for a lot of reassurance that the purchase will benefit the boss. This person may also be a 5,5 buyer, probably a brand buyer with esteem and status needs. You will need to show examples of other successful users. Testimonials are helpful. The key to your success with this personality type depends upon your ascertainment of whom he (or she) is trying to please within the company organization. Who is he affiliated with? Once you know this, you can show him how his boss (group, etc.) will benefit and/or be proud of him. This is his hot button.

The Avoider/Abdicator is a 1,1 buyer with strong safety and security needs. This buyer is very likely to hide behind furniture or be monosyllabic and have retiring body language. You can best handle this person by removing all threats, pressures, or confrontations, and focusing on minor points of your proposal. Use directive questions to obtain commitment. Although you will be obliged to invest a great deal of time and energy on this timid soul, once you have won him over (gained his confidence), he may become a most loyal client. Then he will use all of those evasive tactics on your competitors. *Profitability* is the key consideration here. Is it worth your time to pursue this business?

The Achiever/Craftsman is a 5,5 buyer who is turned on by a challenge and self-actualized by achievement. Because he tends to become

MANIPULATOR/GAMESMAN
9,9

SAY... LET'S MAKE A DEAL!!

CHAM-ELEON

lost in the data, you should use reflective and nondirective questions while providing a lot of statistical information. Offer short-range payoffs, and do your homework.

The Power Boss/Commander tends to be a 9,1 buyer. In this more complex role are mixed esteem and status needs and safety and security needs. This buyer is autocratic and does not require much information to make a decision. "Don't confuse me with facts; my mind is made up!" and "If I want your opinion, I'll *give* it to you!" are typical comments. Although basically insecure, he believes that a good offense is the best defense. He is a legend in his own mind and feels that everyone is entitled to *his* opinion. Be direct, provide options or alternate choices, and let this client decide. This aggressive personality type does not want to be reassured. Give away all the credit for the decision to him, even if the idea was yours. Let him win. Be brief and firm. Do not be afraid to stand up to this dominant individual, but be careful that you do it in private!

The Manipulator/Gamesman definitely is a 9,9 buyer with self-actualization needs that tend to be politically oriented. The higher you go up corporate ranks, the more likely you are to find this type, who will usually be the boss. You must show this game player results for his long-range objectives. Find out what his long-term strategy is, and then show him how he can use you to obtain these goals. This will be a "win-win" relationship for you both.

To build an empathy bond with your customer, you need an awareness of personality role behavior. (Details relating to the various personality theories and behavior clues are shown in Figures 7.3 and 7.4). Review the

Figure 7.3   Psychological customer profiling.

BEHAVIOR NEEDS

Physical Action Clues	Verbal Clues	Other Clues	Behavior Needs	PAC Profile	Motivation Psychology
Friendly but sometimes shy, avoiding eye contact	Fun-loving, uses words like cute, beautiful, wow! sad, funny, nice, fantastic, it's not your fault, poor you, super!	Sociable, cooperative	Affiliator/Pleaser	Usually natural child	A joiner desire for immediate material benefits, recognition and acceptance
		Fashionable	Social or need to belong	Frequently adaptive child or nurturing parent	
Quick to laugh, smile, cry, display temper or quivering lip	Discussions usually centered around material things and people	Craves recognition		Infrequently adult	
		Impulsive, changeable			
Feelings easily hurt		Extravagant			
		Joiner			
Enjoys physical contact		Concerned about people's opinions			
		People-oriented			
		Team player			
		Compromisers			
		Dependent			
		Followers			

	Conservative in speech	Does not take risks	Avoider/Abdicator	Usually critical parent	Fear of loss
Indecisive	Formal	Conservative in dress	Safety or security	Frequently adaptive child	Minimize risk
Conservative manner	Good manners	Displays little imagination in office decor		Infrequently natural child	A loner
Deliberate movements	Didactic	Desk, office neat, orderly		Infrequently natural child or adult	Committee member
Restrained posture	Frequently complains	Attitude: negative, pessimistic, inflexible, unsociable			
Lack of spontaneous, natural emotion	Quick to criticize	Takes very few risks			
Dislikes physical contact	Discussions usually centered around problems	Saves money in a bank			
Pointing index finger	Words like: always, never, impossible, can't, I told you so	Lives within his or her means			
Folded arms		Does not like change			
Stern glances		Low key, sensitive			
Uptight in difficult situations					
Limp handshake					

Figure 7.4   Psychological customer profiling: Behavior chart summary. People tend to have varying degrees of each of these behavioral styles, but most people have a predominant style which causes them to behave in a fairly predictable manner during a given situation or set of circumstances. An understanding of these behaviors can enhance your chances for success during each interaction.

Alert Interested Thoughtful expression Straight Confident	Asks how and why Asks adult questions Discusses goals and objectives Analytical	Positive Logical Open minded Slow to criticize Inspires confidence Loves data Task-oriented	Achiever/Craftsman Self-actualize	Usually adult Rarely critical parent	Problem solver A challenge Contribution to team
Cocksure Strong handshake Definitive gestures Moves rapidly Decisive Aggressive	Discussions usually centered around achievement, ability and adventure *When* is a commonly used word Leads discussion	Competitive Intolerant Forceful Insensitive Creative opinionated Compulsive Somewhat unsociable Takes risks Ego-oriented Likes sincere praise Does not share credit Sexist	Power Boss/Commander Self-esteem or ego	Frequently natural child Infrequently adaptive child or parent	Self-oriented desire for challenge, change, and the opportunity to prove oneself

Eyes alight	Discusses culture arts, society	Resourceful	Manipulator/ Gamesman	Natural or adaptive child	Game player
Interested	Long-range goals	Creative	Self-actualize	Also adult	Personal satisfaction
Continual body movements	Asks why	Takes calculated risks			Contribution to society
Relaxed	Persuasive	Perceptive			Maximum opportunity
		Charming personality			
		Strategist			
		Long-range goal-oriented			
		Sensitive to people			

Figure 7.4   (Continued)

parallel technique of selling (Chapter 6); it will help you comprehend the diverse needs of your buyer within the firm's organization setting. Prepare yourself well in advance for the all-important initial client contact. Remember: the best surprise in selling is *no* surprise. Do your personality role behavior homework first; it will pay off for you.

The *learning objective* of this section on psychological profiling of your customers is being able to distinguish the quick, intuitive decision makers from the crowd of prospects who require extremely detailed information and who consume an inordinate amount of your selling time. Since *profitability* is the key to long-range selling success, the ability to "read" people will help you to narrow the odds in your favor.

Notes

1. J. W. Thompson, *Selling: A Managerial and Behavioral Science Analysis,* 2nd ed. (New York: McGraw-Hill, 1973), p. 261.
2. Ibid., p. 266.
3. Ibid., p. 362.
4. Eric Berne, *Games People Play* (New York: Grove Press, 1967), p. 48.
5. This material has been developed from the following sources: Gerald D. Bell, *The Achievers* (Chapel Hill, N.C.: Preston-Hill, Inc., 1973); Michael Maccoby, *The Gamesman* (New York: Bantam Books, 1978); Robert Blake and Jane Srygley Mouton, *The Grid for Sales Excellence* (New York: McGraw-Hill, 1970); and Robert E. Toliver, president, Leadership Development, Inc., Glendora, California (unpublished Sales Training Workshop manuscript, 1977).

Chapter 8
Figuring Out the Buyer

We have studied several psychological theories of behavior that help us understand why buyers act as they do and say what they say. We must now take one more factor into account in our analysis of the customer, however. That is buyer fear.

BUYERS HAVE FEARS, TOO

You may feel that you have a world monopoly on fear on the day your sales manager sends you out for your first call. But buyers have their own sets of fears, and buyer fear is related to certain buyer behavior, depending upon personality type.

Avoiders/Abdicators

The most obviously fearful prospects you will encounter are Avoiders/Abdicators. Their behavior and communication is reticent and hesitant, and as we have seen, they protect themselves with physical obstacles as well. In a retail setting, they are the customers who mumble "just looking!" and turn their backs before you even open your mouth to greet them. Even professional avoider buyers—those who are paid by their companies to buy—will refuse to buy until actively encouraged to do so. Avoiders/Abdicators in this role particularly fear failure because of their large safety and security needs. They never will buy if not directly asked, or even told to do so. With this type of buyer, as we have seen, your most important effort should be directed toward removing fear by giving constant reassurance and direction. Many times they are relieved when you make up their minds for them. Some buyers abdicate all responsibility for making *any* decision.

Affiliators/Pleasers

Affiliators are caught between two fears. They are afraid you won't like them, which pushes them toward buying, but they also fear their bosses won't like them, which makes them hesitant to make mistakes. Their insecurity makes them shirk from angering anyone, so they must please everyone. Therefore, they cannot make choices. It is important to do your research ahead of time on these buyers; you should know where their strongest affiliation desires lie. Whom are they most anxious to please? Once you determine this, you take the first step toward empathy by showing them that you sincerely like them. Then, you go on to demonstrate how their chief affiliation target will approve of their making the decision that you want them to make.

Power Bosses/Commanders

During your first selling encounters with power bosses, they certainly may seem to have no fear at all. Indeed, you feel that you are the fearful one. The very aggressive stance of power bosses, however, is usually just an armor developed to cover a tremendous insecurity. These customers fear failure. This fear touches all the basic human needs, because these buyers are sure that if they give an inch, you will slaughter them on all levels. In a sense, they are paper tigers, no matter how real the roar sounds to both you and themselves. They believe that a good offense is the best defense and therefore are constantly trying to keep you off balance through intimidation. Learn to let them win. Manipulate them through their egos and you will find them to be the easiest to sell.

Achievers/Craftsmen and Manipulators/Gamesmen

These fairly well-adjusted types have fewer fears, and as a result they are much easier to work with. They are, of course, affected by the fear of not achieving their goals; the manipulator especially wants self-actualization, and a buying mistake could cause a setback on the path to the top. An interesting point about achievers is that they are easily bored when no new challenge presents itself. They fear and avoid boring and repetitive situations. You should be prepared to present them with new ideas and goals. Give the Achiever a challenge, and show the Gamesman how he can reach his long-term goals by manipulating you.

Customer Complaints

If you are on the receiving end of an angry harangue by a livid customer, it is hard to bear in mind that fear underlies this belligerence, but in fact it often does. First, there is the fear that you are not going to listen, care, or do anything about the problem. Then there is the fear of loss of money, prestige, stature, even company reputation, and a job. Bear in mind that a small error on your part can stop a production line in your client's factory, with its compounded costs and subproblems. That scream is less one of hatred than one of pain and fear. (We will cover more on this in later chapters.)

Decisions

Regardless of personality type, one fear seems common to us all. We all hesitate to make decisions. Most people would prefer to put off for tomorrow something that we should have done yesterday. This seems to be true no matter how small the decision: buying a birthday gift causes hesitation just as deciding to spend several million dollars to acquire another company. That is why closing is necessary. It is a method of overcoming a buyer's procrastination, which is simply the natural fear of making the wrong choice.

COPING BEHAVIOR

In handling buyer fear, the burden is once again on you. First, you must learn to recognize underlying fear: listen, observe, and ask tactful questions. Second, use the skill of empathy. Develop sensitivity and perception, and stand in the buyer's shoes. Finally, you must have flexibility of action. The same treatment is not going to work with every buyer, because fears and personalities differ. Do not reassure a power boss unless you want to get insulted by that individual. Power bosses/Commanders do not need or want reassurance even though they might be very uncertain underneath.

It is easy to talk about figuring out buyers, but their real configurations are not always obvious. You remember our disdainful friend, the shoe clerk who was above his work. His "too good" behavior is based on fear, but it takes an experienced and confident eye and ear to guess at his fear of commitment. Imagine yourself being waited on by this person. Would you see through him? It takes practice to do so.

Here is an example in which an astute salesperson sorted out a prospect's true feelings from his bluster.

> George, a rookie salesperson, was sent by his sales manager to try to recapture an old account with whom there had been a lot of trouble. George was scared; he knew his predecessor had been physically thrown out by the purchasing agent three years before, but his boss had only given him a one-way airplane ticket to the client's city.
>
> Sure enougn, Al, the purchasing agent, spent hours raking George over the coals, trying to humiliate and infuriate him by reiterating all the bad experiences he had had: late shipments, defective products, poor service, broken promises, and so on. Although most of these problems had occurred before George was born, Al seemed to hold him personally responsible for them. George was just about to explode and start shouting himself when he realized that Al's aggressiveness was part of a strategy to extract the best deal from him. After all, if Al really did not want to do business with George's company, he certainly would not waste several hours on this sales interview. There must be something in it for him beside a vocal exercise.
>
> Having perceived Al's game, George changed his own behavior. Al clearly had very high needs for esteem and recognition, coupled with strong fears. Taking a tone that would feed Al's ego while not making himself a doormat, George began to take notes, asking verifying questions to pin down facts and dates. Specifics were hard to come by, and Al saw that he could not intimidate George.
>
> In spite of his obnoxious behavior, Al was quite insecure. Off the job, he was a meek little man to whom no one listened at home. Thus he tried to compensate at work by dominating others. Some time later, after the two had become friends, Al confided to George that the initial interview had been ''a test to see what George was made of.'' George passed the test by listening, so Al liked him.

This self-restraint is sometimes called *tension binding,* or the ability to inhibit a motor act (punching Al in the nose) and then making the appropriate adjustments (listening, asking questions, etc.). Remember, the burden of this coping behavior is always on the salesperson. That is what commission checks are made of!

Not all aggressive behavior is of the same type. In the following example, the salesperson finds herself dealing not with a power boss like Al, but with a manipulator.

> Marianne, a management consultant, took Peter, the executive director of a large educational institution, out for an expensive lunch—and was confronted with this monologue:
> ''When I first took office four years ago, I cleaned house—including

that meathead who recommended you to me. I brought in my own gang. They all have worked with me over the years and have a proven record of success. When I delegate work to them, I know it will be well done. I know what they can do, and they're exceptionally good. Now why should I even listen to you, young lady?''

Marianne, perceiving an opening, responded, ''Let me ask you one question, sir. How did these professional associates of yours get started with you in the first place?''

Peter smiled. ''In other words, how can *you* get started with me?''

''That's right,'' she said, ''all I want is a chance. Apparently you gave them a chance years ago, and they proved themselves. I also would like that opportunity. Now, which of my programs would be most appropriate for your organization?''

It turned out that Peter was dissatisfied with the recent performance of several of his outside resource people. He actually was searching for the very services Marianne offered, but he wanted to test her mettle.

It is clear from the experiences of George and Marianne that you will not be able to apply a formula to your buyer and come up with a pat description of that individual's personality every time. You will need to think on your feet, applying the principles of psychology but also using that sixth sense that you will develop as you gain experience. No book ever published could give you these "street smarts." Selling is the operant behavior. You only learn it by doing it.

Part III
SELL LIKE A PROFESSIONAL

Chapter 9
Prospecting and
Sales Call Planning

Will the world beat a path to your door if you build a better mousetrap today? No. In our modern economy this old proverb no longer holds true. That maxim was coined years ago by Ralph Waldo Emerson when our country's industrial development was in its infancy. Quality manufactured goods were at a premium and plenty of buying power existed to absorb a good product. The real problem was in supplying the demand.

Now, however, the supply of excellent goods and services has proliferated to the point that most manufacturers must advertise heavily to *create* a demand for their products. Goods and services must now beat a path to the buyer's door in the form of the professional salesperson who establishes those goods and services high on the buyer's priority list.

ADVANCE RESEARCH AND PREPARATION

Before you set out on this mission, you had better know your destination, your prospective customer, and your presentation. Advance research and preparation are the foundation on which your sale is built. You will not be successful without them. Eighty percent of your efforts will be in the prospecting and preapproach phases of selling. The preparation you do in these phases will pay handsome dividends later when you meet your prospects on a face-to-face basis.

Some of the research is done by your company for you. Some you do yourself. Your firm should study the market; you study your product and your individual customer's needs. This will enable you to separate the prospects from the mere suspects.

Market Research

In Chapter 2 we looked at the structure of the marketing department of a typical firm. One function within marketing is market research. Next to advertising and sales promotion, market research is a salesperson's best business ally. It describes and measures a particular target market or territory, locating prospects who are similar in age, sex, income, ethnic origin, life-style, and so on. It thus generally defines a group of people who might need your product. Identifiable customers are people who have a need that you can fill and they can pay for. These people must have the authority to make or influence buying decisions and be able to receive satisfaction from your product, or they are not really prospects.

Your company's market research should make certain that you are contacting the right people at the right time with the right product or service. It is demoralizing to a sales representative to try to sell to someone who has no need for or interest in the product or service presented. Faulty market research is to blame here.

In addition to locating market segments with the most sales potential, market research analyzes consumer needs and buying behavior. Differences in demographic and economic factors alone do not satisfactorily explain some significant variations in personal behavior. Consumer purchases also are influenced by psychological and social factors. We examine these customer motives and attitudes in Chapter 6. Today, large amounts of statistical data can be compiled quickly by computer to give us a composite profile of our customer. Armed with this valuable information, we are in a good position to understand our customers' needs and help them solve their problems.

Know Your Product or Service

Your company should make sure that it is handing you the right product and aiming you in the right direction, and it can supply you with all sorts of specifications and information, but it cannot make you an expert salesperson. You must take the responsibility of learning as much as you can about your product or service and how to apply this knowledge. Your company can lead you to water, but it can't make you drink.

Be sure that you know all about not only your own product, but also those of your competitors. Read the trade periodicals in your field. Manufacturer and trade association publications, sales magazines, federal and state government publications, and your own suppliers' representatives are all good sources of information. Seminars and workshops can be extremely informative and useful. Talk with more experienced salespeople. Do not overlook the public library; excellent books may be available about various product lines.

You do not always have to set aside blocks of time specifically for this research. Simply be alert for and open to new information wherever you may find it. This process of learning is continuous; there is never a time when you know everything and can sit back and relax. New products, new uses, and new applications constantly appear. It is your job to keep abreast of the latest news to benefit both your company and your customer.

This expertise that you constantly polish contributes greatly to your source credibility. As you remember from Chapter 3, source credibility is your ability to inspire faith, trust, and confidence in the prospective customer. You can be as honest, presentable, and reliable as the best of your competitors, but if you have weak product or industry knowledge, your source credibility will suffer, and so will your sales. You can no more sell a product that you don't know than you can lead people to a place where you have never been. Therefore, you should own and use the products you sell whenever possible.

Know Your Customer's Position

Knowing your own product, important as that is, still is not enough to make you a professional. Up to now, we have discussed empathy mostly in terms of the customer's personal needs and motivations. Let us add some concrete factors to our concept of empathy.

YOUR CUSTOMER'S CUSTOMERS

To know your customer's needs, you must know your customer's product, service, and marketplace. What are the problems of your customer's customers? If your client does not need what you are selling, you cannot give it away. You must study the business to know the prospect's needs.

> David represented a firm that supplied packaging materials to cereal manufacturers. Although he knew all there was to know about his product and his company's abilities and capacities, David was a busy man who felt that he did not have time to keep up with general news and trends outside his own immediate work.

Thus David was completely surprised when Christine, a major food processor's buyer with whom he had dealt successfully for years, switched to another packaging supplier. Being a conscientious person, David called Christine to find out what had happened. Had he misrepresented his product? Had he ever failed to deliver what was promised? Had another firm offered a lower price?

Christine seemed embarrassed. "It's none of those things, Dave," she finally said. "It's just that you've gotten a little out of touch with what our customers are looking for. You know, they want everything to be 'natural' now—and your designers are just not offering us a look that will attract them."

Understanding your customer's marketplace is, of course, most important in industrial sales and at wholesale, but there is a parallel concept in consumer sales. It is not enough to understand only the person to whom you are selling the car, dress, or backpack; you must be able to picture your customer's own surroundings. Who are the people who will be judging and commenting on the newly purchased item? Because we are all selling ourselves and our ideas all the time, your customer is going to have to turn around and sell the decision to purchase your product to people around him or her. Most people seek approval of their peers when making a new purchase, unless they happen to be the decision maker of their particular peer group. Is your product or service going to look right in your customer's own setting? Will the members of the customer's reference group see it as part of their normal life-style? You may feel that your taste or knowledge is better than your customer's, but if you sell that better product to the wrong person, you may end up with a quick return and a lost customer.

Betty, a wealthy woman whose friends had always admired her excellent taste, went to work in an exclusive dress shop to keep busy after all her children had left home. She felt that she had much to offer her customers; after all, she could educate them as well as sell them dresses.

One day, soon after Betty started to work, a very large and flamboyantly dressed and made-up woman came in, saying that she needed a party dress for a big affair, and money was no object, but the dress had to be classy. Betty, overcoming her horror at this gaudy apparition, set about showing the woman elegant dresses in subdued colors with flattering up-and-down lines that would minimize her figure problems, while trying tactfully to explain to her that simplicity and understatement are the foundations of true elegance.

The patron became more and more impatient and finally turned to Betty and said, "But honey, you don't understand! Why, my husband would kill me if I spent 500 dollars and came home with some little gray rag that won't show up in a crowd!"

DEVELOPING YOUR SALES PRESENTATION

In order to succeed in selling, you must convince your prospective customers that it is in their best interest to use your product or service, rather than a competitor's. Therefore, you should develop a sales presentation which is effective in terms of their needs and perceptions. You will begin by taking a deep and sincere interest in your customers' business and the business of *their* customers.

If you are selling subfractional horse power motors to Original Equipment Manufacturers (O.E.M.'s) like digital clock makers or washing machine producers, you should know how your component part fits into their subassembly and why their clients buy these end products from them. What benefits do *their* customers derive from purchasing those clocks or washing machines? What advantages do your O.E.M. customers have in this marketplace because they use your particular brand of motor? Are there fewer breakdowns or cycle failures, and so forth? What problems confront them that you could help them solve, and are there any special product applications that would enhance their product position?

In other words, if you know why *their* customers buy from *your* customers, you can enable your customers to sell more of their products (which contain your products), solve more of their clients' problems, and thereby enhance your overall relationship with your clientele. This is called *consultative selling* and is axiomatic to long-term mutually beneficial client-vendor relationships.

This concept is related to the purchasing pyramid and the parallel technique of selling, which we discussed in Chapters 5 and 6. Now, how can you move from a thorough knowledge of your product or service to the presentation of end-result benefits to your customers? Figure 9.1 shows a chart that you can use to structure your sales talk or presentation to address those needs in a motivational manner. There are five steps in building a persuasive presentation that will identify what our products offer in terms of specific customer benefits.

Starting with the left-hand column, we fill in the features we have learned about our product. *Features* are a special aspect of your product or service that indicates what it is. Your firm's advertising literature, sales brochures, and specification sheets give these tangible properties, attributes, or functions. In this example we shall use a 50 cubic foot, stainless-steel commercial refrigerator.

Moving to the next column, we list the advantages that our refrigerator has as a result of each feature. *Advantages* are the differential between what your customer now has and what your competition is offering. It describes the purpose or function of a unique product feature. Since our patented design handle cannot be made by our customer or a

Features	Advantages	Benefits Gained or Losses To Be Avoided	Your Customer	Buying Motives
50 ft commercial refrigerator			Standard Industrial Classification System (S.I.C.)	
Stainless steel				
Six legs with casters			Industry customer groupings	
Four doors			Client classifications:	
Made in U.S.A.			1. Restaurant equipment dealers	Profit Utility Fear of loss
Fiberglass insulation				
Patented design artistic handle	Exclusive handle design	Ease of use Ease of cleaning Nonbreakable Lower maintenance cost Few accidents Aesthetic beauty Fewer breakdowns Cheerful kitchen environment	2. Restaurant operators	Utility, pride, and/or emulation Fear of loss
			3. Food service consultants	Utility Pride
			4. Specifying architects	Pride Utility

Figure 9.1 Developing your presentation—converting features to benefits.

competitor, it is truly an advantage that we have in the marketplace which no one else can offer. If *features* describe the product itself, *advantages* describe what the features do and why they are there. Can you summarize the advantages of your product to your prospects in one short, simple, crystal-clear, convincing sentence?

In the third column, we translate these advantages into buyer benefits to be gained or losses to be avoided. *Benefits* are what your client will receive from the *advantages*. This is the "payoff" to your customer as it answers the critical question: "What's in it for me?" Some of the benefits to be derived from our specially designed and patented handle are:

1. ease of cleaning *which means* lower maintenance costs
2. nonbreakable *which means* few breakdowns
3. ease of use *which means* efficiency of operation
4. esthetic beauty *which means* cheerful kitchen environment

It is obvious that a single feature frequently has a single advantage but *numerous* benefits. Now you are, in effect, talking your customers' language and relating to their needs, problems, and perceptions. *This translation of your product's features to buyer benefits is the key to successful selling and the crucial link that many salespersons fail to make.*

Furthermore, you do not necessarily give your prospects sufficient reason to buy merely by demonstrating *benefits.* You must be able to explain what your clients get out of each benefit and why they should buy from you *now.* If they respond "So what?" you have failed to make the connecting link between features, and advantages, and their own urgent *needs.* In the preparation of your presentation you can bridge this potential gap by responding to that indifferent "So what?" question with a statement that contains the words *"which means...."*

For example, the patent design handle *means* that no one else offers it. This advantage assures *ease of operation which means* reduced maintenance costs, fewer accidents, and a most pleasing visual appearance. If you cannot answer the "So what?" question, you do not have a tangible customer benefit. A benefit is not meaningful unless it is related to an actual feature, advantage, or client need.

Moving to the fourth column, we identify classifications of prospects (or individual clients) who might want the benefits we are offering. Ask yourself which specific customer will receive the greatest payoff from each benefit shown. In our example we have listed restaurant operators, restaurant equipment dealers, food service consultants, and specifying architects. You can take this analysis one step further by using specific restaurant equipment dealer names such as Edward Don & Company, or Hammond Restaurant Supply, or using Standard Industrial Classification System (S.I.C.) categories by industry.

Finally in the fifth column, we would list those specific buying motives that would "turn on" or excite individual customers whom you had listed in column 4. Here you would indicate the buying motives that would be used to appeal to basic needs in order to trigger buying action. Since there are "different strokes for different folks," this "hot button" column can be used to direct the most meaningful appeals to your various customers' diverse needs structures. In the case of our restaurant equipment dealers, they would benefit most from the *profit* and *utility* values of our refrigerator while restaurant operators might also be motivated by the *pride* of owning such a magnificent piece of modern equipment or of buying one, because a competitor already has a similar unit (emulation). Both may buy through *fear* of food spoilage, which results in patronage loss and poor profitability. Food service consultants and architects may specify our brand of refrigerator for a new hospital wing or industrial volume feeding facility (such as a new cafeteria or satellite kitchen) because they take *pride* in recommending only the best American made products with new innovations (door handle design), or merely because our product fills the essential need for cold storage space.

Thus by fully comprehending your customers' business, you will be better able to individualize your sales presentation to meet their specific needs. The exclusive features of your company's product or service give you a terrific advantage over your competition. These advantages make it easy for you to demonstrate to your clients how your product or service can help them to gain an end benefit or avoid a loss in terms of *their* marketing situation. In this consultative capacity, you will enable them to improve their profit position and embed your products and services into their long-range business plans. That is the bottom line in consultative selling and your objective in developing an effective sales presentation.

ANALYZING YOUR TERRITORY

Let's pretend that you have just landed your first sales job with a manufacturer of food service equipment. After several weeks' training at the East Coast factory, you are loaded up with catalogs and door samples and shipped off to the Midwest, your territory. Arriving in Chicago, Illinois, you discover that your sales manager, who hired you, has had a fight with the company owner and suddenly quit.

What do you do? There is no one to whom you may turn for guidance and support, and the home office is a thousand miles away. You are on your own with your materials and an obsolete list of accounts. You are on straight commission, so you had better find some prospects before your bills start to pile up.

Customer Identification

Who are those prospective accounts, where are they located, and what is the best way to approach them? Three planning steps will prepare you to go out and start selling.

COMPILE A LIST OF POSSIBLE PROSPECTS

From telephone books, trade association listings, and other specialized sources, you can begin to develop a prospect list. Your own company records of present and past customers are the best starting place. Why not solicit someone who already has bought your product, has passed your company's credit criteria, and knows your policies and procedures? It is easier, faster, and less expensive than chasing after elusive new business, although you will do that also.

ESTABLISH CRITERIA FOR QUALIFYING PROSPECTS

For each possible prospect, check out the type of business, its size, and its financial condition. The Yellow Pages of the telephone directory are an excellent source for consumer products; the *Thomas Register* will give you appropriate information on industrial concerns. Dun & Bradstreet, industry and other association reports, and local credit bureaus can supply credit information if you have access to them. Many times, just looking over your prospect's home or place of business will help you to include or exclude a name on your list.

PREPARE AN OPENING STATEMENT

Think ahead about what you are going to say in order to identify yourself and your firm, arouse interest, and establish rapport while you are going around to look over your prospects.

What One Rookie Did

One young man who found himself in exactly the stranded situation we have described got out and got going as follows. First he developed a prospect list from a computer printout of his company's accounts over the past five years. Then he checked the Yellow Pages for each town in his territory for listings under these categories:

restaurant equipment dealers
food service consultants
restaurant manufacturers and fabricators
specifying architects
restaurant owners
food service equipment dealers
commercial refrigeration service companies

In the *Thomas Register* and various government and education directories, he looked for large organizations where mass feeding would occur, most of which would have cafeterias, and found the following:

large companies by geographic area
colleges, universities
state hospitals
other government institutions

He also checked with trade associations and local chambers of commerce and used information from other salespeople, *F. W. Dodge Reports,* and other new construction reports, and current business publications.

Having completed his list and coded each entry as to its source, he made a 3-by-5-inch card for each prospect. He then sorted the cards according to state, city, and neighborhood within large cities.

Finally, in one area at a time, he took his promotional materials and walked up and down streets knocking on doors. At each place he met the prospect personally, introduced himself, dropped off a catalog, and went on to the next call. Soon he had covered the territory and separated the prospects from the suspects at the cost of a little time, a few catalogs, and a lot of shoe leather.

Obviously, he knocked on many wrong doors. Some of the printout addresses turned out to be vacant or incorrect. Sometimes he stumbled into competitors' offices and found salespeople within when they should have been out on calls. He was not surprised later when some lost their lines; he quickly learned that you cannot hustle business while cooling your heels in your own office.

Without realizing it, our rookie did all the right things and added some more significant research; he

sized up the territory
developed a prospect list
determined the competition
established himself as a "go-getter" by covering the territory quickly
did a preliminary credit screening by looking over the prospects
classified his accounts geographically
distributed product literature, which soon generated inquiries

Ranking Customers

Which of your customers are the most profitable to you? To find out, let us extend our young friend's work a bit. Classify your accounts on two sets of cards: present accounts and prospective accounts. Within these categories, classify group accounts by annual volume (or potential volume). If your company can supply computerized figures on account profitability, so much the better. These volume and profitability figures will help you allocate your time. Since the average cost of a sales call is around 100 dollars, you can see that it is extremely important that you spend your time with the right accounts.

To find out who those right accounts are, Porter Henry[1] uses a three-category system. He states that if you rank your customers by either volume, profits, or units sold, you will find that the top 15 percent of your accounts give you 65 percent of your business. These are called class A accounts. The next 20 percent are class B accounts; they give you about 20 percent of your business. Finally, the remaining 65 percent, the C customers, give you only 15 percent of your business. Figure 9.2 shows examples of this breakdown.

Time Management

Studies of how salespeople spend their time have had varying results, but it appears that no more than 30 percent of the average salesperson's time is spent in pure selling activity (see Figure 9.3). The rest is eaten up in research, company paperwork, order expediting, and travel and waiting. Thus you really do not have as much time as you might think to call on your customers. You must make sure to allocate your time in the most profitable way.

First, how much time should you spend with your active regular customers and how much on beating the bushes for new ones? A good rule of thumb is 75 percent of your time for your current clients and 25 percent for the prospective ones. You should be leaving some time in your daily schedule for cold calls and prospecting.

Within the three quarters of your time that you will spend on regular customers, you will have a natural tendency to allot equal time to each customer. It can, however, cost you money to spend too big a proportion of your time with the little guys. Figure 9.4 shows how the numbers work out if you call on your regular customers with equal frequency. The figure assumes that you have 200 customers and arranges them into the A (top 15 percent), B (next 20 percent), and C (last 65 percent) categories we have described. Using these same percentages on the total number of calls you can make in a year (1000 is an easy round number) gives you the annual number of calls in the customer category (column 3). Where did the sales volume figures in column 4 come from? Remember that the top 15 percent class A accounts give you 65 percent of your business, 65 percent of an assumed $5,000,000 total is $325,000, and so on. Finally, you can divide column 4 figures by column figures to get sales volume per call (column 5). Look at what those little accounts are

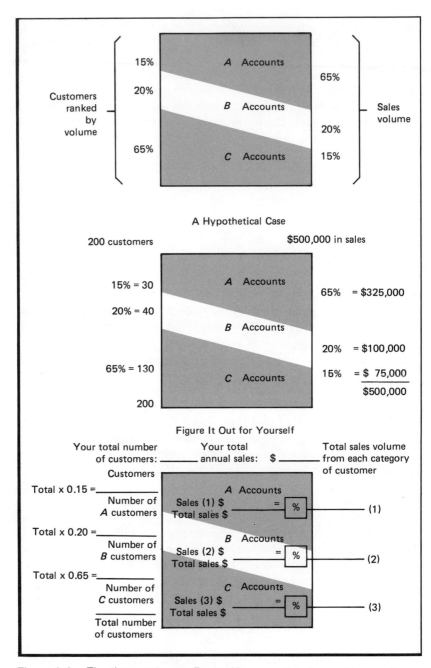

Figure 9.2   The three-category Porter Henry system for ranking customers. (Source: Porter Henry, "The Important Few—The Unimportant Many," *Sales & Marketing Management,* May 24, 1976. Reprinted by permission.)

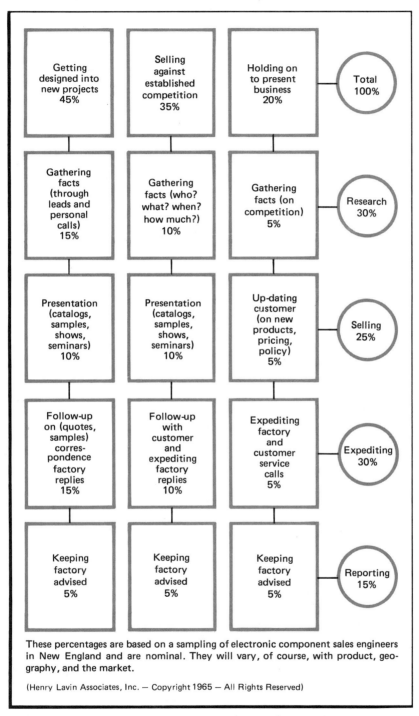

Getting designed into new projects 45%	Selling against established competition 35%	Holding on to present business 20%	Total 100%
Gathering facts (through leads and personal calls) 15%	Gathering facts (who? what? when? how much?) 10%	Gathering facts (on competition) 5%	Research 30%
Presentation (catalogs, samples, shows, seminars) 10%	Presentation (catalogs, samples, shows, seminars) 10%	Up-dating customer (on new products, pricing, policy) 5%	Selling 25%
Follow-up on (quotes, samples) correspondence factory replies 15%	Follow-up with customer and expediting factory replies 10%	Expediting factory and customer service calls 5%	Expediting 30%
Keeping factory advised 5%	Keeping factory advised 5%	Keeping factory advised 5%	Reporting 15%

These percentages are based on a sampling of electronic component sales engineers in New England and are nominal. They will vary, of course, with product, geography, and the market.

Figure 9.3   How does a sales engineer spend sales time? (Reprinted by permission of Henry Lavin Associates, Inc., Marketing Consultants.)

Here's what happens if our hypothetical salesman calls on all customers with equal frequency:

1 Customer Type	2 Number of Customers	3 Number of Calls	4 Sales Volume	5 Sales Volume per Call
A	30	150	$325,000	$2,167
B	40	200	$100,000	$500
C	130	650	$75,000	$115
Total	200	1,000	$500,000	X

Figure It Out for Yourself

$$\frac{\text{Average customer calls per day (not service, prospecting, etc.)}}{} \times 200 = \frac{\text{Total calls per year}}{}$$

1 Customer Type	2 Number of Customers	3 Number of Calls	4 Sales Volume	5 Sales Volume per Call
A		Total calls X.15		
B		Total calls X.20		
C		Total calls X.65		
Total				X

Figure 9.4   Spending too much time with small customers can cost you money. (Source: Porter Henry, "The Important Few—The Unimportant Many," *Sales & Marketing Management,* May 24, 1976. Reprinted by permission.)

doing to you! Given that your sales call costs your company approximately $100, how much time can you afford to spend on $115 calls?

You can easily make up the same chart based on your own particular territory. Porter Henry suggests that you call on class A accounts once a week, B accounts once a month, and C accounts every six months or once a year. Your own decision will vary according to your type of business, but in any case you should concentrate on the larger accounts.

In planning your sales objectives, ask yourself these questions:

Are there any more potential A accounts in my territory?
How many C accounts could I drop without decreasing sales?
Can I cover more of my C accounts on the telephone or by direct
    mail?
What additional A or B accounts could I win over from the compe-
    tition through more calls?

If you are a retail salesperson, obviously you do not go out and call on clients and you cannot ignore anyone who comes into your selling area or play obvious favorites when two customers are present. You should, however, always be developing your own customer list and staying in personal touch with these regular customers. There is no reason why you cannot apply Henry's A, B, and C classification to them and plan your customer contact efforts accordingly.

Are You Breaking Even?

If you are in a business in which you have access to certain figures or your sales manager can supply them, you can figure out what your time is worth and how well you are doing for yourself and your company.

There are two ways to value an hour of your time, according to Dr. Robert L. Vizza.[2] It may be done on a cost basis or on a break-even basis.

DIRECT COST ANALYSIS

Direct costs are those specifically generated by an individual salesperson; if your company did not have you, it would not have these costs. Did you know that, considering commissions and expenses, your company pays approximately twice your annual salary to keep you out there selling? Your sales manager certainly knows, and your results must justify your total cost to your firm. You are a profit center, whether you realize it or not.

Suppose your salary is $15,000 and your total annual cost to your company is $30,000. If you worked 2000 hours (8 hours/day x 250 days/year), your cost per hour would be $30,000/2000 = $15. If you work 250 days a year, 8 hours a day, but only 30 percent of these hours are actually spent selling, your total annual selling hours are 0.30 × 2000 hours = 600 hours. What do you cost your company for each *call* hour? To find out, divide total annual cost ($30,000) by total annual call hours (600) to get a cost per call hour of $50. In that hour, you must generate enough sales to cover your own cost and return a profit. Cost and sales volume are related by the second method of valuing your time, the break-even analysis.

BREAK-EVEN SALES VOLUME CALCULATION

Suppose your company has annual sales of $1,000,000 and manufacturing costs of $800,000. The $200,000 difference left over after the manufacturing costs are paid out is called the *gross margin*, and it has to cover all the costs of fielding all the company's salespeople. In this case, the *gross margin percentage* is $200,000/1,000,000 = 20 percent.

What sales volume must you yourself generate so that your company breaks even on the cost of supporting you? This *break-even volume* is determined by a formula:

$$\text{break-even volume} = \frac{\text{direct costs}}{\text{gross percentage margin}}$$

In this case,

$$\text{break-even volume} = \frac{\$30,000}{0.20} = \$150,000$$

You must have sales of $150,000 per year to justify your continued support. Below $150,000, the company loses money on you. The gross margin on sales above $150,000 contributes to profit.

Doing this analysis using your own real figures will tell you how well you are doing for yourself and your company.

We can go further and calculate the volume you must generate per hour you work to break even. Taking the figure of $15 as your cost per hour, we use a formula:

$$\frac{\text{break-even volume}}{\text{hour}} = \frac{\text{cost per hour}}{\text{gross margin percentage}} = \frac{\$15}{0.20} = \$75$$

You must generate $75 for each hour you work (not just for each *call* hour) to break even.

RETURN ON TIME INVESTED (ROTI)

What do you get from the time you spend on a given account? Return on time invested (ROTI) is a good measure for comparison of accounts. It is a simple ratio:

$$\text{ROTI} = \frac{\text{gross margin}}{\text{direct cost (of time invested)}}$$

For example, if your total sales for the year are $300,000 and manufacturing costs are $240,000, your gross margin is $60,000. The annual cost of your time is $30,000, so

$$\mathrm{ROTI} = \frac{\$60,000}{30,000} = 2$$

A ROTI above 1 is profitable; a ROTI below 1 represents a loss.

You can figure a separate ROTI for each account and compare them. An account with a ROTI of 4 obviously merits more attention than one with a ROTI of 2. You can use ROTI as a guide in forming your sales call plan. Even if your company does not supply the numbers you need to do this calculation, your sales manager may be able to tell you your ROTI scores.

Your Sales Call Plan

Your weekly sales call plan is an action program usually generated by your supervisor, but if you can do it yourself, it will motivate you toward higher achievement.

HOW MANY CALLS?

The plan sets targets for total sales calls and breaks them down by purpose, such as sale, demonstration, and so on. It projects numbers of calls on A-, B-, and C-ranked customers. As you complete the week's work, you enter on the plan the actual totals you have achieved. This method immediately tells you how you are measuring up to your goals. An example is shown in Figure 9.5.

How can you set these targets? To do so, you need to know how many selling days are really available to you. Starting with 365 days in a year and subtracting weekends, holidays, vacations, required sales meetings, office time, and illness, you end up with something like 171 sales days, or less than half. Suppose you drive 30,000 miles per year on business. Subtracting the approximately 83 days you spend driving, you end up with only 88 net sales days. (Other travel figures are given in Figure 9.6.)

How many calls can you make in these 88 days? If you work 9 hours a day, you have $88 \times 9 = 792$ hours; and if a call takes 2 hours, you then can make 396 calls per year, or about 8 per week. (Other possible figures are shown in Figure 9.7.) Now you can decide where to go and whom to see on those eight calls.

THE MOST EFFICIENT ROUTE

Geography now becomes a factor in your planning. You must reach every account in your territory, but the frequency, purpose, and time spent should vary according to their present and potential sales volumes. Start by determining which geographic areas you can cover in a given time period. Parcel these areas like plats on a real estate developer's

Sales Call Plan Week no.: ____________

Salesman: ____________ Planned days: ________ Week ending: ____________

Terr: ____________ Actual days: ________

Total planned calls

Sales calls ____________

Demonstrations ____________

Customer coverage planned

"A" customer calls ____________

"B" customer calls ____________

"C" customer calls ____________

Total completed calls

Call purpose:

Sales calls ____________

Demonstrations ____________

Application ____________

Commercial ____________

"A" completions ____________

"B" completions ____________

"C" completions ____________

Business miles

Calls (company name)	Customer rating	Location (City & State)	Call Purpose
	ABC		SDAC

Figure 9.5 A sample sales call plan. (Source: Charles E. Bergman, "All Out for Productivity," *Sales & Marketing Management,* March 14, 1977. Reprinted by permission.)

map. Some segments represent overnight trips; others, a week or even more out of town.

Begin your trip or "swing" through your territory with the farthest point and work back toward home. In this way you place the most strenuous portion of the trip first, at the time when you are rested, and you will not have to push a long way home when you are tired at the end of the trip. Leave a day early at the beginning, if necessary; it is better to arrive early and get a good night's sleep beforehand than to arrive late and haggard.

CONVERTING RESOURCES TO PERFORMANCE		
Resource-Oriented Operations	vs.	Performance-Oriented Operations
Sales potential		Product/market quotas
Sales territory		Travel time
Customers and prospects		Sales calls and orders
Sales expenses		Cost targets
Promotion materials		Presentations, demos

ANNUAL TOTAL SALES DAYS

Total days	365
Less: Sat. and Sun.	104
Holidays	10
Vacation	15
Total work days	236
Less: Sales mtgs., etc.	10
Reqd. office time	49
Illness	6
Total sales days	171

BUSINESS TRAVEL vs. NET SALES DAYS
Based on 40 mph avg.

Business Travel mi./yr. (OOO)	Total Sales Days	Less Travel Days	Net Sales Days
10	171	28	143
20	171	56	115
30	171	83	88
40	171	110	59
50	171	138	31

Figure 9.6   Calculation of net available sales days. (Source: Charles E. Bergman, "All Out for Productivity," *Sales & Marketing Management*, March 14, 1977. Reprinted by permission.)

NET SALES DAYS AND SALES ACTION CAPACITY Based on business travel				
Business Travel mi./yr. (000)	*Net Sales Days*	*Sales Action Capacity (Calls)*		
		2-hr. avg.	*3-hr. avg.*	*4-hr. avg.*
10	143	644	429	322
20	115	518	345	259
30	88	369	264	198
40	59	266	177	133
50	31	140	93	70

Figure 9.7   Calculation of available sales calls. (Source: Charles E. Bergman, "All Out for Productivity," *Sales & Marketing Management,* March 14, 1977. Reprinted by permission.)

Let your customers know by postcard or telephone that you are coming, and make all local transportation and hotel arrangements. Call ahead for weather reports. Plan ahead, and don't keep your plans secret. Call your home office daily to keep communication clear among it, yourself, and your clients.

Efficient route planning, always important, is becoming even more so as the cost and even the availability of fuel become larger and larger factors in the travel equation. Gasoline shortages are making random drop-in sales calls a thing of the past, which is as it should be.

TAKE TIME TO THINK

A professional salesperson should not need the prodding of a sales manager to analyze and evaluate territory records and client experience as an aid to improving performance. Salespeople who voluntarily do this work are demonstrating sales management potential, as paperwork of this sort is an important part of the job. You must learn to manage yourself and your territory first before you can ever hope to manage others.

Keeping records is sometimes onerous; your own attitude toward yourself and the work must be positive. Frank Bettger provides some suggestions.

One of the greatest satisfactions in life comes from getting things done and knowing you have done them to the best of your ability. If you are having trouble getting yourself organized, if you want to increase your ability to think, and do things in the order of their importance, remem-

If selling isn't a procedure, it shall always be a problem. One of the keys to successful selling is the management of time. The "golden hours" of selling dissipate quickly if you are not aware of the following notorious time traps:

1. The unplanned day
2. The unqualified prospect
3. The haphazard travel schedule
4. The unused telephone
5. The long lunch hour
6. The lunch-time cocktail
7. Inefficiency in paper work
8. The short day
9. The Friday afternoon syndrome
10. Bullshooting

You can avoid these time traps by keeping your sales objective constantly in mind. Ask yourself this question:

"IS WHAT I AM DOING RIGHT NOW CONTRIBUTING DIRECTLY TO MY REACHING THOSE OBJECTIVES? IF NOT, WHY AM I DOING IT?"

Treat your time as the precious, irreplaceable asset that it is, and you will soon find it working for you; not against you. It's time to get tough with yourself.

Figure 9.8   Notorious time management traps. (Source: Edwin C. Bliss, "Why It's Always Later Than You Think," *Sales & Marketing Management,* December 12, 1977. Reprinted by permission.)

ber there is only one way: *take more time to think* and do things in the order of their importance. Set aside one day as self-organization day, or a definite period each week. The whole secret of freedom from anxiety over not having enough time lies not in working more hours, but in the *proper planning* of hours.[3]

In other words, you should *work smarter, not harder.* Try to avoid the notorious time management traps (see Figure 9.8).

Notes

1. Porter Henry, "The Important Few—the Unimportant Many," *Sales & Marketing Management,* May 24, 1976, pp. 43–50.
2. Robert L. Vizza, "Time and Territory Management," *Sales & Marketing Management,* May 24, 1976.

Chapter 10
More About Prospecting

You are an insurance representative in need of business. Somewhere out there in your territory is an underinsured male in his mid-forties with a possible heart condition and a family of youngsters. One Monday morning he suddenly awakens with a start, chokes down his breakfast, jumps into his car, and struggles with the freeway traffic so that he can get to your downtown office. After ransoming his car in a local parking lot, he pounds on your door and begs you to sell him a life insurance policy. Is this a typical sales scenario? Of course not!

If you are lucky enough to locate this desperate prospect, he will probably hesitate and give you a dozen reasons why he should *not* buy that needed insurance policy now. Since he won't come to you and ask you to sell, you have a two-step selling procedure on your hands. First you must *locate* this hot prospect, and then you must *sell* him.

THE NUMBERS GAME

As previously stated, your first step is to develop a prospect list. You would then try to reach this potential customer by using a qualified lead source such as new telephone listings and new home owners. Many of these lists can be purchased on the open market. Once you begin dialing these telephone numbers, you are participating in a lucrative numbers game.

Let's say that of 20 prospects you call, one makes an appointment. Out of 10 appointments, on the average, 1 person buys. This means that out of 200 people you originally called, 1 ends up buying. Of course, this system does not work on a schedule; sometimes you call 40 or 50 people in a row and not get an appointment. At other times, 10 calls will produce 3 appointments. The numbers in this game, however, conform to your averages over a longer period of time. The rules for winning this game are simple:

The more people you call,
the more appointments you will sell,
the more sales you will make, and
the higher will be your commissions.

LEADS AND REFERRALS

In Chapter 9, when we discussed the compilation of a prospect list, we said that company leads and customer referrals were among the best sources for this list. What are leads and referrals and where do they come from?

What Is a Lead?

In its simplest form, a *lead* is merely a place to go. It might be a name and address or just a name and telephone number. Leads come from many sources. The best lead is the *referral*, which occurs when one satisfied customer provides you with the name of another potential one. Leads also come from responses to direct mail and other advertising materials in which the prospect clips and mails a coupon making an order, asking for a salesperson's call, or requesting more information. Examples are shown in Figures 10.1 and 10.2. Obviously, in Figure 10.1 or in a case where a buyer requests a specification sheet, price list, and salesperson's visit, you have a tight lead; whereas the respondent to Figure 10.2 is a loose lead, perhaps more of a dreamer than a buyer. Some people just like to receive mail.

Leads also are culled as we described in Chapter 9 from telephone, business, and government directories and sorted out by cold canvasing. To be efficient with your time planning, you must *qualify* leads, or make judgments on their order-generating potentials. In general, although you want as many leads as possible, their quality is more important than their

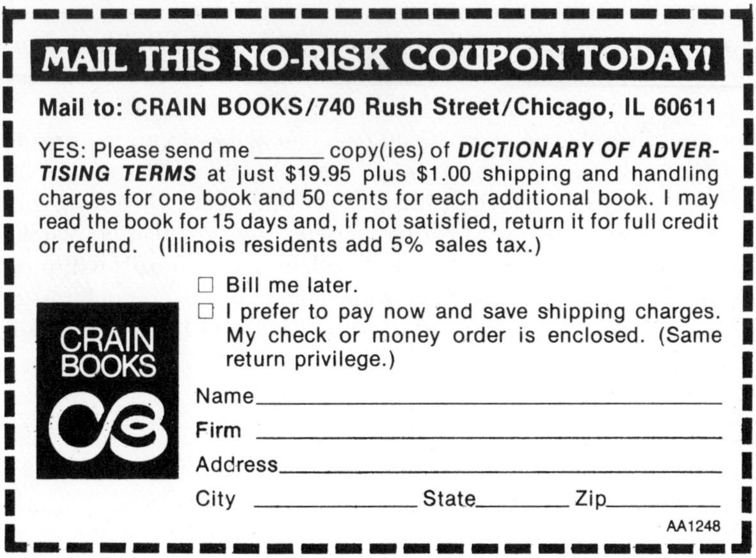
MAIL THIS NO-RISK COUPON TODAY!

Mail to: CRAIN BOOKS/740 Rush Street/Chicago, IL 60611

YES: Please send me ______ copy(ies) of ***DICTIONARY OF ADVERTISING TERMS*** at just $19.95 plus $1.00 shipping and handling charges for one book and 50 cents for each additional book. I may read the book for 15 days and, if not satisfied, return it for full credit or refund. (Illinois residents add 5% sales tax.)

CRAIN BOOKS

☐ Bill me later.

☐ I prefer to pay now and save shipping charges. My check or money order is enclosed. (Same return privilege.)

Name ______

Firm ______

Address ______

City ______ State ______ Zip ______

AA1248

Figure 10.1 A tight sales lead. (Courtesy of Crain Books, Chicago, Ill.)

quantity. Ignore crank responses on coupons or leads from children interested in premiums or in just receiving mail.

When you are canvasing on the telephone, certain questions will help you to qualify the lead and decide whether it is worthwhile to pursue. Experience will teach you to sense a weak lead. In the beginning, it is better to pursue too many leads than too few. You must learn from your mistakes.

Proven Referral Methods

An old customer can help to get you new customers. Some consumer-oriented businesses where the product is a permanent investment depend heavily on these referrals.

DIRECT REFERRALS

If your customer believes a friend or associate can benefit from your product, and *if you ask for these names,* he or she may give you referrals or introductions. Unless the recommender actually has bought your product or service, the referral will not be good, because the new prospect will be influenced by the fact that the recommender has bought the product and recommends both the product and the salesperson.

Such referrals are best asked for immediately after you have made a sale, for reasons we shall discuss in Chapter 18, and they should be followed up immediately, while the recommender has you and the pur-

Let us introduce you to
<u>Kia Ora Royale.</u>

**10 days to Papeete
and Kia Ora Villages
on Moorea
and Rangiroa**

$1,169

8 days on Papeete and Kia Ora Village on Moorea.	$ 949
10 days on Papeete, Bora Bora and Kia Ora Village on Moorea.	$1,240
2 weeks on Papeete, Bora Bora, Huahine, and Kia Ora Villages on Moorea and Rangiroa.	$1,444

For more information on this all-inclusive 3-island package and the other packages as well, please send me some brochures.   CHECK NUMBER

Name

Address

City_____State_____Zip_____

First Class
Permit No. 697
Van Nuys
California

Business
Reply Mail

No postage
stamp necessary
if mailed in the
United States

Postage will be paid by

UTA French Airlines
P.O. Box 9000
Van Nuys
California 91406

Figure 10.2   A loose sales lead. (Courtesy of UTA French Airlines, Van Nuys, Calif.)

chase fresh in mind. Good regular customers, however, can keep on bringing in referrals. You should regard all your satisfied customers as people who are out there working for you to bring in leads. Supply your buyers with promotional materials and arrange finder's fees and gifts if that is the accepted practice in your field. Help them to do a good job for you.

THIRD-PARTY LEADS

If your product or service lends itself to this technique, you can use a direct mail campaign in which a recommending third party suggests your product to potential buyers and shares in the proceeds of the sales. Figure 10.3 shows an example in which the product is a book. Similar letters could go out from local banks or savings and loan associations or private groups such as alumni associations or other fund-raising groups.

TESTIMONIALS

More than just a letter of introduction, a testimonial states the benefits that the product user has received. The testimonial may or may not be addressed to a particular prospect. Used at the right time, these letters are very effective in helping you to close orders. Testimonials are also heavily used in advertising through mass media (radio, television, and magazines).

Your First Referrals

Everyone loves a winner, and bandwagon psychology is based on this principle. A prospect who has doubts about buying from you may change his or her mind if someone else is seen to buy. This is particularly true of Avoiders/Abdicators, Affiliators/Pleasers, and Achievers/Craftsmen.

When you are getting started in sales, you can use this reality. In insurance, financial, or other service sales, your sales manager probably will ask you to start off by listing all your relatives and friends, who form your personal *sphere of influence.* Your manager may regard this as an ideal prospect list, but you, a rookie, have qualms about approaching these people who are close to you and may not have approved of your becoming a salesperson anyway. They might feel that you are taking advantage of your relationship to them.

Do make up this prospect list—but do not sell to these people! Just ask each one to give you referrals, and sell those. Your friends and relatives will be happy to get off the hook by giving you as many names as you want. Once you have sold the friends and relatives of your friends and relatives, the situation will change. You have become established as a successful professional and not a beggar. Your own friends and relatives will start to hear from their friends about what a good salesperson you

Sherman Oaks
Chamber of Commerce

14652 Ventura Boulevard — S201
Sherman Oaks • California 91403
Phone 783-3100

Dear Chamber Member:

You will be pleased to know that arrangements have been made with SOLDADO
PUBLICATIONS to make available the new San Fernando Valley History Book direct
from the publisher at a pre-publication discounted price. Proceeds will go toward
the Chamber's Bicentennial projects in the Sherman Oaks Park.

A DECADE IN THE MAKING!

This first comprehensive history of the San Fernando Valley is a magnificent
9" x 12" volume, handsomely bound in a choice of the rich blue royaltex, white
imperial or leather cordoba bindings with an embossed metal-lay heirloom seal, and
was created by the noted sculptor, George Smith. It is designed to be a family treasure;
a fascinating perusal of the past; a reference book, and is richly illustrated with old
and new photographs of various exciting Valley localities.

Dr. E. Caswell Perry and his expert editorial staff have compiled 31 chapters of
documented historical and geographic facts from the days of the early settlers to the
present modern era. Among the topics included in this unique publication are: Mission
San Fernando, Mexican Rule and Secularization, Downfall of the Mission, Last of the
Ranchos, the Boom of 1887, the Valley in World War I, the Motion Picture Invasion,
the Great Crash, Building Boom of the 1940's, Population Explosion and the Hidden
Metropolis.

RESERVE YOUR COPY NOW!

Just fill out the enclosed reservation card so that a representative from the publisher
can give you all the details of this exciting pre-publication discount offer. If you act
now, you can save as much as 20-25% off of the established retail price.

Cordially yours,

R. J. Wagenbach
President

/ys

Enclosure

Figure 10.3   A third-party lead. (Courtesy of Sherman Oaks Chamber of
Commerce.)

are and how much they have bought and benefitted from the purchase.
These first customers will thereby help you to come back and sell your
original prospect list, who have become affected by "bandwagonitis."

Your situation here is the same as that of our American opera sing-
ers, who until recently had to go abroad and establish a European repu-

tation before anyone would listen to them at home. Sing to a foreign audience first. You will be far more successful that way.

Leads from Dormant Accounts

Going through a dormant account to a live prospect can also result in a bandwagon sale.

> Tony, a Century City stockbroker, was having a hard time reactivating a large individual investor. After trying every motivational tactic he knew, he was about to give up when an idea occurred to him. It arrived on his desk in the form of a brief report on an obscure over-the-counter security with a small initial investment requirement but a good profit potential.
>
> Tony dashed off a note to his former investor and enclosed the stock prospectus:
>
> > Dear Mr. Big:
> > This is *not* for you. Can you recommend five small investors who might go for it?
> >
> > Sincerely yours,
> >
> > Tony
>
> The affluent customer did provide the five names, and these prospects bought. Afterward, each one called Mr. Big to thank him for giving the profitable tip and sending such a competent agent to call. Learning of this financial success, the large investor decided he also wanted a piece of the action!

Bandwagon psychology combines the buying motives of profit, fear of loss, pride, and emulation. Affiliators/Pleasers cannot resist this group appeal ("Everyone's doing it!").

Analyze Your Order Sources

It is a good idea to know how many orders you are getting from what lead sources so that you can plan to concentrate your prospecting efforts in the most effective ways. List the various methods you have used and the number and percentage of total orders that each has generated. An example is shown in Figure 10.4. Possible sources of your orders might be as follows, depending on your product:

Referrals from Existing Accounts
unsolicited
pursued

Code	Title	January 1981 % of Total	Fiscal Year to Date % of Total
1	Telephone promotion	1.6	1.4
2	Referrals	8.5	5.8
3	National advertising	36.4	38.0
4	Direct mail	1.0	3.3
5	Exchange lead getting	.2	.2
6	Pass out cards	4.8	4.3
7	Exhibits	2.6	3.9
11	Deleted leads	1.5	2.5
12	Paid ups	.2	.2
13	School carding	1.9	1.8
14	Third party	26.8	25.6
15	Prospect list	2.0	.5
16	New birth names	1.9	2.1
17	Miscellaneous	6.1	6.0
18	Free drawing	4.5	4.4
	Total	100.0	100.0

Figure 10.4   Source of order analysis.

Referrals from Influential Nonaccounts
Direct mail responses
   individual mailings
   local circulars
Cold call canvasing
   telephone
   door-to-door
Community contacts
   club membership and participation
   chamber of commerce
   service organizations
   politics, school boards, etc.
Bid business
   public agency contracts
   private contracts
Advertising other than direct mail
   Yellow Pages
   radio and television
   trade journal ads
   easel, "take one," untended displays
   bag stuffers, publication inserts

Occasionally, an overzealous salesperson has found an unusual lead source.

> Barry, an unemployed movie actor, started a rumor that he and a famous film producer had been seen having lunch together at the Polo Lounge of the Beverly Hills Hotel. Soon the grapevine carried the story throughout the industry. Everybody wanted to know what the two had been talking about and, specifically, which part the young man was going to have in the producer's new multimillion-dollar film. By the time the tale reached the front page of *Variety,* Barry had completely forgotten starting it. But when he saw his own rumor in print, he believed it and got all excited about its possibilities. He was ready to sign a contract. He immediately telephoned his agent and urged her to follow up on this hot lead!

Lead Action Generates Sales Action

Your success in selling depends not only on your persuasive powers, but also on your prospecting skills. Regardless of the type of selling job you have or what industry you are in, your earnings always will be directly related to the intensity with which you work your territory and your attitude toward prospecting. If you believe that leads are available, you will get them; and if you believe a particular lead can be converted to an order, you will make it happen.

> Jerry is a general insurance agent. Early one morning, as he entered the elevator in his midtown Manhattan office building, he overheard two executives discussing the need for increasing their life insurance coverage. Rather than follow the executives to their office and write up the order himself, Jerry had a better idea. When he arrived at his office, he immediately summoned his sales staff and announced that there was someone in their office building right now who was ready to purchase an insurance policy. Jerry then repeated what he had overheard in the elevator and concluded by offering a cash prize to the first representative who could find these prospects and sign them up.
>
> All his salespeople charged out of his office and nearly tore the building apart in their frantic pursuit of these easy orders. By the end of the day they had set an all-time agency record for the greatest number of new orders written in any single day. After all the orders were tallied and entered into the books, Jerry observed that the original hot prospects, who were ready to be closed, were not among the new orders. His sales staff had missed them completely! If he had told them to go out and cold canvas the office building for business, the motivational response of his sales force and their results would have been considerably different.

TELEPHONE CHALLENGES AND TECHNIQUES

The single order source that gives salespeople more challenges and opportunities than any other also gives them the most self-induced problems. It is the telephone.

The objective of your telephone approach should be to sell an appointment, not a product. Selling appointments is the secret of getting many productive sales interviews.

Practical Tips

The use of the telephone is an exercise in self-discipline. Establish and faithfully follow a daily telephone schedule. Include this time in your weekly action plan.

If you tend to avoid the telephone out of fear, remember that the tiny holes in the receiver are too small to allow an angry fist to come flying through and hit you in the face. You can never get hurt using the telephone, but you could get rich. Certainly there are days when your prospects are so uncooperative or abusive that they give you a headache or a cauliflower ear. These times try your patience, and you may want to quit. At this point maturity and self-restraint separate the professional salesperson from the amateur. Patience and persistence with the telephone will put money in your pocket in the long run.

WHEN AND HOW TO CALL

If possible, send a letter or piece of promotional literature before you call. It will give you and your prospect a point of reference before you launch into your telephone sales talk. Be certain this piece goes to the person with buying authority.

Collect everything you need: telephone call sheet, monthly work card, pad, and pen. Make yourself comfortable and arrange for as much privacy as you can. Begin early and avoid distractions of any kind.

Plan on spending about two hours daily to make a set minimum number of calls. Less than two hours is inadequate to generate enough business, but more than two hours is tiring and ineffective, because your voice begins to sound flat and boring. After two hours, all the voice qualities that arouse curiosity and excitement are gone.

Never let the telephone ring more than five times, as you might anger prospects by catching them at inconvenient moments. The best times to call various types of people are shown in Figure 10.5. When you call a prospect at a bad time, such as during a meal or a business meeting, nothing you say can bring a favorable response. When this happens to you, determine a more acceptable time to call back.

Whatever business you are in or whenever you call, keep your mes-

SOME GENERAL HINTS ON WHEN TO CALL	
Accountants	Usually not between January 1 and April 15 Otherwise, anytime during the day
Bankers and stockbrokers	Before 10:00 A.M. and after 5:00 P.M. (Eastern time)
Chemists and engineers	Between 1:00 P.M. and 5:00 P.M.
Clergymen	Between Monday and Friday
Contractors and builders	Before 9:00 A.M. and after 5:00 P.M.
Dentists	Before 9:30 A.M.
Druggists	Between 1:00 P.M. and 3:00 P.M.
Executives, merchants, store managers, and department heads	After 10:30 A.M.
Homemakers	Between 11:00 A.M. and noon Also between 2:00 and 4:00 P.M.
Lawyers	Between 11:00 A.M. and 2:00 P.M.
Physicians and surgeons	Between 8:30 A.M. and 11:00 A.M. and after 4:00 P.M.
Professors and teachers	Between 7:00 P.M. and 9:00 P.M. (at home)
Publishers and printers	After 3:00 P.M.
Retail butchers and grocers	Before 9:00 A.M. and between 1:00 P.M. and 2:30 P.M.
Salaried employees	At home in the evening

Figure 10.5   The best time to telephone various categories of prospects.

sage brief and businesslike. Don't fall in love with your own voice, let your prospects do that when they meet you in person!

TELEPHONE SELLING STYLE

Within a short time and without the advantage of being face to face, you must get the person you call to think and feel as you do and to act as you want—by giving you an appointment.

Mood selling is the essence of telephone solicitation. The human voice is a powerful and persuasive instrument. Try to establish an appropriate selling atmosphere through your voice tone and inflection. You must sound both seductive and authoritarian while playing on your prospect's imagination. Make the prospect curious enough about you to want to meet you.

The ideal voice projects warm sincerity, forcefulness, and enthusiasm. You can help to achieve this ideal by smiling, raising your eyebrows, and talking slowly and distinctly while keeping your sentences short. Don't talk with anything in your mouth, and keep the mouthpiece about an inch from your mouth to be heard clearly. Use your normal speaking voice, and be careful of your enunciation and diction. Speak as if the prospect were sitting across the desk from you. Don't shout into the receiver on long-distance calls because of an unconscious delusion that one must speak louder if the other party is farther away. By the same token, do not speak louder to a foreign person. Instead, be careful to use simple sentence structure and no slang, and speak slowly with clear diction.

You can never speak too slowly over the telephone, and you should plan to pause now and then, since to speak without pauses sounds unnatural and "canned." When asking a question, you should pause long enough to give your prospective customer time to answer. Silence or a long pause is an important psychological tool because most people feel uncomfortable when confronted with silence. They feel that they must talk to fill the void.

Imagine a pleasant, smiling face on the other end, and smile back. Somehow your voice will convey this expression, and smiling influences your own attitude. Be positive and confident. If you expect the prospect to say "Yes, come on over!", it is more likely to happen. If you really want to see people, they somehow also want to see you; but if your voice is expressing your inner feeling of "I hate this!", your prospect will hear an undercurrent of "I hate *you!*"

What to Say

Before you dial the first number, you have to define what you want from the prospect, what you are going to say, how you are going to say it, and how you are going to close. In other words, you must have clear objectives and a reliable, proven telephone script.

SCRIPT PREPARATION

In preparing your telephone talk, ask yourself four questions:

1. What benefits can I promise to gain interest?
2. What objections can I anticipate?
3. What words will I use in answering objections?
4. How will I close for the appointment?

Don't plan to tell your prospects too much over the telephone. Offer good reasons for listening. Prepare a series of questions that will get them involved, but avoid questions that can be answered with a flat "yes" or "no." Ask "How do you use product X?" rather than "Do you use product X?" Plan to use feeling-finding questions so that you can see whether your message is being received and accepted.

"Does that make sense?"

"What do you think of that?"

Use descriptive words, and leave space to use your customer's name often. Research has shown that you will keep prospects' attention for at least eight seconds after you mention their names. If you have difficulty with a name, ask the prospect to pronounce it for you, and write it down phonetically.

Never argue with a prospect or become abusive. If a prospect starts name-calling, do not lose your composure and prove that you deserve it. Do not let anyone but yourself control your emotions. Conduct yourself with dignity and self-assurance, and you usually will be treated accordingly.

THE TELEPHONE TALK

Start by immediately identifying yourself and your firm. Be courteous and pleasant and try to establish rapport with your prospect. Four openers have been suggested by Robert W. Chernow.[1]

1. The *benefit opener* is direct and shows the prospect how he or she can specifically benefit from your product or service.

   "Ms. Purchasing Agent, I want to speak with you about our new machine, which pays for itself within the first year."

   "Mr. Buyer, my firm has a special 30 percent discount during March on all office equipment repairs."

2. The *question opener* attempts to relate your proposal to your customer's specific situation.

   "Mr. Client, would you like to be able to cut your bad debts in half?"

   "Ms. Dealer, how would you like to make more profit selling one 35-mm camera rather than the dozen that you are carrying in stock now?"

   The immediate appeal to the profit buying motive is both arresting and interesting. Most prospects will respond favorably.

3. The *news opener* is a timely approach to a prospective customer's situation. Much research and advanced preparation are required to make this approach truly effective.

   "Ms. Prospect, perhaps you saw the latest *C. W. Dodge Reports* regarding new construction in your area. You will probably want to get your bid in on the new hospital wing before the August 1 deadline."

You are selling equipment which this buyer either specifies or subcontracts. This piece of news could be worth money in the bank for both of you.

4. In the *problem-solving opener,* you have ascertained your prospect's problem through advance preparation and probing questions and have devised an appropriate solution built around your product or service.

In addition to these proven attention-getting openers, you can use a direct or indirect approach. For the *direct approach,* you should tell only enough information to determine whether the prospect wants to hear more. Normally, you should use this technique when you have a large territory and can afford to see only those prospects with definite interest. You are, in effect, qualifying their interest level.

For the *indirect approach,* you spell out benefits without revealing the product or service, and you then ask for an opportunity to explain how the prospect can obtain these benefits.

"Ms. Prospect, this is Sam Salesperson. My firm specializes in ways to save storage costs and make your valuables more secure. All I'll need is 15 minutes to explain what we offer. Naturally, there is no obligation on your part. Would Tuesday at 2:00 P.M. or Thursday at 10:00 A.M. be more convenient for you?"

Avoid answering too many questions. If your objective is to obtain an interview, you shouldn't give your full story away beforehand. If your prospect asks for more information, say "That is a point I would like to explain in an interview," or "I will be glad to explain that when I see you. What is the nearest cross street to your house or office?"

If you tell all now, your prospects will have time to build up defenses or withhold the appointment altogether. You want them to build up interest and curiosity instead.

After the opener, make comments that create interest and ask fact-finding and feeling-finding questions. The next step is to deliver your sales message. At least in the beginning, use a previously rehearsed script. Finally, ask for an appointment, giving the prospect a choice of dates or times. This approach tends to prevent the idea of refusing an appointment. Overcome any objections. Confirm your understanding of the objection, prepare your prospect for your answer, answer the objection, and try another close to get the appointment. Once you have the appointment, confirm it, perhaps by asking for directions to the prospect's location.

Here are some sample scripts for telephone talks.

AGENT: Mr./Ms. Prospect, I am Sam Salesperson, with the XYZ Life Insurance Company, and I have no way of knowing whether my services as a life underwriter can be of any value to you at this time. But I do have an idea which has proven so valuable to other people in positions similar to yours that I think it can be of value to you. It will only take a moment of your time for you to decide whether this idea may be useful to you. Would it be convenient for me to stop by tomorrow at 10:00 to show this to you, or would Tuesday at 2:00 be better?

AGENT: Mr./Ms. Prospect, are you free to talk for a minute? My name is Connie Closer, and I'm in the life insurance business with XYZ Life. I had planned to stop in to see you for about 10 minutes tomorrow morning. The purpose of my visit is, first, to introduce myself, and second, to hand you some information that I think will be of value to you in the years ahead.

My visit won't last over 10 minutes, and you can time me. But I did want to phone you first rather than barge in. Could you work me in for about 10 minutes tomorrow morning or would some other time be better?

AGENT: Mr./Ms. Prospect, this is Sam Salesperson of the XYZ Life Insurance Company. I am calling at the suggestion of Carl Client, for whom I have recently done some work. May I see you tomorrow afternoon at 4:30, or would 9:00 Friday morning be more convenient?

PROSPECT: What do you want to see me about? [or] Is it about life insurance?

AGENT: It's about an idea involving life insurance that has proved to be very interesting and helpful to people like you.

AGENT: Mr./Ms. Prospect, do you have a moment to speak on the phone? My name is Connie Closer, of the XYZ Life Insurance Company.

(Then select the most appropriate statement:)

Fellow Member

I have several friends and acquaintances who are Alma Mater High/College graduates/members of Rotary/other, and I have heard about you, and while you . . .

Neighbor

I am a neighbor of yours, Mr./Ms. Prospect. That is, I live in Precinct Heights, too, and I've heard about you and while you . . .

Move In

I have heard about your moving here from Othertown, and while
you . . .

Prospect Letter

I have in front of me some information and a brochure that my
home office asked me to give you and while you . . . may not even
want to talk about insurance, Mr./Ms. Prospect, I would like to
meet you. If you have no objections, I'd like to stop by tomorrow,
say about 9:00. Will that be OK?

(Listen to response; then answer objection. // means pause.)

AGENT: I realize that my my wanting to meet you doesn't call for too
much enthusiasm on your part, so I'd like to make it worth your
while in this way—I have access to information that might be
worth money to you even though you never buy more insurance,
and if I may drop in and meet you, I'll take // well I tell you,
Mr./Ms. Prospect, I'll take less than three minutes.

PROSPECT: Can't you just mail me the information?

AGENT: If it were possible I would, but to be of value, this information has to be based on certain facts that only you can furnish.
Would next week be more convenient than tomorrow? How
about Monday at 1:00? Or would Tuesday afternoon be better?

PROSPECT: I'm not in the market for life insurance right now.

AGENT: I can understand that, Mr./Ms. Prospect. That's perfectly all
right, and even if you were, I'd be the most surprised person in
town! Would you be willing to take just 10 minutes' time to see
what this unique service/idea could do for you?

PROSPECT: I'm too busy to see you. I don't have time to talk about it.

AGENT: I can understand that, Mr./Ms. Prospect. That is exactly
why I phoned. I know you would have been courteous enough to
see me if I came over, but I want to see you at *your* convenience
when I won't interrupt you at your busiest. Would this afternoon
be okay or would tomorrow morning be better?

SALESPERSON: Good morning. Is Mr./Ms. Prospect in? This is Sam
Salesperson calling. I'm with the Valley Book Company. You
know, the book that's being promoted through the Anytown
Chamber of Commerce?

The reason I called is that I'm going to be in your area tomorrow morning and I'd like to stop by and give you the details on
our discount prepublication offer. Would 10:00 be OK, or would
the afternoon be more convenient?

PROSPECT: Can't you send it in the mail?

SALESPERSON: My job is to explain the prepublication offer and leave some information if you are interested. OK with you? I'm hopping around the county like a grasshopper, and I want to be sure that you receive the information in person. Rather than stick it in the mail and have someone throw it in the wastepaper basket, I'm willing to take a few minutes of *my* time to make sure that you get the program straight. OK?

ENROLLMENT COUNSELOR: Hello, Mr./Ms. Prospect, this is Connie Closer from the HMO Medical Group. [*Smile!*] I think that you are going to find the purpose of my call a little bit unusual. You see, we are conducting a neighborhood survey about the health and welfare of your family, and how your health problems are handled.

This health care study will help in planning and delivering better medical services to people like yourselves and your neighbors. Everything that you say will remain completely confidential. OK?

1. Are you familiar with federal, state, or local government-sponsored health plans?
2. Are you familiar with the Medi-Cal State Health Plan?

[*and so on to qualify prospect*]

Would you be interested in a State of California sponsored program that would give you and your family free medical and dental service at no cost to you? We will even check your eyes.

PROSPECT: I'll think it over and call you later.

ENROLLMENT COUNSELOR: I can understand how you feel, Mr./Ms. Prospect, but not everyone is eligible; only certain people can qualify. I would like to leave some literature with you in case you might know someone who qualifies and who would like information about this new health service.

PROSPECT: Are you selling something?

ENROLLMENT COUNSELOR: No, Sir/Ma'am, the program is absolutely free. The state of California pays everything. It doesn't cost you a penny. You still live at 1000 Any Street, don't you? Is that a home or an apartment? The reason I ask is that I'm not familiar with the area and I'll be in the neighborhood this afternoon, or would tomorrow morning be better for you?

Don't overqualify. Some salespeople try to find out too much over the telephone. They get lazy and seek a sure sale before they will plan to leave the friendly confines of their warm offices for the great unknown. They want prospects to say "I'll take it!"—or they will not budge.

Remember that the telephone receiver's little holes will not allow a purchase order to squeeze through any more than they will accommodate that flying fist. Don't overqualify your prospects on the telephone. Sell appointments and then get out and sell your product in person.

Rejection and the Numbers Game

No matter how good you are, you are not going to sell them all, or even most of them, and on some days you will not sell any of them. On those days, remember that selling appointments is a numbers game, and your score will average out in the end if you keep your attitude positive. The harder you work that dial, the luckier you will get. The next person you call can make your day!

Notes

1. Robert W. Chernow, "Phone Selling Is No Time to Play It by Ear," *Marketing News*, American Marketing Association, October 8, 1976, p. 9.

Chapter 11
New Account Strategy

Let us imagine that you are about to go out for the first time and call on a new prospect for your company. Although in Chapter 9 we made a general plan for finding customers and figuring out how to present products and services to them, we now need a strategy specifically designed for this particular prospect.

RESEARCH PROSPECTS AND THEIR ENVIRONMENT

Find out as much as you can about your prospect's personality and organization role. You will be much better prepared for whatever may happen in the sales interview if you know ahead of time what your prospect's psychological profile is. Is this customer an Avoider/Abdicator or Affiliator/Pleaser, or are there clues that you will be facing a Power Boss/Commander? Will you be lucky enough to deal with an Achiever/Craftsman, or will you need to keep alert as you sell to a Manipulator/Gamesman?

Try to talk to people in the prospect's environment as well as those in your company who may have information about this buyer's behavior.

An Affiliator/Pleaser contact is your best starting point. Put together a picture of this personality beforehand, and you will have a smooth interview with few surprises.

Sometimes the personality of the buyer's secretary may be a clue to that of the boss. An Avoider/Abdicator boss who is able to put up little defense against an aggressive salesperson often installs a strong secretary to guard the door, much as Dante's Cerberus guarded the entrance to hell. Even if you have not been able to find out much about the buyer beforehand, this fierce guardian immediately tips you off to watch out for an avoider.

Experienced door-to-door salespeople know that a "No Solicitors" sign is a similar indication that an avoider lurks within. That sign, the only defense that the prospect can offer, exists to be bypassed, just as the fierce secretarial guardian does.

Sometimes you can learn about a prospect's personality by looking for the buyer's assistants' cars in the parking lot. Perhaps you find a shiny late-model Porsche. In this case, one of the buyer's assistants is a Manipulator/Gamesman, while the other assistant drives an old, dusty Dodge Dart with rust holes. Obviously, you would make your first company contact with the Manipulator/Gamesman assistant, because this individual would know everything that is going on within the company and a great deal about the buyer's life-style and decision-making process. This information will enable you to develop an effective strategy within that target account.

In addition to personality groups, industrial buyers tend to fall into one of two other categories, according to Hersker and Stroh.[1] There are *methodical* and *creative* buyers. Methodical buyers simply fill requisitions from middle managers and others within their companies to the best of their abilities. These individuals search for alternative sources of supply, write detailed specifications, and get competitive bids. They keep records on each supplier and often on each sales representative to see who keeps promises and who does not. This bookkeeping is merely another form of stamp collecting, and it will be cashed in at the appropriate time. These defensive attitudes (9,1 or 1,1) represent methodical buying at its worst, and many procurement officers remain at this low level throughout their careers.

Creative buyers, on the other hand, do not just fill requisitions. They ask a lot of questions beforehand to determine why a manager wants to buy something, and they often use value analysis to discover where substantial savings can be realized. They do not just place orders and expedite deliveries, they consult with management before requisitions are drawn up. They keep management posted about new products, price fluctuations, and other supply conditions.

These creative professionals (9,9 or 5,5) want ideas, suggestions, and solutions to problems, and they are willing to pay for them with purchase orders. They do not necessarily get competitive bids, but often will reward the sales engineer who provides cost-saving ideas and other services. Alert sales engineers recognize and respect these creative buyers and have little trouble closing them. The goals that buyer and vendor attain together in this way do a lot for each person's self-esteem, reinforce empathy, and help to foster a lasting business relationship.

Your advance research on your new prospect should go beyond personality to his or her real position in the organization. A buyer's official title may not reflect strong influences that other people inside and outside the company may have on the buying decision. The same is true in consumer sales, where the official user or wearer of a product may be strongly influenced by a friend's or relative's opinion.

YOUR SALES PRESENTATION STRATEGY

Think carefully through your sales presentation before you go to see your prospect. You must plan what to say and how to say it to this particular buyer.

Focus your attention on the prospect's needs and problems. In the context of personal needs, your dialogue with the buyer must satisfy

the Avoider/Abdicator's need for security
the Achiever/Craftsman's need for data
the Affiliator/Pleaser's need for reassurance
the Power Boss/Commander's need to be right
the Manipulator/Gamesman's need for long-range results

Moving to business-related needs, ask yourself these questions. How can my product or service help my client to

reduce costs
improve profitability
increase inventory turns
communicate more effectively
develop cost-effective alternatives in the manufacturing process
improve purchasing activity
secure and hold key employees

With this particular customer in mind, move through the chart of features, advantages, and benefits that we developed more generally in Chapter 9. Carefully think through the essential points of your message, and then write it out word for word. Keep it simple. Do not try to cover too many points all at once, or you will lose the main issue and confuse the customer. The PAPA formula offers a simple clear-cut approach.

P   romise a benefit
A   mplify the promise
P   rove it
A   ction

Your verbal *promise* should relate your product's problem-solving attributes to a specific client need. The *amplification* of your promise is structured by facts that demonstrate the want-satisfying nature of your sales proposal. You can *prove* your promise with testimonial letters from satisfied users, visits to installations where your products are now performing, and any statistical data or test results that verify performance. Finally, the *action* you desire is either a commitment to proceed further in the negotiation or a purchase order.

Bear in mind that the central issue you are addressing is *what does my proposal mean to my customer?* Other questions that prospects will be mentally asking are:

What's in it for me?
Why should I even listen to you?
So what?
Prove it!
Why should I buy it *now?*

How can you prepare yourself in advance so that all of these bases are covered? After you have completed the *features-advantages-benefits-customer-buying motives* exercise in Chapter 9, you should gather all appropriate product literature, samples, testimonials, and other relevant data to be used during your presentation. You would naturally vary the amount of input depending on the psychological type of customer with whom you are interacting. For example, Avoider/Abdicators and Achiever/Craftsmen demand a great deal of data (although for different reasons), while an Affiliator/Pleaser is indifferent to statistics, and the impatient Power Boss/Commander is angered by this information. "Don't confuse me with facts, my mind is made up!" is a typical response.

Plan ahead for customer participation. You do not want to sustain a monologue during your entire visit and then find out that you lost your customer near the beginning. Your presentation should be based on a series of modules or units, each with its own close. You cannot pass from module A to module B until you have asked for and obtained agreement on the values or solutions expressed in module A. If you are to be using a standard presentation or "canned pitch" supplied by your company, be sure that you understand where these modules and their associated closes occur, so that you will not fall over backward in surprise if your customer suddenly buys in the middle of your talk.

Learn the presentation thoroughly. Memorize the benefits that your product or service has *for this customer*. If you do not memorize them, you will not be able to remember these benefits during the give-and-take of the sales interview.

PLAN THIS SALES CALL

Exactly what are you going to do when you arrive at an office or home or when your customer comes to see you? You must have clear-cut call objectives. You must know why you are calling on this particular customer and what you hope to accomplish.

Before the call, ask yourself these questions:

What are my objectives on this visit?
   sell
   get decisions
   influence
   inform
Is this person the correct one to contact? If not, who should be contacted?
Who is this prospect or client?
   name
   position, authority to decide
   peculiarities, habits
   personal profile
What does this client want? What are the needs, problems, and buying motives?
What benefits and solutions can my product or service offer?
What points should I make to support these claims? (Evidence is especially wanted by Avoiders/Abdicators, but also by Achievers/Craftsmen and Manipulators/Gamesmen.)
What objections is the client most likely to make? (Power Bosses/Commanders and Avoiders/Abdicators will have the most objections.)
How will I answer these objections? (We shall cover objections more thoroughly in Chapter 16.)

Note

1. Barry J. Hersker and Thomas P. Stroh, "The Purchasing Agent is No Patsy," *Sales & Marketing Management*, June 13, 1977.

Chapter 12
The Outline of a Sale

In Chapter 1 we said that selling is persuading people to think and feel as you do so that they will act as you want them to act. How do we actually go about this persuasion?

Each time you communicate successfully with other people to obtain acceptance of an idea, you do so through seven distinct steps. Most people go through this stepwise persuasion process intuitively and are never aware of the pattern. Understanding and using it, however, can make you more effective in selling

SEVEN PSYCHOLOGICAL STEPS TO A SALE

During the selling process, you take your customer through these seven steps:

1. contact
2. attention
3. interest
4. desire

5. conviction
6. resolve to buy
7. purchase order or sale

Customers act as you want them to act when they finally buy, but the processes of learning to think and feel as you do correspond to three steps apiece.

Think
    contact
    attention
    interest
Feel
    desire
    conviction
    resolve to buy
Act
    purchase order or sale

Obviously, your goal is the sale, but you cannot get there without going through all the steps. You must lead your prospects through the thinking and feeling stages before you can expect them to act. You cannot just bounce into a prospect's office or home and announce yourself thus: "Good morning, I'm Jane Salesperson. Want to buy?" There is something to be said for shock value here, but the most likely responses are three orders: get out, stay out, and don't come back!

Think As You Think

Your customer certainly is not thinking as you think when you first appear, but in three steps you will bring that about.

INITIAL CONTACT

Your first few seconds with a prospective customer can determine your fate. Thus your approach is by far the most important step. If you cannot get past this step, you have no chance for a sale. You must present an appropriate appearance, behave in a businesslike but courteous manner, and have an air of professionalism and enthusiasm.

ATTENTION

Your sudden appearance before your prospect is not the major event of the day for that person. Your visit probably will be viewed as an interruption rather than as the coming of the new Messiah! Until you appear on the scene, your prospect's minds are filled with other matters. They all have other interests and distractions that will cause them to be less than enthusiastic about your presentation. You must allow time for their minds to slow down and refocus on your ideas. Various methods are used to encourage this refocusing, but your main concern is awareness and flexibility of behavior during this step.

INTEREST

Attention can be held only a short time unless you quickly capture the prospect's interest. Interest should be a logical extension of attention if you can show that your product will provide a benefit, prevent a loss, or solve a client problem. Your prospects are not the least bit interested in what your product is, but rather in what it will do for them.

Do not tell a farmer about the length of a cow's horns, the color of its hide, or its number of teeth. What the customer wants to know is whether it gives milk.

By putting product or service benefits in terms of needs and wants, you have led your client to think as you think. Now you must move the buyer along gently to the point of feeling as you feel.

Feel As You Feel

Do people spend money out of interest alone? Could you skip the next three steps and ask for the order? Of course not! You must take each step in order, or the process will surely fail. Sometimes you can achieve several steps in quick succession or even simultaneously in the buyer's mind, but you cannot skip any one step and still get the order.

DESIRE

If you have done well in explaining what your products or services will do for the customer, you will find a sense of desire developing. In this step you sell the concept or idea of the generic product or service, but you do not yet differentiate your product from those of competitors. You make the customer feel as you feel about this product or service as a general class. The customer may be thinking along these lines:

> "Yes, I like the idea of owning a widget some day. Now, let's see— there are 34 brands of widgets on the market. You come back in about 10 years, after I've had a chance to check them all out. Thanks for making me aware of their existence."

In marketing, the establishment of a new product concept is called creating *primary demand,* and it must precede the selling of a particular brand of the item, or the creation of *secondary demand.* For example, when television sets were first put on the commercial market, people had to be sold the concept of television in general before they could be sold specific brands of televisions.

CONVICTION

Moving on into the sale of your particular brand or product line, you want your prospects to develop a conviction that they want your product more than others on the market. Here you create secondary demand for your widget, bumping the other 33 brands from the buyer's consciousness. Here, the customer wants *your* brand of product or service.

RESOLVE TO BUY

To turn the customer's feeling of conviction into more than a brush-off, you must develop a pressing reason for acting now. If you are persuasive and tactful, you will cause the feeling of conviction to ripen into a resolve to buy.

At this point, you might think that your journey toward the sale is over and the buyer will live up to that title and buy. After all, the buyer thinks as you think and feels as you feel . . . isn't the next logical step to act as you want?

A psychological stumbling block that we have mentioned before occurs between the resolve and sale steps. It is called *excuses and objections,* and it is based on the natural hesitation that everyone has about making decisions. Logic gives way to emotion and procrastination. People would rather put off until tomorrow what they should have done yesterday. They miss other people's birthdays, the last opportunity to buy theater tickets, and the ends of clearance sales this way. Everyone does so to some extent, but with some customers it is a way of life.

PURCHASE ORDER OR SALE

Hesitation, although emotional in nature, usually takes a logical form when voiced. In Chapter 16 we shall discuss the handling and answering of objections. Once they are resolved to the mutual satisfaction of you and your customer, the sale is made.

SIX STRUCTURAL STEPS TO A SALE

Although the seven steps we have been discussing are a good description of the psychological process of the sale, it is more convenient for us to break our own action during the selling process into six stages: the approach, warm-up phase, bridge, presentation, objections, and close. If we now line up all three descriptions of the selling process, we can get a rough idea of the buyer's mental patterns during our actions. Note that there is no clear point at which interest occurs: it builds from the bridge into the presentation.

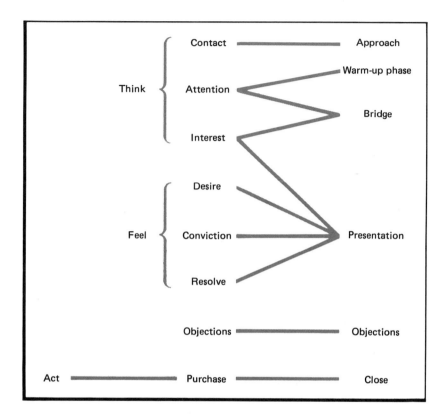

The approach can be regarded as a complete sale in itself, during which you sell yourself and your own source credibility to the customer. Also, you should compare the steps of the sale to your telephone method of prospecting, which is nothing more than the sale of an appointment. We shall discuss the six structural steps to the sale in Chapters 13 through 17.

Chapter 13
The Approach

Your initial approach is already partially complete when you arrange an appointment with a prospect over the telephone. Your first approach is still to be made, though, if you are in a line of selling that requires cold call approaches either to consumers at home or to industrial buyers in their offices.

The object of this part of the sale—the approach—is to sell the interview itself, because as we pointed out in Chapter 12, you certainly cannot sell to a prospect if you cannot get in to see him or her. During the approach you are selling *only* the interview, and to do so, you must arouse curiosity in the prospect. You must create desire in that person to hear the rest of your presentation.

SOURCE CREDIBILITY

In Chapter 3 we defined source credibility as the ability to inspire faith, trust, and confidence in the prospective customer. We added to our understanding of source credibility in Chapter 9 by discussing its basis in product, market, and customer knowledge. Now we need to add another important component—your first impression upon the customer. You do not have a second chance to make a first impression, so your nonverbal communication had better be working for you and not against you.

How You Look

You must appear as your prospects expect you to appear so you can get them to think as you think and feel as you feel. The basis of this need to harmonize is that people look at other people to determine whether they are members of the same "tribe" or social group. Appropriateness is the key. People are more likely to empathize with other people who appear to belong to their own social group or to look up to those who appear to belong to a slightly higher social group, and you want to create empathy and respect for yourself.

It goes without saying that no matter whom you are approaching, you must be clean. You will make a better impression on prospects if you are in good health than if you are not, because your skin and hair texture as well as your physique can show the effects of too much eating, drinking, or smoking and not enough sleep and exercise. No one trusts a person who appears to have crawled out from under a pile of decaying leaves or who appears to have spent the previous 48 hours in a smoke-filled room or a garlic packing plant.

Your choice of dress, accessories, hairstyle, and so on have been shown to be crucial to the impression you make. John T. Molloy has done considerable research on the subject and has written two books on his findings.[1] Molloy believes that a person can sell himself "through the adroit manipulation of his clothing more effectively than he can by any other means."[2] Your wardrobe is a weapon that carries a message, and it can open and close doors for you.

Central to Molloy's research results was the discovery that most salespeople are dead before they open their mouths because their clothing represents them as not likable, dishonest, not trustworthy, and insincere. It is impossible here to convey all or even a good part of Molloy's material, and his books are required reading for anyone who is serious about selling. The basic ideas, however, are that you must look conservative and appropriate to the situation in which you sell—neither overdressed and too superior to your clients nor disheveled. Men should not wear any facial hair, especially goatees. Women will find their authority greatly increased if they wear skirted suits or dresses with jackets. Some additional tips are given in Figure 13.1.

In marketing terms, clothing yourself is like packaging a product. After all, you are the product that customers must buy during the approach, before they ever see what you are selling.

DRESS RULES THAT ALWAYS PAY OFF

In addition to the general guidelines involving size, age, sex, race, socioeconomic background, geography, occupational orientation, and product significance, there are some rules that all sales representatives should adhere to, all the time. They are:

1. If you have a choice, dress affluently.
2. Always be clean; it is not always necessary to be obsessively neat, but it is always imperative to be clean.
3. If you are not sure of the circumstances of a selling situation, dress more—rather than less—conservatively than normal.
4. Never wear any item that identifies any personal association or belief, unless you are absolutely sure that the person to whom you are selling shares those beliefs. This rule includes school rings, masonic rings, ties that are connected with a particular area, political buttons, religious symbols, etc.
5. Always dress as well as the people to whom you are selling.
6. Never wear green.
7. Never put anything on your hair that makes it look shiny or greasy.
8. Never wear sunglasses, or glasses that change tint as the light changes. People must see your eyes if they are to believe you.
9. Never wear any jewelry that is not functional, and keep that simple. Big rings, jangling bracelets, and gaudy cuff links are absolutely taboo.
10. If you are a man, never wear any item that might be considered feminine.
11. Wear, do, or say something that makes your name or what you are selling memorable.
12. If it is part of your regalia, always carry a good attaché case.
13. Always carry a good pen and pencil, not the cheap, junky ones.
14. If you have a choice, wear an expensive tie.
15. Never take off your suit jacket unless you have to. It weakens your authority.
16. Whenever possible, look in the mirror before you visit a client.

Figure 13.1   A summary of dress rules that always pay off. (From the book *Dress for Success* by John T. Molloy. Copyright © 1974 by John T. Molloy and Thomas Humber. Reprinted by permission of the David McKay Company, Inc.)

An experienced sales manager once hired a bright young man who seemed to have all the traits and abilities needed to sell the product except for one thing: he wore a single gold earring in his left ear. The sales manager, knowing what would happen, wisely said nothing, but let his new recruit go out on his first day of sales calls sporting the earring.

The young man was quite bright and observant. It did not take him long to figure out what was causing the odd looks he was getting. The next day the sales manager noted that the earring had disappeared. The young man apparently had decided that sales goals were more important than individuality.

Perhaps the best guideline for women on the subject of appearance is the response that Mary Wells Lawrence of Wells Rich Green gave to a question about how she dressed. "The Mary Lawrence that my clients see is a rather carefully structured image. It's looking the way I think my clients think I should look—feminine but businesslike, pretty but not whistle bait."[3] Dressing the way clients think you should *not* dress can be disastrous, as we saw in the case of the flashy shirt that was related to a $19-million loss in the mind of a consultant's customer (Chapter 7).

Other Nonverbal Signals

A person to whom you are making an approach is not looking at a still photograph but at a body moving in space and time. As we saw in Chapter 4, you are communicating in nonverbal ways from the moment the prospect first sees you, and this kind of communication outweighs whatever remarks you may make as the prospect forms a first impression.

What is your body saying to the client? Is your posture poised, open, and confident, or is it defensive or overly aggressive? Watch your gestures. What do they convey to the prospect? Try your approach out in a mirror or with a critical friend to find out how it appears to someone else.

Space language in the approach stage can portray you as diffident or overly aggressive. We have seen a purchasing agent gradually back all the way down a long hall as he unconsciously tried to maintain a comfortable distance between himself and a saleswoman whose comfort zone was smaller than his. She appeared highly aggressive to him. Be observant, and note the distance your prospect chooses as a comfortable one. Do not cross the imaginary lines that prospects draw for you, even if they are not where you would have drawn them.

We already have mentioned the importance of time language. Do not set the buyer against you by being late. If you keep clients waiting, you prejudice them before you ever appear. Buyers, of course, may keep you waiting for legitimate or game-playing reasons: a Power Boss/Commander wants to control you, and an Avoider/Abdicator doesn't want to see you at all. In any case, you should use the strategy outlined in Chapter 7. Wait a few minutes; ask the secretary to remind the buyer that you are there, but will have to go on to another appointment soon; and if this tactic does not get you in to see the buyer, leave politely. Do not wait beyond 15 minutes unless the buyer has given you a legitimate reason for the delay. You will not lose much business by leaving a game-playing buyer; this prospect was not going to be a profitable customer anyway.

The Buyer's First Impression

It is worth your time, money, and effort to learn how to make a good appearance and to acquire the necessary props, including clothes, hairstyles, gold pens, leather attaché cases, and even glasses and cars. Ask your sales manager to give a critique of your appearance, and listen objectively to what is said. You have the right to dress in any way you wish, but you must balance your rights against your chances for success. Ask yourself this question: do your clients smile when you appear—or when you disappear?

GREETINGS

Greeting prospective clients should be no different from meeting friends in a social setting, although a first meeting between strangers is more formal than one where there is an established relationship. In both situations you exchange greetings, introduce yourself, shake hands firmly, and do everything possible to put the other person at ease.

> Meg, an industrial salesperson, has a well-earned reputation for her perpetually cheerful countenance and disarming manner. Whenever she appears in a dealer's office, everyone there feels good. These visits give her clientele a lift, and they always look forward to her next appearance.

> Werner is well known in his trade for his enthusiastic salutelike greeting. "Whenever he appears in your presence," says a friend, "he acts as if you are either a flag pole or a taxicab driver whom he is hailing. There's never any doubt of his getting your attention!"

Act as if you are genuinely interested in meeting your prospects and clients. Nobody likes a dud, but people usually respond to warmth and enthusiasm. You are in the people business, and you should act accordingly.

A final word about greetings: if you are a retail salesperson, never, never approach your customer with the time-worn phrase, "May I help you?" This opener begs for the equally trite answer, "Just looking!" or just plain "No!" Try these openers instead:

"Hello!"

"Good morning! I'm Les Ades, and you are . . . ?"

"Hi! I'm John Doe. What size suits were you looking for?"

"Those hot trays are so convenient when you're giving a dinner party!"

"Hi! I have something special I want you to see."

"Aren't those great looking? They just came in today, and I don't think they'll be around long!"

If your customer gives defensive signals or claims to be only looking, say something like this: "Please do. The sports clothes are on this side, and the dresses are over there—and the new bathing suits are on the far wall. Have fun!" Then beat a retreat before the prospect takes fright and flight. Appearing to be just passing by on your way to hang something up a little later, pause and ask, "Was there any certain *type* of thing you were looking for?" By this time the customer either has been reassured by your low-pressure attitude and has taken stock of the surroundings or has left because she or he really *was* just a looker, in which case you have lost nothing.

PENETRATING THE FIRST LINES OF DEFENSE

Getting past a prospect's receptionist or secretary can be a sale in itself. These alert personnel can be like Dante's Cerberus. Bear in mind that, as we mentioned in Chapter 11, the secretary's personality may offer you a clue to that of the boss. This guardian is worth careful observation and handling.

How To Handle Buffers

Although some secretaries and receptionists feel that it is their sacred duty to get rid of salespeople, trickery is not the way to handle them. In the long run, the best approach is to take them into your confidence, be honest and sincere with them, and show respect for their position. Many times they will help you out in unexpected ways.

If you have frequent contact with buffers, learn their names and use them as often as possible. Even if they do not remember your name, they will be pleased that you found them memorable. (This technique is particularly helpful with surly waiters or gas station attendants, also.) The most beautiful word in the English language is *your name* on someone else's lips!

A secretary or receptionist can turn the buffer zone that occurs between your entrance and your prospect greeting into an end zone if you are not well prepared. To penetrate this first line of defense, you must make the receptionist think (as you think) that what you have to offer will benefit the boss. Secretaries must be made to feel that you have some information or business that they cannot receive and communicate for you. They must like you and your manner of presentation. Using your charm and personality can help, but remember that you are there to pitch the bosses, not the secretaries. Your aim is to make these buffers feel that they will not place themselves in unfavorable positions with their bosses if they let you get by them.

A word of warning: do not make the assumption that all bosses are male and all secretaries female. The person in charge of executive personnel recruitment for one large California department store chain is a woman, and her secretary is a young man. It is obvious that a tactless assumption or remark in a situation like this one could put concrete on your casket well before you began your presentation. It is also foolish to venture an opinion on a subject unless you know the listener's views. You have everything to lose and nothing to gain if your opinion is opposed to your prospect's.

Helpful Tactics

After greeting the buffer courteously and introducing yourself, you might refer to a personal letter that you previously have sent to the prospect, or you might tell the secretary what your service does, but not what it is.

> "I have some information regarding a personal matter which I'm sure Ms. Prospect would want treated confidentially . . . It is a special service that could be of very real importance and benefit. Is she in?"

If you must explain your service and its benefits to the buffer, show only how you can relate these benefits to the boss's special needs. In some cases you might want to ask the buffer's opinion and then sell the desirability of allowing your prospect to see you.

> "I know that Mr. Prospect is very busy [with a pleasant smile], but I wonder if I might see him for about 10 minutes one day this week. Is he in now? Do you think that this would be a convenient time—as long as I'm here now?"

Some sales representatives send in their business cards with notes written on them to stimulate prospect interest. Others obtain newspaper clippings about prospects or about matters of interest to them and then write appropriate comments on these.

Buffers always should be thanked for their courtesy and given a word of appreciation as you leave. For a regularly visited office, cards or small gifts at holidays may enhance your standing with the corporate watchdogs. By following a few common sense rules and treating the buffer as a person on an equal footing with yourself, you can avoid the ill-fated lobby interview, because Cerberus is on your side.

PROVEN APPROACH TECHNIQUES

Whether you are making a cold approach to a buffer or a prospect at home or you are seeing for the first time a person to whom you have sold an appointment by telephone, the first few things you say and the way you say them are of equal importance.

How You Say It

Most people overlook the effective use of their voices in selling situations. Many men, in particular, tend to use only the lower register of the voice, with the result that vocal intonation becomes monotonous. Women, on the other hand, can make more effective use of their lower vocal ranges than they do.

Some salespeople tend to talk too loudly. Keep the volume of your voice down to a conversational level, but make certain that you are using your entire vocal range. In particular, when you ask a question or make a compliment, use the upper ranges of your voice. This makes you sound interested in what your prospects may have to say. They, in turn, become motivated to give you the attention and interest that you seek.

Make the quality of your voice responsive to the emotional content of what is being said. If your prospect reveals a recent unfortunate occurrence, your voice should take on a sympathetic tone. If the customer divulges something of a personal nature, your voice should reflect an understanding or intimate quality. Complete responsiveness can have a powerful effect on your customers, making them not only willing but anxious to meet with you more often.

You can, however, overdo vocal inflections and colorations. Avoid any intonation that borders on the unctuous. This tone makes you sound insincere and may alienate rather than attract. Generally, however, most salespeople err on the side of too little expressiveness rather than too much. Listening to yourself on tape can be a difficult experience, but you should do so. You may be surprised at what you are saying and how you are saying it. Study your habits and make corrections.

Facial expression as well as vocal expression conveys meaning to your prospect. You can improve your facial expressiveness by raising your eyebrows frequently and smiling often. You should raise your eyebrows when asking a question. The resulting expression makes you appear receptive. It helps your prospect to open up to you; and, incidentally, behaving in a receptive way has the feedback effect on your brain of making you feel more receptive than you would otherwise.

Obviously, it is not desirable to sit like a grinning idiot throughout the sales interview. Do, however, let a half smile (not a smirk!) play around your lips often, particularly when asking probing or "hard" questions. The personal edge is taken off this kind of question when your smile and raised-eyebrow expression soften it.

No one wants to talk to a stone-faced individual. We like to talk to someone whose face reflects our views and who seems to understand and appreciate what we are saying. Some salespeople are so good at appearing to be understanding, sympathetic, and receptive that they are able to keep their prospects talking at times by facial expression alone. Again, you should correct any stone-faced tendency on your part by practicing with a mirror.

Do not overdo these techniques to the point where they become obvious; they then make you appear artificial and insincere. The more intelligent, sophisticated, and sensitive the prospect is, the more restrained you must be. Such a person will tune you out if you overdo. However, most salespeople tend in general to be under- rather than over-expressive.

Bear in mind the basic rules that you should maintain eye contact, that you must remember and use people's names, and that you can do almost anything with a smile!

Keep your pace slow. Salespeople tend to speed up because they are afraid of hearing "no" from prospects. As we have said before, speed is threatening to prospects because they are afraid of being buried under an avalanche of words without having a chance to protest. If you want to sound natural, slow down and use pauses. No one naturally speaks in a continuous, rapid stream. Salespeople seldom speak too slowly, although others may drive them crazy by doing so.

What You Say

Several scripts will help you get ideas about what to say. For a cold approach at a home, try these.

"Good morning, I'm Sam Salesperson from the Blank Company, and I'm calling on families in the neighborhood. May I step in and visit with you for a moment?"

"Good morning, Mrs. Homemaker? I'm your neighbor, Jane Parttimer, and I'm visiting busy mothers with young children. May I visit with you for a moment?"

Effective actions should precede and accompany your words. Walk directly up to the front door, ring the bell, and then step back a pace. Look around nonchalantly. You should appear casual and not terribly interested in going inside.

When your prospect opens the door, smile and *step backward* as you give your approach talk. This technique causes the customer to relax. If you step forward, the prospect will feel defensive and perhaps close the door.

After you finish what you are saying, lower your head, wipe your feet on the doormat, and walk forward into the house. By wiping your feet, you show respect for the prospect's house and furnishings. Dropping your head makes an objection difficult. Have you ever tried talking to the top of a head? Most people do not like to do so. Silence gives consent, and you enter.

Obviously, if the prospect is defensive and bars your way, you do not use physical force to enter!

Although these techniques are most clearly related to the sale of goods and services from door to door, they are good to know even if your selling takes place in other settings. After all, if you are involved in community or political affairs, which is highly advisable, you are bound to end up canvasing for a charitable fund or walking precincts for a candidate. You will find these methods very helpful in these endeavors.

In general, residential door approaches are much easier for a woman or sales teams consisting of both women and men than they are for a man or a sales team of men only. If the prospect is a woman, the element of fear is greatly reduced by the presence of another woman.

Suppose you are making your approach to a business or professional person or an industrial buyer. While drop-in calls are not generally advisable, in some lines of selling they are required. What should you say? Here is an approach to someone who has answered an advertisement:

"Mr. Prospect, I'm Connie Closer. I have the information booklet that you requested. May I step in?"

In the case of a cold call, try this:

"Ms. Prospect, I'm Vern Vendor of the Widget Company. Are you free to speak for a few moments?"

Suppose you have written the prospect a letter in advance.

"Good morning, Mr. Prospect. I'm Paula Persistent, with Patience & Persistence, Inc., and I'm following up on the letter that the Chamber of Commerce sent you on the short program they're sponsoring. Have you had a chance to read it? [handing prospect the letter] Just as the letter says, the seminar is being held on two consecutive evenings, January 14 and 15, from 5:30 to 9:30 P.M. The purpose of my visit today is to give you some information on the background of the speaker and explain what she plans to cover and to determine the number of people in your organization who would benefit from taking the program."

If you *must* drop in on a purchasing agent, try the "driving by" approach to the buffer.

"Hello, my name is Sam Salesperson. And you are . . . ? You know, Mr./Ms. Buffer, I've been driving by this building several times now, and my curiosity just got the best of me. Is this the Zilch Corporation that's affiliated with the one in Minneapolis? No? Well, just what type of business do you have here? Is that right! And the chief purchasing agent's name is . . . ? Does he happen to be in? When would be the best time to catch him in? I'd sure like to meet him. Would you tell him that I'm here to see him?"

When you meet the purchasing agent, use the same "driving by" story with him.

How about a life insurance opener?

"If I could show you the finest program for accumulating money you've ever seen—you're to be the sole judge—would you be in a position to put away, say, $25 to $100 a month for the next 10 years if it were something you really wanted?"

Here is a simple one for business and professional sales:

"Ms. Prospect, I'm Richard Rap. I've been asked to see you about the new widget program. It has meant increased profits (savings) to other companies in your industry. I wonder if I could have about 10 minutes of your time?"

All these different approaches have one common objective—an appointment *now*. All you are trying to sell is the interview. Whether you are using the lobby telephone, or receptionist or switchboard operator, the procedure is still the same. Ask enough questions to disturb the person you want to see, and then back off. You seek to make that person curious enough about the idea you have to offer to set up an appointment now, or at some later date. If this technique is to work effectively for you, you must continually ask questions to gain attention and interest. A survey of your prospect's needs could open the door to the main sale.

Some Power Phrases That Work

"Let me put it together, and then you can take a look at it."

"You're a business person, and I'm a business person." [This is equivalent to saying "My Adult is talking to your Adult."]

"I work with some of the top legal and accounting talent in this part of the country in my business practice."

"The *worst* thing that can happen is that you'll make sure everything is OK."

"If my ideas make sense, I would of course expect to represent your interests in implementing them. Is there any reason why I shouldn't?"

"My instructions are to give you your free brochure and then give you a brief preview of the program. When I am finished, I'll ask you just one question—have we done a good job? Fair enough?"

Answering Objections in the Approach

What happens if your prospect responds with an objection or question? A "no" response cuts off the interview; but a question gives you a second chance.

PROSPECT: Well, what is it all about?

SALESPERSON: You *are* Johnny's mother, aren't you? [*smiling*] He's a preschooler, isn't he? What I have to discuss with you will benefit Johnny. May I step in?

PROSPECT: What's it about?

SALESPERSON: We are talking to neighbors about their health, the welfare of their families, and how their health problems are handled. May we step in?

PROSPECT: Are you selling something?

SALESPERSON: Mr. Prospect, my call is to acquaint you with a service. It will require only a few minutes, and I'm sure you'll consider the time well spent. May I step in?

PROSPECT: I'm very busy. What is it about?

SALESPERSON: You must be very rushed, Ms. Prospect. I'll come back another time. Is morning or afternoon better? [*Do not discuss the purpose of your call.*]

PROSPECT: I'm really rushed, I don't have time. What's it about?

SALESPERSON: It's just a few questions. [*show questionnaire*] It's going on all over the country. You wouldn't mind answering a few questions, would you?

PROSPECT: I'm not interested in buying anything.

SALESPERSON: Fine, Mr. Prospect. You've every right to hesitate. I wish more people took your attitude of caution. You can benefit from these ideas, however. You do want to know about things that can help you, don't you? May I step in?

PROSPECT: I'm very busy. Can't you just drop your booklet in the mail? I'll get back to you later.

SALESPERSON: Yes, I certainly could do that, but you are entitled to a brief preview of the program, also. It'll only take 10 minutes of your time.

PROSPECT: Just send me the stuff in the mail and I'll look it over, OK?

SALESPERSON: Yes, Ms. Prospect, I could do that, but there are a few points of interest to your new job application that could best be discussed in person.

PROSPECT: What's this all about? I'm just going into a meeting.

SALESPERSON: Mr. Prospect, I've been reading about you in *Dun's Review*, and what I see looks very good. Now I might have called you on the telephone or sent you a letter, but I wanted to pay you the courtesy of a personal visit so that I could meet you and you could meet me and we could determine whether or not our Business Service would be of some help to you. I think we both can decide that pretty quickly if I could ask you a couple of questions.

PROSPECT: I have a friend in the business.

SALESPERSON: Is that a $5000 friend or a $10,000 friend? [*Whether or not prospect asks you what you mean, say:*] You're probably wondering what I mean. Well, you're a business person and I'm a business person. I imagine that you do a lot of business on a bid basis. So as one executive to another, if I were in a position to save you $5000 to $10,000 on the books of your business, would you have any objection to discussing it with me?

PROSPECT: I have all that taken care of.

SALESPERSON: By whom? When did you last see her? Did she do a good job? [*If the answer is yes, you should prospect on that basis, saying:*] Having this work done, you are in a position to appreciate the tremendous value of planning your affairs. I wonder if you could think of any other business persons who are as financially successful as you are, and who might have a need for this type of planning service. For example, who is your best competitor? If you had to pick and choose one person who is really going to rise to the top in your profession, who would that be?

As you can see, objections generally fall into the same common categories. You will not be able to gain an interview every time, but a good response will help to get you past procrastinating objections on the part of people who really might be interested. Persistence is important, and a little humor can help, too.

> Ron, a high technology salesman trying to get in to see a busy specifying applications engineer, sent his card in via the secretary, but was not admitted to the inner office.
> "Well," he said to the secretary, "could you get the card back for me then?" The card came back torn in half—a most emphatic objection to his approach.
> "Hey," he said, "would you tell your boss that these things cost money." The embarrassed secretary disappeared and then reappeared with a nickel. "Mr. Hotshot says this is to cover it."
> "Well, in that case, you had better take him another one," said Ron, getting one out and handing it over. "I wouldn't want to cheat him—they're two for a nickel."
> His persistence and humor finally got him through the door.

HANDLING APPROACH FEAR

On the first few times out, every new salesperson confronts approach fear. With some people it is so bad that if they had cymbals on their knees they could be heard in the next county! Even veteran salespeople have to admit that there are times when they drive around and around an industrial park trying not to find a parking space, hoping the buyer will not be in, or wanting to hear just one more song on the radio.

What is approach fear? It is the fear of rejection and humiliation that we discussed in Chapter 5. Coping behavior for these fears is the same as that for others. First, name and face up to the fears. Use visualization techniques to envision successful outcomes. Remember that you are playing a numbers game in which eventually you have to win because each rejection makes winning on the next approach more likely.

YOUR FIRST IMPRESSION

Your appearance is important because the customer will receive a first impression of you and your company from it and will judge you accordingly. You should not do likewise, however; never judge your customer by appearance. It is too often deceiving, as one man's experience shows.

> Leo was working his way through college by selling part-time at a stereo store in the Loop in downtown Chicago, only a few blocks east

of Skid Row. Occasionally a derelict from this area would wander across one of the Chicago River bridges and gape at the store windows or even come in and pretend to be shopping. Usually these characters were quite harmless and could be funny as they imagined aloud that they had a million dollars and were going to buy out the store. However, the regular clerks on straight commission did not find the resulting waste of their time amusing, so one day when a hobo appeared and swaggered in, Leo found the floor suddenly deserted except for himself.

The unshaven and shabby bum announced that he was interested in seeing only the best equipment or he would not waste his time in this establishment. He was, he said, a "high roller" and would only patronize the store if it would accept a one-thousand-dollar bill in payment.

Leo almost burst out laughing, but he restrained himself and replied that he would accept any money that the prospect had as cash payment. Thinking that he would get in some valuable practice with the better merchandise, he proceeded to explain the advantages and disadvantages of all the better components on display. When Leo finally finished his sales presentation, the nonchalant hobo produced not one, but five one-thousand-dollar bills to purchase over $4,700 worth of equipment. To the chagrin of the regular clerks, this "derelict" turned out to be an eccentric inventor who liked to masquerade as a bum.

Although you should qualify prospects to see whether they are serious, never be an armchair qualifier. The fact that you dress for success does not mean that your prospect does also. Prejudging a customer can lose a big sale. That very large older lady wandering through the junior dress department might need a birthday present for her niece or granddaughter. The stammering boy who answers the telephone could be a senator's son—or even the senator. The man casually kicking tires could be an authority on engines. And the bum could be a millionaire.

Notes

1. John T. Molloy, *Dress for Success* (New York: McKay, 1974); and *The Woman's Dress for Success Book* (Chicago: Follett, 1977).
2. Molloy, *Dress for Success*, p. 118.
3. Interview of Mary Wells Lawrence, *Vogue*, February 1978.

Chapter 14
The Warm-up Phase

Many of us are tense and self-conscious when we meet others for the first time. Through nervousness or fear we build a protective wall to shield ourselves from possible hurt. Naturally, the wall also stops both effective communication and relaxation that results from an easy and casual relationship. This stiffness is as common at the beginning of a business association as it is at a cocktail party. As a professional salesperson you are responsible for breaking down that wall between you and your new client.

For until everyone is relaxed, good interaction between the two parties is unlikely. Needed is an interim following the approach to foster relaxation.

The *warm-up*, the second stage in our selling process, is that warm-up or transitional period. It helps set the mood for the actual sales presentation to follow.

Casual confidence is the key to a good transitional bridge. As you talk, adopt a generally relaxed and easy manner and do everything you can to put your prospects at ease. Start a light conversation about anything from the weather to recent athletic events. The length of this conversation can be as little as five minutes, though the time varies with regional customs and your client's personality. (Some high-intensity Achiever types will be impatient to start talking business in two minutes; more laid-back Affiliator-type customers could easily spend the afternoon in small talk!) When your prospects are relaxed and start to talk freely, though, you can launch into your presentation.

I know of one high-technology sales manager who puts all incoming calls on his telephone squawk box and does paperwork for the first five minutes of each telephone conversation. He says that it does not matter whether it is a local or a long-distance telephone buyer or whether the caller is an account or one of his salespeople. The end result is the same. It takes people about five minutes to get warmed up before they ever come to the main reason for their call. "By talking to them over the squawk box, I can get a lot of my own work done before I finally have to devote my full attention to their call. You multiply that five-minute 'warm-up factor' by all of the various incoming calls and you can readily see how much work I can accomplish over a year!"

THE PATH TO THE SALE

Where are you along the psychological path to the sale as you start this small talk? You have made the *initial contact.* By the end of it, you had started to gain the prospect's *attention.* Now you must consolidate attention on yourself and move on to the beginnings of *interest.* You must move the prospect's mind from his or her own concerns to yours, which means you must start out by talking about something that is close to this person.

In terms of the prospect's desired path from thinking as you think through feeling as you feel, you are just beginning the thinking stage. That is why your first topics of conversation are conventional and not emotional. You never talk about sex, politics, or religion.

SET THE STAGE, TAKE COMMAND

Unless you are selling at retail, you are a guest in your prospect's office or home, but you should assume the role of host or hostess and adroitly control the proceedings. The setting becomes your space module, and you are the astronaut who directs its course.

If you are to gain control, you must place yourself and others correctly and arrange a setting that is conducive to buyer attention to your performance. This arrangement includes changing the sound and lighting conditions if necessary.

Do not be afraid to move furniture or people around to achieve the best arrangement. People are used to being told what to do, and most will not take offense. The exception is the Power Boss/Commander, who will probably try to place *you* where *he* or *she* wants—an immediate clue to personality.

When you are presenting materials to several people and both sexes are present, the rule of seating is to place the person of your own sex next to yourself and the others beyond. Thus if you should happen to touch the person next to you unintentionally, neither that person nor the others in the group will be distracted by wondering what your true intentions are. If you are right-handed, seat your prospects to your left side. The key point is that if you feel uncomfortable, you will make your prospects feel nervous or uncomfortable, too.

If you foresee that it will be difficult to retain control in the prospect's surroundings—if ringing phones, people popping in and out, and other interruptions are a problem—try to change the environment by taking the client out to lunch, to coffee, or even just to your car for whatever sort of trip is appropriate. (Drive the client to the airport, for example.)

In any case, you must eliminate as many distractions as possible. How do you gain attention in an office when the purchasing agent is on the telephone or is signing or dictating letters or allows interruptions? What do you do in a home where the television is on at full volume, a baby is crying, and two other children are fighting under the kitchen table?

Almost anything can be done with a smile. Try smiling and asking the purchasing agent to hold all incoming calls for the next 10 minutes or so, or smiling and asking the home prospect if it is all right to turn off the TV set—*as you in fact do so.* This bold sweetness approach works in some very difficult situations because although you are in effect directing others, the smile takes the hard edge off your commands. This is *action language* at its best.

As an alternative, you might try dropping your voice to an almost inaudible level. This may cause the prospect to recognize and correct the distractions, the purchasing agent might close the office door, telling the secretary not to allow any interruptions.

Another effective technique is silence. Stop talking suddenly and wait for the prospect to realize that you are being treated rudely. This Friendly Silent Questioning Stare (FSQS) technique works with mature prospects, but with others there is a risk of never regaining full control of the situation.

As you take command, do not hesitate. To do so makes you appear not to believe in what you are doing. Hesitation asks for objections to the interview. It communicates an alternative response to your desired action.

PROVEN BRIDGE TECHNIQUES

What do you do or say to start building the bridge and moving your prospects' minds from the "small talk" (warm up) to the "big talk" (presentation)? You can use one or more of the following techniques.

Object Language

Survey your prospect's surroundings. What is the furniture and how is it arranged? What is sitting on the shelves and hanging from the walls? Don't be afraid to glance around—these things were put there to be seen. Comment on the most impressive object you see. It is an excellent clue to a prospect's interests.

> Jack is an avid fisherman who has a huge fish stuffed and mounted on a plaque above and behind his desk. He uses this fish to sort out the salespeople who approach him. "Nine out of ten salesmen notice the fish," he says. "I wouldn't buy anything from the person who didn't. Of the nine remaining vendors, four will tell me how they caught bigger fish in the same location. They are dead ducks, too. Thus, only five, or half, of the salespeople who call on me have a chance of selling me their products or services."

Your observant attitude should make that prospect's mounted minnow seem like the whale that swallowed Jonah. Even if you caught a 40-foot shark called Jaws, you must not put down this fisherman. You may win the bragging contest, but lose the sale.[1]

Different personality types provide different object language clues. The Power Boss/Commander may have nothing on the walls, but 1½ inches may have been sawed off your chair legs to put you physically beneath the buyer. She will have a squawk box and other symbols of power on the bare surface of her desk. The Avoider/Abdicator has stacks of papers on his only chair—you are not welcome here. The Affiliator/Pleaser's surroundings are soft and comfortable, inviting you to stay and be friends. He will have photos, awards and other trivia around his office. The Manipulator/Gamesman has a bare desk. She may have oil paintings and an enclosed bar in her office. This buyer wants to pick your brain without giving you any clues in return. The Achiever/Craftsman doesn't care much about the appearance of surroundings. He will have charts and graphs and maybe a prototype product model on his neat desk.

On the subject of object language, we should mention that the most sacred chair in the corporation belongs to the president. Don't sit in it!

Mention a Referral

Mentioning the name of the satisfied customer or mutual friend who referred you to the prospect can provide a bond between you or can give you a clue to the prospect's motivations. Is there evidence of emulation or other needs?

Give a Compliment

A sincere compliment on the prospect's home, office, neighborhood, or business progress will draw a favorable response. Compliments should be related to the interests expressed by the prospect through object language if possible. The Avoider/Abdicator and Affiliator/Pleaser love compliments; the Power Boss/Commander likes them if they are kept short. The Achiever/Craftsman and the Manipulator/Gamesman do not care for them; one knows, and the other does not care!

Discuss a Subject of Mutual Interest

From your precall research or from observation of such clues as radios tuned to ball games during business hours, you can start your conversation off on something that you know interests the client. Be sure to let the prospect talk. Do not take over the conversation yourself, even though you may know more than the customer does about the subject.

Offer a Survey

Depending on the nature of your product or service, you can offer to make a survey of your prospect's situation to obtain information that ultimately could benefit the client firm. Avoiders and achievers respect this tactic.

Product Samples

Showing product samples gives you an opportunity to either demonstrate or discuss this product conversation piece. A refrigerator door sample or a publisher's prospectus is an effective attention-getting device. Many times, your complete sales talk can be built around your product samples or visual aids. Achievers prefer this approach, if you can document your product claims with facts and figures.

The Bridge

Some sales executives bridge the gap between small talk and sales talk with transitional statements like these:

"I guess you're probably wondering what this is all about. Well, you are certainly entitled to know. [*Produce read-off sales presentation notebook or flip chart.*] This little booklet tells you the reason for my stopping by to see you today. Now, if you'll sit over here, Mr. Buyer, and you over there, Mr. Assistant, we can run through this together. [*Seat prospects and arrange furniture.*] The booklet begins by asking you a very important question: [*open book and indicate first page*] 'Are you satisfied with your present health care coverage?' "

"Based on the information derived from my previous survey of your situation, our engineering department has drawn up a special set of specifications for your consideration. Now, if you'll sit over here, where the light is better, Ms. Buyer, we can run through it together. On page 3, I'd like to direct your attention to the following features. . . ."

"Here's the information that you requested. [*Show, but place on table out of their reach.*] In addition, you are entitled to a brief pre-view of the new Fall line of merchandise. Now, just make yourself comfortable here, while I show you what's new and what's selling well."

"Just as the letter indicates, the seminar is being held on two consec-utive evenings on March 1 and 2 from 6:30 to 9:30 P.M. The purpose of my visit today is to give you some information on the speaker, ex-plain what she plans to cover, and determine the number of people in your organization who would benefit from taking the course.

Incidentally, I'm new in town, and I don't know very much about your organization. Exactly what do you do here? . . . Are all of your people here or do you have other locations? . . . Approximately how many full-time employees do you have now? . . . Of course, how many are in supervision or involved in customer contact?

Well, fine, Mr. Prospect, from what you tell me, I believe that we have a program here that may very well benefit you and your people. Let me tell you a little about Ms. Wordsmith, who teaches this course. . . ."

MORE ABOUT COMMUNICATION

What should you say to a customer during the bridge and what should not be said? How can you find out whether this client has a good chance of being truly interested in your product or service? For what should you listen?

Statement of Interest

You will find it very effective to make an opening statement that you are interested in serving your customers' needs. This kind of remark enhances your source credibility, because many clients expect salespeople to serve only themselves. To the Affiliator/Pleaser, point out how the boss will benefit. The Avoider/Abdicator should be assured that you will help make a safe choice. Show the Power Boss/Commander that you want to help him or her win. Point out that you want to present challenges to the Achiever/Craftsman and long-term benefits to the Manipulator/Gamesman.

Positive and Negative Words

During the bridge and throughout your presentation, you should be aware of the words you choose. Certain words are known to evoke positive responses in listeners no matter how they are used. A sample of these words is given in Figure 14.1. In preparing your sales talk, ask yourself which words will best arouse the emotion with which you wish to motivate your customer.

The use of such words is not a sophisticated technique, and it works better with less experienced buyers than with more experienced ones. It is a simple stimulus-response technique, but customers often are complex. You cannot ring their doorbells and expect them to buy immediately, unlike the situation with Pavlov's dogs. However, use of a few such words can help you to size up your customer if you listen and watch for responses.

Negative or "hard" words should be avoided. They are such words as *sale, sign, buy, sell, contract,* and so on. They evoke defensive reactions that originate in the Parent of the buyer, which has been taught to recognize these words as threatening—particularly to an Avoider/Abdicator.

What Not To Discuss

Few of us would be so foolish or tactless as to start out a conversation with a new prospect with the topics of politics or religion. It is not difficult, however, to make a remark that offends your hearer without realizing it until afterward. An example is the mention of a new development in medical or surgical techniques to a person who is a Christian Scientist and does not believe in conventional medical practices. While you cannot always know such facts ahead of time, be careful: tactlessness often can be avoided. You have nothing to gain by offering an unsolicited opinion—but everything to lose.

WORDS THAT BRING POSITIVE RESPONSES

1. Truth (attracts immediate attention)
2. Let's (contraction of two words: *let* and *us*. Implies togetherness—"Let's see why you will get more value for your money. . . .")
3. Fun
4. Value
5. Time-saving
6. Recommended
7. Successful
8. Efficient
9. Durable
10. Bargain
11. Stylish
12. Elegance
13. Necessary
14. Growth
15. Scientific
16. Youth
17. Genuine
18. Love
19. Excel
20. Enormous
21. Beauty
22. Independent
23. Tested
24. Tasteful
25. Home
26. Mother
27. Qualify
28. Progress
29. Guaranteed
30. Safe
31. Stimulating
32. Health
33. Appetizing
34. Affectionate
35. Clean
36. Popular
37. Modern
38. Ambition
39. Reputation
40. Economical
41. Warrantied
42. Status
43. Courtesy
44. Personality
45. Relief
46. Admired
47. Sociable
48. Thinking
49. Low-cost
50. Expressive
51. Up-to-date
52. Hospitality
53. Sympathy
54. Amusement
55. Pride

Figure 14.1   Words that bring positive responses.

When discussing Chet's ex-professional basketball coach, Len almost introduced the subject with an opinion. Instead he asked Chet—now a purchasing agent—what *he* thought of Coach Jox. "That miserable bum! He's about to lose his present coaching job too. He was a flake when I played for him, and he still is today!"

A young man hired as a clerk in a grocery chain store was standing in the produce section one day when a well-dressed gentleman approached him and asked the price of a head of lettuce.

"Three dollars," the clerk responded.

"Three dollars for a head of lettuce!" The man was outraged. "Young man, I'll take half a head."

"Well, I'll have to ask the boss," said the clerk, and he headed through the swinging doors into the back area, unaware that he was closely followed by the customer.

"Boss," he said, "there's a meathead out there who wants to buy *half* a head of lettuce!"

The boss's face paled as he gazed over the boy's shoulder at the enraged customer. Becoming aware of the situation, the clerk added brightly,

"And this gentleman wants to buy the other half!"

Impressed with the young man's quick thinking and competence, the boss, after several months, called him into his office and told him that a new store was to be opened in Toronto and he would be promoted from clerk and sent there as manager.

"But sir!" blurted the clerk, "There's no one in Toronto but prostitutes and hockey players!"

The boss drew himself up and puffed out his cheeks.

"I'll have you know that *my wife* is from Toronto!" he said.

"Oh, really? What position did she play, sir?"

Unfortunately, most of us are not so good at retrieving our feet from our mouths. The solution is not to place them there in the first place.

Qualify Your Prospect Further

If your company has done an acceptable job of market research, or if you have done your own precall research and planning well, you should not find yourself trying to sell baseball bats to little old ladies or cold rolled steel to bubble gum distributors. Individuals within targeted groups do, however, vary from company norms. Before you have spent much time on a presentation, you should find out whether this particular prospect has a fair chance of becoming a buyer. This process is called *qualifying the buyer* from a suspect to a prospect.

Dan, who represented a company that sold solar swimming pool heating systems, got an appointment from a telephone call to a Ms. Peters who appeared on his company's list of prospects. After a string of rejections on the telephone, Dan was delighted and relieved to get this appointment, and he certainly did not want to jeopardize it by questioning the lady too closely over the telephone.

Arriving at the house in the evening, Dan was very warmly welcomed by Ms. Peters and her sister, both of whom, it turned out, were elderly widows living together. They pressed tea and cakes on Dan and listened attentively throughout his long and somewhat technical presentation. Finally he got out the necessary measuring equipment and flashlight and stood up.

"And now could you ladies show me where the pool is?" he asked.

"Oh, dear, we don't have a pool!" replied Ms. Peters. "We just thought your idea sounded so interesting—and we are lonely and love to have company—so we invited you over to tell us about it!"

It is a good idea to start out by asking qualifying questions that seek information. The answers will quickly help you to decide whether you have a live prospect or a Ms. Peters.

"So that I can determine exactly how much savings the use of my product/service could mean to you, Ms. Prospect, I will need to have some information. . . ."

"Tell me, are you satisfied with your present services in this area?"

"Let's say a miracle occurred and you suddenly owned this product/service. Say someone gave it to you. Would you use it? Or would it wind up gathering dust in the attic or down in the basement?"

An answer of "yes" to the second question or "no" to the third indicates no need on the part of the prospect—and *no need* is an objection that cannot be overcome. You should extricate yourself gracefully from the situation and spend your valuable time elsewhere.

You may not even need to ask any questions if you watch and listen for the prospect to self-qualify. Remember to observe gestures and facial expressions. They can reveal more than the prospect's words.

A prospect who does not already know what product or service you represent might respond to your initial comments or questions with solid information:

"I'm sorry, but I've already purchased your product recently."

"I do use your type of product, but a friend handles my account."

"I know about your product/service and I like it and intend to buy it some day, but I simply can't afford it right now."

Now you are in a stronger position than you were before, because you know the prospect's position and can speak to it. In the first case, turn the exchange into a request for referrals:

"You should be congratulated on your good judgment in selecting our product line. I've sold these fine products for a dozen years now to knowledgable people like yourself. If you ever need service or have a question, please don't hesitate to call me. By the way, since you have a high regard for our products, would you recommend any of your employees or associates who might be interested in enjoying their benefits?"

In the second case, try selling the idea of service:

"I'm glad you're benefiting from our product/service, even if it's from a competitor! But I know we offer some very special services that you may not be enjoying now. To demonstrate them to you, I'll need to know some information about your present program objectives. . . ."

The third case is ideal because the product/service has already been accepted. You are much further along toward the sale than you might have realized.

"If I could show you how it could be installed now on a lease basis, and you could save more in the long run than it would cost you now, could we count on your cooperation? It will only take a few moments to show you. . . ."

Introductory Remarks and Indirection

The technique of *indirection* is a strategy of asking questions and making comments that *indirectly* present your solutions to prospect problems. It is a method of arraying forces within the prospect's mind so that he or she identifies the problem and chooses the solution you offer without your ever having to assume an authority's position and give commands. Buyers in this case feel that they have clarified their own needs and solved their own problems with little help from you, so they never develop defensive feelings of confrontation with you.

Indirection is powerful, but you will need practice to learn it. It is worth the effort, however, especially when you find yourself dealing with Power Bosses or Achievers, both of whom respond very well to it. Power Bosses/Commanders especially like to take credit for all successes, and with this approach you should encourage them to do so.

At the bridge stage of the interview, indirection takes the form of open-ended questions that encourage the prospect to start talking and thus produce the information that will allow you to understand the problem and guide the client toward understanding it.

"How's it going? Is the new product line moving?"

"How's business? Does the next year look bullish?"

"How's your new irrigation system working out?"

"How are your teen customers taking to the shorter dresses?"

"What's the outlook for business in the do-it-yourself market?"

Of course, indirection and the customer's interpretation of it can be taken too far:

Two psychiatrists crossed paths between buildings at a large medical center.
  "Nice day!" said one, and hurried on.
  "Hmm, I wonder what he meant by that," mused the other.

Remember To Listen

Especially as a beginner, you may have a tendency to cover nervousness at the beginning of a sales interview with a stream of chatter. Actually, it is much easier just to ask a few questions and let the prospect talk, and it is much more helpful to you, as well. Train yourself to listen. If you do not, you can lose the sale very easily.

> Gus was a faking listener: he always responded with the words "Great! Great!" whenever a purchasing agent would manage to squeeze a few words into the conversation. Once a buyer told Gus that his wife had just died.
> "Great! Great!" was the inevitable response. To this day Gus does not know why he lost that account.

Note

1. Joe Girard and Stanley H. Brown, *How to Sell Anything to Anybody* (New York: Simon & Schuster, 1977), p. 164.

Chapter 15
The Presentation

Now we arrive at that time for which you have prepared so well for so long: you are going to make your sales presentation to the customer. What is this sales presentation going to do? It will explain the product or service to the buyer; it will identify buyer problems and propose solutions; and it will create need, use, and value for the product in the buyer's mind before price is brought up.

It is impossible to overemphasize the fact that you are to sell solutions, not hardware. You sell benefits, not generic products. You do not push a product; you solve a problem.

GAUGING THE CUSTOMER'S PROGRESS

During the presentation, which is the heart of the entire selling process, you will move the buyer through several psychological steps. If the bridge has been correctly negotiated, *interest* will already be developing. You will confirm interest in the buyer's mind and move along to *desire*, *conviction*, and *resolve to buy*. You also will move the buyer from thinking as you think, which is complete with achievement of the interest step, to feeling as you feel, which encompasses desire, conviction, and resolve.

INDIRECTION, EMPATHY, AND PERSUASION

Persuasion is a matter more of strategy than of manipulation. Professional selling is a process of arraying logical forces so that people themselves decide to do what you want them to do, rather than a process of changing minds. Any effort to get buying actions by tampering with people's emotions not only encounters the psychological limitation of resistance, but also can be prohibitively time consuming and expensive.

A well-planned approach to selling recognizes that rational motives are often the best persuaders. You must become aware of your customers' motives in order to adroitly move them in the desired direction.[1]

Most people have healthy minds; they like to buy. Everyone experiences pleasure with each new acquisition. Irrational resistances, even if in the subconscious, can and will be handled by healthy prospects themselves if they are provided with a sufficient rational motive as incentive. Such selling is not manipulating people behind their backs; it is giving them rational motives for doing what is in their own best interests as individuals and as members of society at large.

As we have said, you must empathize with customers. You must find out what their concerns are and walk in their shoes. But you also must bring them to empathize with you—to think as you think and feel as you feel. Indirection, which we discussed at the end of Chapter 14, is the tool for persuasion and establishment of empathy.

ENTHUSIASM

When we listed the qualifications of a good salesperson, we included enthusiasm. If you want to see people, they will want to see you; and if you believe that your product or service is the best of its kind, and you let them know it, they will tend to feel that way too. Cynicism or a holier-than-thou attitude has no place in selling. Have you ever asked a waiter or waitress in a restaurant to tell you what is good today and received the reply, "I don't know—I don't eat here myself!"? What kind of buying mood does that produce?

ACTION LANGUAGE

Nothing is more boring than a person who acts like a zombie. Keep moving during your presentation, especially if you are standing and speaking to a group. You should convey conviction in both word and deed. If the words of your presentation are exciting, you get *excited!*

Touching people can be very effective. You must, however, develop a sense of appropriateness concerning touch. Depending on social conditioning and personality, some people like to be touched and others find it offensive. In some situations, touch symbolizes a relationship that you do not intend. You should never stand behind a seated corporate president and place your hand on his or her shoulder while looking over at what he or she is writing or reading. It is not a good idea for a man to place his arm around a woman's shoulders unless he is sure she will react positively; this gesture is regarded by feminists as demeaning, however innocently it is intended.

SOURCE CREDIBILITY IN THE PRESENTATION

During the approach, warm-up phase, and bridge, your appearance has indicated to the customer that your source credibility may be good. Now you must back up your appearance with knowledge and skill. You must *be* as well as *look* professional.

Company Knowledge

In addition to knowing all about your products and about what services your company provides, you must be prepared to apply this knowledge for your customer's need. It is better to underpromise than to overpromise. If you know that delivery is averaging about six weeks right now—say seven to eight. Then the customer will be pleasantly surprised if the merchandise arrives earlier and will not be annoyed by a slight delay. Leave a margin of error around your promises. Then, if there is an emergency, you will have a little slack to take up.

Accept blame for mistakes, even if they are not your own. Why lose a good account by quibbling over whose fault caused a misdirected shipment? Unless the problem is large and you are being asked for compensation, just apologize and leave the issue behind.

Protect your customer from price or availability changes. If you see a price rise coming, let the buyer know in case he or she wants to beat it. And, of course, never quote a current price when you know a future price will apply. If an item is to be discontinued, let the buyer know. Do not let a customer design a production sequence around a unit that is about to become unavailable. You may lose an immediate sale, but you will gain permanent good will. This is the crux of buyer-vendor empathy.

Industry Knowledge Through Commitment

As a sales professional, you know your industry backward and forward, and you become a source of information for both your clients and your company. Your clients may rely on your expertise because your knowledge is of a specialized sort that they do not have the time, inclination, or ability to acquire. In some cases, clients even pay for such expertise. Agricultural chemical representatives, for example, often receive from the farmer a flat fee per acre just for their information and advice. This is *consultative selling* at its finest. Your company, on the other hand, receives valuable feedback through you on up-to-the-minute conditions in the marketplace. This information helps in the areas of new product design, product pricing, sales predictions, and long-range market planning.

As an industrial sales engineer, what you have to offer is technical competence. If you know all about your product, you will not have to bluff if a customer asks a question to which you should know the answer.

> Pat, a new salesperson, learned this lesson from the chief procurement officer of a large corporation. After Pat failed to answer satisfactorily a few direct product-related questions, the old buyer stopped abruptly.
>
> "Look here," he said, "you can afford to make some mistakes with me on your first visit, but by the time you return, I will have studied up on your product line and its applications. If I know more about your products than you do by then, you won't be welcome here, because I won't need you."

A seasoned buyer is nobody's fool. These professionals, in fact, often are consulted by sales managers and others when sales territory changes are to be made. Don't go unprepared to such a meeting. You must be able to give the buyer whatever is needed.

You can continually increase your knowledge by joining business-related organizations such as the American Marketing Association, local chambers of commerce, and the Sales and Marketing Executives Club. Continue your education through books, seminars, and local educational institutions. Also, speech improvement classes and organizations such as Toastmasters can help you gain poise and confidence.

Be honest about your products and services. Do not pretend that faults do not exist. Every buyer, whether a consumer or an industrial purchasing agent, knows that nothing is perfect, and if you pretend that it is, you will lose source credibility. People buy when the advantages of a purchase outweigh its disadvantages in relation to other alternatives.

Always conduct your affairs in a professional and businesslike manner. In selling there is no place for clowning, begging, or playing around. Make understatements rather than exaggerations. Do not malign your competitors; doing so reflects badly on you as a person. You can get your fair share of business without losing your dignity. Who knows? Some day you might end up working for one of those competitors. What would you say to a customer then?

Product Knowledge Through Ownership

Where possible, you should purchase, own, and use the products and services you sell. If you cannot own a product such as a die-stamping machine or a personal airplane, you should at least know how to operate it so that you can demonstrate its features to customers and answer their questions intelligently. If you do not own or use the product, conviction will be lacking in your delivery.

Know Your Customer's Position

As we emphasized in Chapter 9, you must understand your customers' markets and their customers' problems. Sell to your customer's needs. Do not just try to sell the largest dollar amount; such a move is short-sighted. Resist the temptation to sell the most expensive item in your line, or your buyer will soon learn that your recommendations are self-serving. Do not load a buyer up with $10,000 worth of equipment when the budget is $5000 or pass off slow-moving items just to make your sales quota.

Treat your large and small customers with equal fairness. Although A accounts will receive the largest share of your time, you should not be less honest, less helpful, or less empathetic with your small customers. After all, some of them will grow into large ones, and you want to be on excellent terms with them when they do.

SELL BENEFITS, NOT GENERIC PRODUCTS

Consultative selling is a humanistic and problem-solving approach to customer welfare. As we have said before, the problem-solving approach to selling focuses on your customers' wants and needs and on how your product or service can fill them. This philosophy should permeate the sales interview. Remember that you must try to enter the sales pyramid (Chapter 5) as near to the top as you can.

In most situations, your prospects are unaware that they have a particular problem until you bring it to their attention. It is your job to identify the area of improvement that their company has not considered. Perhaps they should purchase new equipment, modify old equipment, or develop a completely new product. You have to give them headaches before you can provide aspirin.

Once customers recognize a problem or need, they often become motivated to buy, so you should try to identify your product or service with the successful solution to their problems. Sometimes, however, the proper solution does not include your product. In these cases, you have acted purely as an advisor. Don't be afraid to say, "Don't buy now!" Your consultative services will not be forgotten. Sometimes you have to cast bread upon the waters in the hope of a subsequent return.

In any case, be aware of the true benefits or solutions you are offering. The concept of selling benefits was most clearly expressed in a famous statement by Charles Revson, the Revlon magnate: "In the laboratory," he said, "we make cosmetics; in the store, we sell hope."

Think about your product or service. What is your customer really buying? If you don't know, perhaps you should do again the features—advantages-benefits exercise in Chapter 9.

THE SALESPERSON AS EDUCATOR

Until you explain them, customers know very little about your products or their applications. You perform a teaching function as you sell ideas and knowledge along with your product line. The better you are as an educator, the more successful you will be as a purveyor of the knowledge, concepts, and ideas in your sales talk.

Learning takes place through our senses and through doing, and an effective sales presentation is a teaching and learning experience for both buyer and seller. You need to develop good verbal communication skills to pass on ideas clearly, concisely, and persuasively to your buyer. You should back up your own teaching with visual aids.

The main methods of education are lecture, discussion or participation, demonstration, and performance.

Lecture

The lecture is one-way communication with no provision for feedback. A radio commercial or a printed advertisement is a good example. A lecture can give a lot of information quickly, but it is the weakest of the four teaching methods. Any lecture over eight minutes long bores the audience and is ineffective. In selling, a lecture is called a canned pitch.

Discussion or Participation

Any form of teaching or selling that encourages two-way communication between student and teacher or between buyer and seller is better than a straight lecture. Material that is interesting to both parties, such as samples or visual aids, will encourage discussion. Most current sales presentations are structured around the discussion method.

Demonstration

Demonstrations increase the credibility of both the sales presentation and the salesperson. They break the monotony of a sales talk, and hold the prospect's attention, and they help you to tailor your sales talk to the individual customer's needs. Demonstrations show how the product works.

Performance

The best way to learn any new skill, whether how to sell or how to operate a new piece of equipment, is to try it. No one learns by watching; you cannot learn to swim without getting wet. Next time you are demonstrating a product, remember that demonstration is an excellent sales tool, but if you want your clients to operate your equipment after you depart, let them perform. Put them into action; let them operate it to learn. In doing so, they are trying out the role of ownership. Let your customers help you make the sale. If they can perform, they have learned it. Performance thus serves as positive reinforcement to the buyer.

Does your sales talk encourage your customers to participate physically in the proceedings? Is a demonstration included? Don't make customers sit still for an hour or longer listening to you. At least plan to have them hold or examine visual aids or samples, actually operating them if possible. Do not, however, hand out literature for customers to read and then talk while they are reading. Most people cannot take in two inputs at once.

Three Psychological Learning Principles

There is a difference between understanding and remembering, and the object of your teaching is to impress the benefits of your product on the buyer's mind, to be remembered at least until after the sale is made.

You can use three methods during your presentation to help customers learn and remember your main points: they are *summation, reinforcement,* and *repetition.*

Summation occurs when you stop periodically, recapitulate the major points you have made in brief form, and then obtain agreement. Reinforcement is the giving of a reward of some kind for desired behavior. This procedure tends to cause the behavior to recur. For example, you can reinforce customers' statements that move them closer to buying by complimenting their judgment. Repetition needs no explanation. It has been widely used in advertising. Note, though, that repetition on the customer's part leads to much faster learning than does repetition on your part.

PRESENTATION STRATEGY

Your actual presentation procedure should follow a plan based on a series of modules, each with its own close.

Modular Plan

Under this plan, you do not proceed from module A to module B until you have persuaded the customer to accept the salient points of module A. Otherwise, you will find yourself completing the entire sales talk only to have your proposal rejected because of an objection that should have been overcome during an early module of the presentation.

Variations on this theme go by different names, but the principle behind them is the same.

GATE THEORY OF SELLING

Envision yourself starting off on the path to your sale down a road with a series of stoplights which are connected with gates. Your sales presentation is a series of modules that are separated by these gates. You must gain commitment at each gate before entering the next module. As you approach the first one, it is red. You ask the customer, "Does that make sense?" If the answer is "Yes!" the light turns green, the gate swings open, and you may proceed to the next light. This is known as gaining a positive commitment to continue. If the answer is "No!" the gate stays shut and you must stay at that point until you can change the no to a yes. (Proceeding to the next module despite a red light is high-pressure selling.) Only then may you move forward. If you fail to do this through listening, observing, and adroit questioning, you might receive an objection in the last module that you failed to answer or clear up in an earlier module. The buyer's mind had closed against you at that point.

BARRIER SELLING

A manipulative version of the module strategy is barrier selling, in which *you* establish barriers in your prospect's mind in the course of your sales presentation. Each barrier represents something that your prospect desires. You build these barriers by phrasing your discussion topics in such a way that you elicit favorable responses or admissions from your prospects and they are forced to indicate their desires. Thus if at the end of the sales talk your prospects decide not to buy, they must, in effect, contradict all their earlier statements. Encyclopedia salespeople use it as follows:

> "Mr. and Mrs. Buyer, you can always buy these books at this regular price, but for your favorable decision *tonight*, we shall ask you to do some things for us, and we shall make some concessions to you—including a substantial price discount. And when we are finished with our presentation, we shall ask you just one question—did we do a good job? In other words, we shall ask for your immediate acceptance or rejection. Is that fair enough?"

Agreement from this prospect family unit establishes the barrier of making a decision beyond *tonight*. The salesperson has, in effect, taken away the "I'll think it over" objection. This technique is highly manipulative and can be demeaning to a sophisticated buyer. It is better used as a strong *closing* technique.

Mood Selling

A famous Bible salesman once said that he had to make his prospects laugh and cry before they would buy. He was depending on mood selling.

Most radio broadcasters will tell you that the human voice is by far the most persuasive selling instrument because it plays upon the listener's imagination to create a mood that is conducive to buying. This phenomenon can be used constructively in selling. You can convey the appropriate mood through warmth, sincerity, and the conviction that comes from product knowledge and belief. Mood selling is most effective with Avoiders/Abdicators, Affiliators/Pleasers, and, surprisingly, Power Bosses/Commanders.

Avoid mood selling just for mood's sake. Creating a mood is like setting a stage for a grand performance. Your performance, of course, is your sales presentation. It does not have to win any Academy Awards— only a purchase order. Mood selling has its place, but it is not the whole show.

Using Questions and Comments

To avoid misunderstandings as you proceed from one module to another, you should seek clarification of the customer's needs and position. Here the art of indirection becomes extremely helpful. Questions should be introduced into your sales talk naturally and so subtly that they seem to flow logically from what has gone before. As your prospect relaxes and continues to talk, you should establish a warm and friendly atmosphere by giving frequent praise (to Avoiders/Abdicators, Affiliators/Pleasers, and Power Bosses/Commanders), playing down unfavorable information or comments, and injecting a little humor into the conversation. These transitional questions and remarks help to avoid the impression that your sales interview is segmented or disjointed and give it a pleasant and friendly tone.

Be sure to keep listening. Listening to people has three effects:

They like you.
You learn.
They tell you what they want.

A Few More Tips

Keep your presentation short. Remember that any monologue over eight minutes long is boring. Tailor the material for *this* customer; don't cram in everything you know.

Avoid jargon or abstruse technical terms. You don't impress others with how "in" you are by using these words; you just confuse and alienate them.

Watch your selling syntax. Through trial and error you will learn to select some selling appeals over others, change a few thoughts, or alter the tone or length of your sales talk to harmonize with customer perceptions. Sometimes a minor sentence change can decide the fate of a sale. Active verbs are more effective than passive ones.

A picture is worth a thousand words; a participatory demonstration is worth a thousand pictures.

Keep it simple. Too many words and too many ideas can strangle a sale. Present just one main selling idea rather than many telling points. Speak simply. Do not repeat yourself or use cliches. The memorable acronym for this rule is KISS: Keep It Simple, Stupid.

Personalize your message. A sale is made not by one company to another, but by one person to another. Always try to personalize the vendor-buyer relationship. When all other things are equal, *you* make the difference.

THE PRESENTATION AT RETAIL

After greeting and chatting briefly with your customers, you should try to find out answers to the following questions:

Why are they here?
What are their requirements?
What type or style is right for them?
What characteristics appeal to them most?

To get this information, listen carefully to what they say and observe their reactions. Ask a minimum of questions. Once you have two or three facts, show some stock items. Customer reaction to the merchandise will tell you more than a lot of questioning. Do they smile or frown when you show an item? Often the information that a customer volunteers will give you a lot of facts.

Customers often do not know what they want, partly because they do not know what is available. In any case, start showing merchandise as early in the interview as you can. Show a few (for example, three) items in a medium price range, watch and listen for reactions, and then move on toward the style and price level that seems more suitable.

Always remember that with each customer you are building the basis for a longer relationship and repeat sales. You cannot usually tell at a first interview whether this customer will end up in an *A, B,* or *C* category, so you must maintain an equally helpful attitude toward all. Do not try to push off unbecoming, slow-moving, or unsuitable merchandise on customers. They will be much more appreciative and thus more likely to return if you say honestly, "That one really doesn't do much for you. Why don't we try this one?"

If you do not have what the customer wants, suggest a substitute and explain its good points, but be open about the fact that it is a substitute. If the customer is not interested in it, recommend another department or another store. Your helpfulness will be remembered after the item itself is forgotten, and the customer will return to you later for merchandise that you do have.

There are many poorly trained retail salespeople of low self-esteem who have the negative attitude of the disdainful shoe clerk we met in Chapter 3. It is easy to take advantage of this fact and make yourself the exceptional, professional retail salesperson who enjoys the creative and problem-solving work of selling. Customers like to do business with this professional. Be proud of yourself and your work and they will come to you.

THE CANNED PITCH: SHOULD YOU USE IT?

The memorized sales presentation, or "canned pitch," is widely used, and its value is controversial. Those who favor it say that its virtues are completeness, logic, and efficient use of time. It gives the confidence of preparedness to the veteran salesperson and makes a decent presentation possible even for a rank beginner. It covers all selling points, some of which a salesperson might later regret having forgotten. Its structure builds from basic ideas to more complex ones, ensuring customer understanding. It keeps the salesperson from going off into a boring monologue or taking a one-sided emphasis.

Opponents of the canned pitch, however, say that the canned pitch, like a recorded announcement, tends to reinforce mediocrity, is not personalized, and leaves the salesperson off stride if there is an interruption. It may turn a human being into a parrot and destroy initiative.[2]

A Practical Approach

Actually, few canned presentations are entirely mechanical and inhuman. This structured presentation is very useful when salespeople are new or underconfident or lack training. The canned pitch usually anticipates and answers questions that might daunt such a representative.

More experienced salespeople, however, usually use the canned presentation as a starting point or a track to run on until customer responses alter their paths. These professionals use the prepared presentation much as a teacher uses a lesson plan, a speaker uses notes, or an entertainer uses a prompter. If you start off using a canned pitch, you should eventually make it your own. An experienced sales manager once declared that he would fire all of his new recruits if they did not use the company's standard pitch by the end of their first month in the field; but he also would terminate their employment if they were still using it by the end of their third month!

How To Give Life to a Canned Pitch

With such a reliable method, all you will need is an animated, convincing delivery, and that will come with practice. You can perfect your "platform presence" through the following means:

> Read the lines through once in your training class and then repeat them at home and during subsequent practice sessions.
> Decide what the lines are meant to convey.
> Practice incorporating that meaning into your tone of voice a few times until it comes naturally.
> Recite the lines of your presentation to several prospects. What happens? Almost immediately it becomes the real *you* speaking, not because you wrote it, but because you understand it. Musicians are paid handsomely for their interpretations of other people's work. Why should selling be any different?

After you have used the material several times, you will know what to say and how to express it as you turn each page of your flip chart or sales presentation read-off booklet. Here are a few pointers to help you liven up a canned sales pitch:

> Always lower your voice at the end of each sentence. This helps to create an intimate mood.
> Watch your bark! Keep your voice down and be aware of its pitch.
> Vary your tone of voice frequently. Pausing now and then makes you sound natural.
> Use physical and vocal expressions that suit your words. If the words are exciting, you should get excited.
> Vary the position of your visual aids. You should handle them as an artist uses a palette: hold them in front of your prospect, place them on the table while turning pages, and so on. A good sales presentation can be a real work of art.

To develop a sales presentation delivery that makes prospects sit up and listen, follow the three P's: *practice, participate,* and *perform.*

Practice not only during training class time, but also make "live" presentations on your own time.

Participate willingly and enthusiastically in discussion and learning sessions with fellow students and trainees.

Perform for your peers at every opportunity. As you perform, you learn by doing. Performance will build your confidence by helping to get rid of "opening night performance" butterflies. Also, you might write some orders by accident.

As children we all learned that practice makes perfect. We learn to sell not by being told, but by doing. You cannot learn how to swim without getting wet.

HANDLING INTERRUPTIONS

How do you handle an interruption such as a telephone call or a visitor who walks in during your presentation? Several techniques are used by professionals.

Verbal Techniques

Try any of the following verbal tactics:

Repeat the last statement that either you or the customer made before the interruption.

Review some of the high points from your discussion up to the interruption.

Ask a question that calls for the customer to make a judgment or leads into further development of your presentation.

Make a forceful statement (not criticizing the interrupting party, however!).

Discuss a subject of mutual interest, then move back to your presentation path.

Start over from the beginning. This technique should be used when the interruptor is a visitor who is a buying influence and decides to stay. In this case, highlight your main features and benefits, encouraging the initial prospect to participate. Often one prospect will help to sell the other.

Nonverbal Techniques

Use visual aids. Hand the prospect a sample, a picture, a few notes on the meeting so far, a written proposal, or anything that will refocus attention on you.

Put yourself in motion. Any appropriate action will draw attention to yourself.

Write down or draw something concerning the previous discussion and show it to the prospect.

Sit patiently and silently, a clue to the prospect that you are waiting for attention.

When Nothing Works

You can use these techniques singly or combine them in any way you like. If, however, the customer remains distracted or the interruption continues, excuse yourself and ask for a later appointment. Of course, if the interruption brings disturbing personal news to the buyer, you should not even try to reestablish the sales interview.

PRACTICE, PARTICIPATE, AND PERFORM

Now that you have read about and understood the sales presentation, you are ready to begin really learning about it—by doing. As we have said before, it will take a lot of time and effort and many presentations before you become a good salesperson.

Whether you are a beginner or the veteran of many sales calls, you will find it instructive to practice your sales talk while being videotaped. If taping is not possible, use a critical friend or even a mirror. At least listen to your voice on a tape recording. You may be embarrassed by your own mannerisms and the strange mutterings or squeaks of your voice, but these honest reflections show you what your customers are seeing and help you to correct your habits. To gain practice in public speaking, join a group such as Toastmasters.

Your first few sales presentations will not be good. In fact, not until around the fiftieth one will you become competent. After that, through trial and error, you will polish your presentation and adapt it and yourself to the needs and expectations of customers. The rough edges and blunders will gradually diminish and disappear.

That is why you must practice your sales talk in front of a live audience as often as you can to improve it. Participating in the give and take and shared experiences of sales meetings will stimulate your desire to perform. Through persistence, you will have the thrill of getting an order—and you will be hooked on selling.

When Liz applied to Mike, the sales manager, for a job selling toothbrushes from door to door, Mike hesitated to hire her because it was a tough job and he wasn't sure a woman was up to it. But Liz persuaded him to let her try just for three days, and with one eye on the federal government, he decided he would have to give her a chance.

"OK, you'll have three days to prove yourself, and you'll have to reach a quota of 25 toothbrushes a day by the third day, or I can't keep you on," he said.

The first day, Liz went out full of vigor and pep with her case full of toothbrushes. Mike shook his head knowingly. Sure enough, just after five o'clock, she stumbled back in, bedraggled and haggard.

"How many toothbrushes did you sell today?" Mike asked.

"Five."

"I knew you weren't going to be able to do it," he said. "Look— why go through another day like this? Why don't you quit while you're ahead?"

"No!" Liz pulled herself up straight. "You promised I could have three days."

The next day the performance was repeated, except that Liz came in looking much worse. She had sold three toothbrushes. Mike felt sorry for her.

"Look, kid, why do this to yourself? You could be home baking cookies. You'll never make it at this rate. What do you say to knocking it off now?"

"You said—three days!" mumbled Liz, and she dragged herself out the door.

Once again, on the third day, Liz went out, and again Mike waited to hear the results, though he suspected she would not return at all. It was too bad, he thought, that she hadn't done better. He really had to admire her spunk and persistence.

Sure enough, five o'clock passed, and then five thirty. Mike stuck around, just in case—well, anyway, he had some work to do.

At six fifteen, Liz came through the door, so tired she could not stand up or talk. After sitting her down in a chair and getting her some coffee, Mike brought himself to ask, "How many today, kid?"

"Six thousand, four hundred and seventy-two," Liz croaked.

"What! How did you do it?"

"Well, I went to the airport and set up a chip and dip stand. When someone walked by, I'd say, 'Free chip and dip?' and they'd try it.

'Yuck!' they'd say. 'Tastes like mud!' And right away I'd say, 'It is! Do you want to buy a toothbrush?' "

Notes

1. Edward C. Bursk, "Opportunities for Persuasion," *Harvard Business Review*, September–October 1958.
2. Frederic A. Russell, Frank H. Beach, and Richard H. Buskirk, *Textbook of Salesmanship*, 10th ed. (New York: McGraw-Hill, 1978), p. 245.

Chapter 16
Handling Objections

The successful salesperson masters the art of overcoming objections. The objection phenomenon occurs between resolve to buy and the purchase in the seven psychological steps to the sale. It also is the point at which most sales talks break down. If you do not receive *any* objections during your sales presentation, you are not really selling. Most likely the sale will not stand up afterward.

OBJECTIONS AND EXCUSES

An objection is not the same as an excuse. When prospects raise objections, they are not reacting negatively to your proposal, but rather are seeking clarification of it. Unless the objection is an outright "no," they are really saying, "Help us to buy—we need more information. Tell us more, *sell us more*, because we are not sold yet!" A solid objection makes your job easier because it shows you how to direct your selling effort; you are aiming all your force at a well-defined target. Through objections, buyers may seek your help in convincing themselves—or ammunition to use in convincing their superiors. Objections are your leverage for closing orders.

An excuse, on the other hand, is a delaying tactic. It seeks to avoid a decision or the necessity of saying "no." As you might imagine, Avoiders/Abdicators and Affiliators/Pleasers are prone to excuses. The Affiliator/Pleaser certainly does not want to lose you, the salesperson "friend," by saying "no."

Thus an excuse seeks a delay in or avoidance of the buying decision, while the objection merely seeks more information. To succeed in selling, you must not only understand these differences, but also develop the appropriate behavior to cope with them.

THE REAL OBJECTION

The objection that your customer presents may not be the real, underlying objection. J. Pierpont Morgan, Sr., once said, "A man generally has two reasons for doing something—one that sounds good and a real one." The customer may or may not consciously know what the real objection is. We shall see how to deal with this situation after we have seen what some common objections are and how to handle them.

WHY DO PEOPLE OBJECT?

As we saw in Chapter 5, most people have a natural hesitation when confronted with a decision. This hesitation is based on the fear of commitment and of making an irretrievable error. Procrastination sets in, and objections result. Prospects at this point are looking for a way to justify the purchase or for reasons why they ought not to buy. Either way, they want more information and expect you to provide it. This preliminary weak "no" is an invitation to further discussion, a stepping stone to an order. A strong or final "no," of course, ends negotiations at this point.

Objecting is completely automatic to some people, no matter what the proposal. Some Midwestern farmers are so cheap that it must be in their genes (jeans). They will always protest that your price is too high. An extreme situation occurred during a roadside demonstration of Yamaha motorcycles.

> Keith stopped alongside a rural highway to demonstrate his motorbikes to a farmer. He discussed all the benefits the farmer would receive from it, demonstrated it, and even persuaded the prospect to try it out. Returning the motorbike to the salesman, the farmer asked, "How much is it?"
>
> Just as Keith named the price, a tractor-trailer rig whizzed by, with a deafening roar that completely drowned out what he said. But that didn't stop the farmer's automatic reaction:
>
> "Your price is too high!"
> "By how much?" responded Keith.

"Aw, you've gotta come down at least $25.00 on that motorcycle."
"How much did I quote the price?" asked the bewildered Keith.
"I don't know!" was the puzzled response.
They both had a good laugh as Keith wrote up the order.

THE ETHICS OF PERSUASION

Some people have a negative set against the idea of persuasion, feeling that to try to get others to do what they don't seem to want to do is somehow unethical. Let us set this matter straight before we continue.

You cannot *persuade* people to do what they really do not want to do. You can only *coerce* them to do these things. Persuasion works when people want or need but are not aware of their existing wants or needs. Persuasion brings this preexisting want into the customer's consciousness. It gives the buyer a rational basis on which to overcome hesitation and do what he or she really wants to do.

Even under hypnosis, people will not do what is suggested if it is against their principles. Don't be afraid to persuade.

THE SIMULTANEOUS SALE CONCEPT

A sale is made in every interview. Either you sell your product or service, or your customer sells you an objection or excuse. While you are selling them on need, use, and value, they are selling you the idea that they don't need, won't use, or can't afford the product or service.

At the end of the interview, one of these sales will have been made. If they buy your product, it is your sale. If you accept their objections, then you have bought their sad stories. You didn't get their business; they gave you the business!

Only one of these two sales will be made, and it should be yours. This fact of sales life should give you a new perspective on objections.

TRANSACTIONAL ANALYSIS

We now have come to the part of the sale during which communication between you and the buyer must remain clear and open, or the interview will break down and you will lose the sale. Transactional analysis, which we introduced in Chapters 4 and 6, can help you to keep the lines of communication open.

Complementarity of Transactions

As you remember, the unit of social intercourse was a *transaction*—a stimulus and a response between two people. Either the stimulus or the

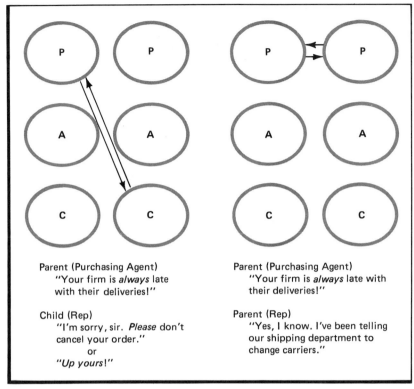

Parent (Purchasing Agent)
   "Your firm is *always* late
   with their deliveries!"

Child (Rep)
   "I'm sorry, sir. *Please* don't
   cancel your order."
          or
   "Up yours!"

Parent (Purchasing Agent)
   "Your firm is *always* late with
   their deliveries!"

Parent (Rep)
   "Yes, I know. I've been telling
   our shipping department to
   change carriers."

Figure 16.1   Complementary transactions allow continued communication. (Adapted from *Games People Play* by Eric Berne, New York: Grove Press, 1967.)

response may originate in any of the three ego states: Parent, Adult, or Child.

Communication will proceed smoothly between two people as long as the transactions are *complementary*. As is shown in Figure 16.1, complementary transactions follow normal human relationships: a stimulus from the Parent state is complementary with a response from the Child state, and vice-versa. A Parent-Parent transaction may also be complementary, as may an Adult-Adult or Child-Child transaction.

If, however, one person's Parent addresses the other's Child but receives a response from the other's Parent, the exchange is a *crossed transaction*, which blocks communication. Examples of crossed transactions are shown in Figure 16.2.

Complementary transactions allow communication to continue, but this communication may or may not be effective. *Only Adult-to-Adult transactions are truly effective.* You must learn to recognize the state

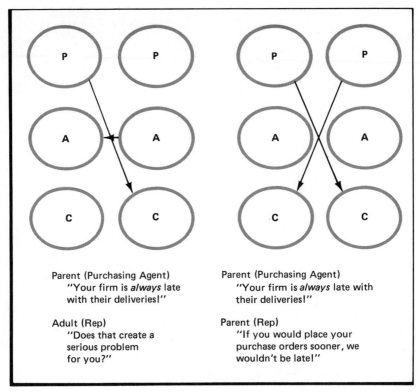

Figure 16.2   Crossed transactions block communication. (Adapted from *Games People Play* by Eric Berne, New York: Grove Press, 1967.)

from which the customer is speaking and either complement it or try to shift it.

For example, suppose a salesperson presents a stimulus directed from his Adult to the Adult of the customer: "My factory just informed me that shipment of your merchandise will be late." If the customer is operating strongly in the Child ego state, a Child response may be directed to the salesperson's Parent: "How come you guys always pick on me?" Your choices as the salesperson at this point are to end this blocked transaction, shift yourself into the Parent state (which is called allowing your Parent to be "hooked"), or try to involve the customer's Adult.

If you let your Parent be hooked ("Don't criticize what you don't understand!"), communication will continue, but it will not produce solutions to your problems. If, on the other hand, you are able to bring out the customer's Adult ("I know you are a reasonable person and you've had experiences like this in your firm, too."), then communication can continue and the problem may be resolved.

Shifting a Parent or Child state customer into the Adult is by no means easy, and you will not always be able to do it. If you cannot make this shift, it is best to end the transactions. Communication is broken off when a crossed transaction occurs, leading to a game of uproar in which the salesperson is sure to lose. No communication can occur until one person stops playing the game. If the buyer will not stop playing, there is nothing you can do but withdraw.

Transactional Analysis and Objections

Applying this theory to the phenomenon of excuses and objections, we can see that an excuse is most likely to originate from the customer's Child or Parent, whereas the objection tends to come from the Adult. An excuse from the Child represents the Child's tendency toward avoidance and irresponsibility. It is the Child who hesitates out of fear. An excuse from the Parent, on the other hand, represents commands such as "Don't make snap judgments!" and "Always have your attorney look at everything you sign!" which were recorded into the Parent during the customer's formative years.

It is the Adult who offers the true objection. The Adult's unemotional computer simply needs more information to synthesize an accurate picture and grind out a decision, and that is what the objection seeks.

The function of your persuasion is to remove the Child's fears and hesitation on the one hand, or to get the customer's Parent to turn the decision over to the Adult on the other. The Adult is the only one with whom you can deal in facts and figures. Therefore it becomes obvious that if you can detect the ego state that is making the excuse or objection, you have a better chance of determining which it is and responding to it in a way that brings about a successful outcome.

Excuses and objections, as we shall see, may sound exactly alike. You will need to rely on nonverbal cues as well as verbal ones to decide whether you are being addressed by a Parent, Adult, or Child state; that is, whether you are hearing an excuse or a true objection. Since relatively few people operate out of the Adult at all times, it is more likely that you are hearing an excuse from the Parent or Child, but you still need to determine which of these two is speaking.

If you already have selling experience, you know that you see more Avoider/Abdicator (1,1), Affiliator/Pleaser (1,9), and Power Boss/Commander (9,1) types than you do ideal 9,9 Achievers/Craftsmen and Manipulators/Gamesmen. Thus you are dealing with more Child and Parent ego states than Adult states. It is interesting to note, while we are making such comparisons, that the Adult-Adult transaction is nothing other than a transaction between two 9,9 types. It is the ideal communication toward which you should aim.

COMMON EXCUSES AND OBJECTIONS

What do excuses and objections really sound like? Here are some of the more common ones.

No Need or Interest

In this category you may hear

"We don't use those any more—changed our process."

"My doctor doesn't let me wear high heels."

"Unfortunately we're going out of business next month."

"We don't have any children, so I don't think we'd use these books."

"Your company just gives us too many delivery hassles. I can do without that kind of problem."

No Money

"I can't afford it."

"Your price is too high."

"We don't yet have a buying budget this year for this agency."

"We just can't take it under these payment terms."

No Hurry (Procrastination)

"My boss/husband/wife will have to decide. I'll tell him/her about it and get back to you."

"I'll think about it. We'll probably do it next year."

"I've got to sleep on it/get my attorney's approval/talk to my CPA."

HANDLING EXCUSES AND OBJECTIONS

When you get an excuse or objection, you must decide which it is and how to deal with it. Of course, the best method is to avoid hearing it or having to handle it, which you can often do by preparing ahead of time.

Anticipate and Cover the Objections

As we noted in Chapter 11, while you are doing your preapproach re-search, you should think ahead to what objections are likely to be made by customers. Design your presentation so that it answers these objections. In doing so, you are applying the inverse of barrier selling. You prevent customers from taking stands from which they would be reluctant to back down. If they have not voiced excuses, no one need know they have changed their minds. With a little practice, you will be able to sense objections toward which customers are tending and cover them in your presentation even if you have not anticipated them during precall preparation.

This approach works with Achievers/Craftsmen, Avoiders/Abdicators, Affiliators/Pleasers, and Manipulators/Gamesmen but is less successful with Power Bosses/Commanders.

Ignore the Objection

Sometimes the best way to handle the first and sometimes even the second voiced excuse is to ignore it. Elmer Leterman says that his hearing is very poorly attuned to the word *no*.

> The first three negative responses go past me completely unnoticed, making no more impression than if they had not been uttered at all. With the fourth no, I begin to be aware of a vague vibration in my ears. It conveys some sort of message to me. It is a message that seems to say: "I'm not sure I'm interested, but I'd like to hear a little more from you." This is all contained in the two-letter word *no*. It is then, and only then, that I become convinced that I may have a real selling job ahead of me.[1]

In some cases where the excuse is simply a Child procrastination, it is even possible to laugh it off:

> Bill, a securities agent, called on a wealthy Beverly Hills widow. As the butler ushered him into the foyer of her plush mansion, Bill noticed a Jaguar and Mercedes Benz parked in the driveway and that expensive oil paintings and art objects were everywhere in the house—certainly six-figure object language! The bejeweled matron appeared in a St. Laurent gown and offered Bill a cocktail. The sales interview proceeded amicably until they reached the close. When the young man asked for the order, however, the widow replied, "I can't afford it!"
> Bill laughed out loud, ignored her objection, and wrote up the order. He had correctly perceived her remark as an automatic Child procrastination and treated it as a joke rather than a serious objection. They both had a good laugh over her sense of humor.

You cannot laugh at every objection or at each kind of customer, however. This ignoring technique is most effective with Affiliators/Pleasers and Power Bosses/Commanders. Achievers/Craftsmen are highly offended by it.

Answer the Objection

J. Pierpont Morgan's famous observation, quoted earlier, makes it clear that you must know the real objection before you can answer. To find out the real objection (and to determine that it really is an objection and not an excuse), use the tools of indirection and probing questions.

For example, suppose prospects have just told you that they cannot afford your service. Your question should be, "Tell me, is there any reason other than money why you would not want to go ahead with this program now?" or perhaps, "In addition to that, what else makes you hesitate?"

If the customer really meant the objection, it will be repeated; but if not, you will hear a different one or a whole string of different ones, which you should now reclassify as excuses.

If the customer appears to be the victim of fuzzy thinking, you can use your own lack of understanding as a way to seek clarification tactfully:

"Could you run that by me again? I must be a little dense today."

"Could you elaborate a little bit on that point so I am sure I understand what you mean?"

"Would you repeat that? I was distracted there for a moment."

If you have not successfully anticipated or ignored an objection, you must answer it. Several methods may be used.

SMILE AND AGREE

The best method for answering an objection permits you to try it out for validity at the same time. It consists of four steps: smile and agree, turn the objection, show more value, and close again differently.

It takes two parties to make an argument. Thus it is disarming for you to agree with your prospects. Expecting an argument, they will be thrown off balance by your apparent concurrence. They probably will relax and be more receptive to your ensuing comments. For this reason, the first step—*smile and agree*—is the most important.

Next, *turn the excuse* around and make it work for you. If the prospect claims not be able to afford your product or service, you should make a response something like this one: "Yes, Mr./Ms. Prospect, I can see how you feel about it. You certainly know your situation much better than I do, and perhaps you really can't afford it. But have you thought about it this way?"

You now return to the benefits that the prospect will gain or lose. An excellent approach here is to point out that the prospect is going to pay for the product or service one way or the other: either directly, or by loss of benefits through not having it. Continuing from the point where you left off, *show more value*, and then *close again differently.*

DIRECT DENIAL

You may decide to meet the objection head on, with a direct denial. Here you try to show clients the error of their ways. This technique is good only when you have made a particularly strong selling point and the objection is either unrealistic or weakly voiced. Direct denial is most suited to Power Bosses/Commanders and Affiliators/Pleasers.

INDIRECT DENIAL

If you do not want to risk an argument, you might try an indirect denial response. Here you attempt to correct the false statement without a direct confrontation. This method is more diplomatic, less forceful, and occasionally more effective than is a direct denial. Use indirect denial with the Avoider/Abdicator, the Affiliator/Pleaser, and the Achiever/Craftsman.

COMPENSATION

If the objection to a feature of your product is valid, use the compensation method. Here you present other factors that either justify or offset the objection. This method, sometimes called the "yes—but" technique, is characteristic of salespeople who can think on their feet and adapt to any sales situation without being at a loss for words. It is effective with Achievers/Craftsmen, Manipulators/Gamesmen and Avoiders/Abdicators.

BOOMERANG

The Boomerang tactic endeavors to convert the prospect's statement into a reason *for* rather than *against* buying. "Mr./Ms. Prospect, *that* is the very reason why you should buy it now. If you look at it this way, you can see what I mean. . . ." The boomerang is most likely to hit the Power Boss/Commander, Affiliator/Pleaser, or Manipulator/Gamesman.

These four rebuttal techniques (direct and indirect denial, compensation, and boomerang) can be quite effective, but you must use them with great care or you will antagonize your customers. Forceful selling does not have to be high-pressure selling. It is not your job to argue or antagonize; it is your job to convince your clients that they should have your product or service *now.*

In answering objections, remember to use "soft" rather than "hard" words. In our examples, you should note that we have said such things as "Would you go ahead with it?" instead of "Would you buy it?" We said

"I must be a little dense," not "You haven't made this clear to me." Soft speech and tact are important with all buyers, but they are vital with Avoiders/Abdicators.

If you are reluctant to use a rebuttal in answer to an excuse, try a third-party testimonial. A direct testimonial from a satisfied customer will help you to close the sale. You can present supporting letters from third parties, or you can even call them on the telephone during your presentation. Sometimes the buyer will be more impressed by someone else's praise of the product or service than by yours. Testimonials are most effective with Avoiders/Abdicators, Affiliators/Pleasers, and Achievers/Craftsmen. Whether or not you get the order, always remember to thank the third party by letter, phone call, or visit.

Suppose that your customer offers not an objection, but a flat "no" without explanation. What do you do to answer? The best thing to do is to ask simply "Why?" or "Why not?" You may very quickly draw out the true objection this way, and it may be a weak one.

Accept the Objection

Are some objections valid? Yes, there are some that you should accept. Although this is the least desirable way of handling objections, sometimes it is the only acceptable way of interacting with your customer.

What is a valid objection? Some are obvious, some more subtle. The most clear-cut and unanswerable objection is shown in Figure 16.3. Sometimes people just dislike each other on sight. You might remind the prospect of a relative whom they dislike. Therefore no matter how good you are, or how well you do your job, you will never succeed with this individual. If you can do so at this point, you should turn the customer over to a different salesperson. In retail selling, this is called TIO—turn it over! Here is an example of where you shouldn't let your ego get in the way of your sales object—a half a loaf of bread is worth more than no slice at all.

BUSINESS AND PROFESSIONAL SALES
In business sales, the following objections are valid and should be accepted:

> recent purchase of a competitive or substitute product
> moving or going out of business
> change of merchandise or clientele
> governmental agency without buying budget at this time
> wrong product or specifications
> delivery difficulties on your firm's part
> bad credit or impossible buying terms

"You've overcome all my objections except one, Ades. I object to you!"

Figure 16.3 The unanswerable objection.

reciprocity (arrangements with another firm to "trade" sales of about equal value)

CONSUMER SALES

breadwinner unemployed, or family on relief

overextended in time payments (look for object language: new house, car, furniture, clothes)

breadwinner illness; recent death in family

any objection repeated three or four times in a row

complete consumer apathy

In these cases do not embarrass yourself or anger your customer by entering into a dispute that you cannot win. Use tactful persistence.

Turn the objection a few times during your presentation to test its validity. If it is sincere, legitimate, and adamant, do not waste your time. Get out and look for a more promising prospect. Keep your positive mental attitude intact.

CALLBACKS AND THEIR MEANING

A *callback,* or second or subsequent visit to sell to the same prospect, has different meanings depending on its setting. In consumer selling, the prospect's demand for a callback is an attempt to sell you an excuse. Do not buy this excuse. Remember that a callback is really a charge-back on your precious selling time. With in-home consumer sales, this ploy is usually tied to an "I have to persuade my wife/husband" type of statement. Actually, except in some first-generation immigrant or ethnic families, the housewife usually is the official purchasing agent for the home. She should be able to make a buying decision on the first call. Because of television, her children are called *consumer trainees.* They strongly influence the purchasing decision.

At retail, a similar psychology appears in the use by customers of "holds" or "on approvals" to escape from the necessity of a one-call decision. Most holds are excuses. Try to get a decision, most of your holds will never come back.

In industrial sales, on the other hand, the negotiation process leading up to a large or complex sale involves more than one corporate executive level and several different personalities. In this case, it will take several calls and a lot of time to achieve the sale. The selling process is more involved, and the period of negotiation is longer.

Even when you are selling less complex products to corporate purchasing agents, you may make several calls to establish yourself and your firm in a buyer's mind before you get an initial order. This pattern is to be expected, and you must persist optimistically until the buyer accepts you.

CAN YOU AVOID OBJECTIONS?

Would the best of all possible sales situations be one in which your entire presentation went off with no interruption and no objection by the customer? Not really—because at the end this prospect might say "no," and you would have no idea why or where you got off the track.

If you do not get an objection or an order, you are not selling. You must face your objections, and you must arrange to get them out as early as possible if you see that anticipating and covering them is not going to work. Early objections are splendid qualifiers—and an early close gets an early objection, something we shall discuss in Chapter 17. In the game of bridge there is a saying that you should lose your losers first—don't hold weak cards until the final tricks, because you will lose control of the hand if you do. Objections work the same way.

Notes

1. Elmer G. Leterman, *The Sale Begins When the Customer Says "No"* (New York: Manor Books, 1976).

Chapter 17
Closing Techniques

We have defined salesmanship as the art of persuading prospects to think and feel as you do so that they will act as you want them to act. With practice you can learn to influence people to think and feel as you do. However, until their signatures are written on purchase order forms or their checks are in the cash register, they have not acted the way you want them to act. This last step of the sale is the ultimate objective of the whole interview, the step that produces the order. This step is called the *close*.

Closing is asking for the order, in one way or another, and getting it. Many beginning salespeople approach the close with great trepidation. Although this feeling is natural, it is not usually justified. A good close is the logical finish to a good sales talk, and the serious client *expects* you to wrap up your presentation in this way. The prospect who is interested in buying wants detailed information about such things as price, terms, quantity discounts, delivery, and so on. These are the facts usually contained in the close. Give them to your customers and you give them an opportunity to say "Yes!" Like selling itself, closing is an *attitude*—it starts in your own head. You must *believe* that you will get that order *now,* that you cannot fail. Don't be satisfied with merely your fair share of the business. *Want it all,* and try to get it all—*every* time. This positive expectation of success will enable you to overcome objections and close orders.

Closing is not the art of getting a decision, but the art of *making a decision that your buyer will approve.* Using indirection, you influence your buyers' problem-solving and decision-making processes by introducing ideas in such a way that they believe these ideas are their own. If you don't ask them to buy, they won't.

> A certain buyer who was known to want and need an item for her company nevertheless did not buy from a young salesperson who came to show her an excellent line. Asked by a colleague later why she had not bought, the buyer replied, "He never asked me!"

This is the *main reason* why most salespersons fail to obtain orders.

CLOSE EARLY AND CONTINUALLY

Sales can be closed much earlier than you might imagine. You should start closing early in your presentation because you have no way of knowing your customer's readiness to buy (Figure 17.1). Some buyers may require less proof of value than you plan to supply. Some may have been partially sold by advertising before your call. Most orders, however, are not written until the fourth or fifth close. Getting started with closes early in the presentation enables your prospects to start overcoming their natural hesitations early, so that by the time you complete your presentation they are ready to buy. The trial close plants the idea of immediate ownership. Each successive close conditions their thinking toward making a decision to buy.

You cannot see the buying readiness curve in your buyer's mind. If you close only once at the end or only twice, you are much more likely to miss your buyer's readiness peak than you are if you close several times (Figure 17.2).

Results of the Trial Close

Closing early gets one of three results: an order, an objection (which you then answer), or a qualification of the buyer. In the last case, the buyer's response to your close narrows the range of topics to be discussed and frequently leads to an order.

Closing Cues and Comments

Buyers give both verbal and nonverbal signals that they are approaching readiness to buy. You must not rely entirely on verbal cues; nonverbal

Figure 17.1

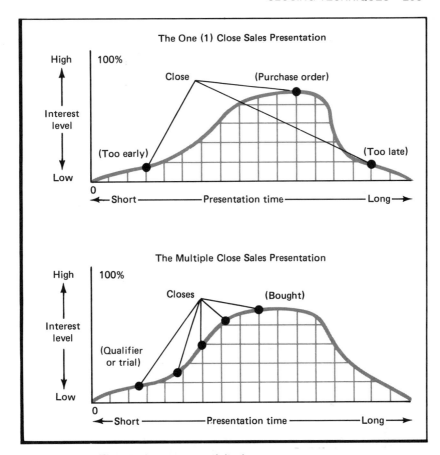

Figure 17.2   The closing curve revisited.

ones are equally or more important, since most people do not know how to conceal them.

NONVERBAL CUES
In these action or gesture clusters, prospects nod their heads in agreement to your presentation, examine prototype models or a proposal, or actually try out an item. Department store customers try on garments; new car customers test drive vehicles. Watch for a purchasing agent to open and study a sales brochure, take notes or sketch a schematic diagram, or handle your product. The customer may lean forward and appear very attentive or have a facial expression of obvious interest.

VERBAL CUES
Your customers usually indicate their resolve to purchase by asking questions you would normally expect toward the end of negotiations.

Verbal buying signals usually follow nonverbal ones and are more obvious and more committing. They range from the subtle ("How is it packaged?") to the very strong ("When can I get delivery?"). Questions may focus on any of these areas:

price and terms
trade-in values
delivery schedule
contract details
design or technology
maintenance
quality and service
trial order possibilities
installation procedure
product performance and availability
shipping method

The most subtle, yet most revealing, question concerns a nonessential part of your product or service. Here your customer is asking you for help with the decision in the least self-threatening way possible.

Referring again to Figure 17.1, we can interpret our buyer's position on the commitment curve from the type of question asked. Questions like "How long will it take to install it?" or "When would it be available?" are low on the commitment curve. Your client has not fully bought yet. Thus your trial closing question "When do you need it?" is nonthreatening and allows you to find out what further data are needed.

Should your customer ask, "Does this feature come with the equipment?," your response might be, "Do you need this feature?" or "What did you have in mind?" This nondirective question would encourage your buyers to tell you what they really want.

"When can I have this system in operation?" is higher on the commitment curve than "How soon can you have the system in operation?" "When will my people be fully trained to operate the equipment?" is higher on the commitment curve than "How soon could you train my people?" Both questions are higher on the curve than "How long does it take to train operators?"

Thus a question on your firm's ability to deliver your product can be interpreted one of three different ways, depending on the way your client asks the question. For example:

"How long does it take?" means that your client *could* buy.

"How long would it take?" means that the client *might* buy.

"How long will it take?" indicates that your client *will* buy.

If you know these verbal buying signals you will know when to close (see Figure 17.3).

VERBAL CLOSING CLUES

Figure 17.3

THE TRANSITION FROM SALES TALK TO CLOSE

Make the transition from the main body of your sales talk into the close through the use of questions. Use leading questions in this decision-making phase wherever possible. A leading question puts the answer into your prospect's mind and emphasizes what you have been saying. You can accomplish this desired result by simply making a statement and turning it into a question with a slight change of syntax and vocal inflection.

"This is Friday the 13th, isn't it?"

"Looks pretty good, doesn't it?"

Try to word your questions in such a manner that you get the answers you want.

"Do you see where this new layout would save your company half the purchase price within the first three years?"

"Does the competition have feature A, feature B, or feature C?"

You and the prospect both know that they are exclusive features of your product.

Because closing is more emotional than presenting, you should develop an emotional relationship between your questions and what you say. The following question and comment appeal to emotional buying motives.

"How would you like to make as much as 20 percent more on each camera you sell?" [profit motive]

"This installation will become a showcase in your industry." [pride]

We have said before that the art of selling is the art of transition. Through the adroit use of questions and comments, the evolution of your sales presentation to the closing phase can be achieved both smoothly and effectively.

MAKE IT EASY FOR THE CUSTOMER TO BUY

Besides creating a positive and accepting atmosphere, you can make it easy for your prospects to buy through the use of "soft" closes. A soft close makes a hard decision seem easy for your prospect. Instead of directly asking for the order and risking either a confrontation or a rejection, you *assume* that your prospect is going to buy. It is no longer a question of whether or not the customer wishes to buy, but of how that individual wishes to place the order. *Assuming the sale is axiomatic to closing.*

Here are a few examples of soft closing questions that make it easy for a prospect to buy:

"Just your name and address, please." [You indicate where.] Sometimes you may write up the order blank, application, or contract in advance, even though you have only the prospect's name and address on it.

"If you'll just OK the shipping instructions, I'll be on my way." [Make a large X at each place where the prospect is to sign.]

"This is where my autograph goes," [you sign] "and this is where yours goes." [Place the contract directly in front of the customer. If you are in a standing position, place the unfolded contract in the buyer's hands and look expectant.]

"I'll need your John Hancock here." [Indicate the place and slip your pen into the customer's hand. You will be amazed how mechanically buyers will respond.]

Always carry at least two pens with you. If someone accidentally pockets your pen, you will not be without one at your next interview. How would you feel if you lost an order because you had nothing with which to write it up?

These soft closing questions are definitely preferable to the clumsy alternatives:

"Sign the contract now!"

"Press down hard, there are four carbon copies and yours is the bottom one."

"Do you want it or not? Speak up!"

Make it easy for the prospect to buy. After all, isn't that what this selling business is all about? You are paid to sell, and buyers are paid to buy.

HOW TO CLOSE: BASIC TECHNIQUES

Most new representatives look upon closing as a mysterious process in which the master salesperson, through some sixth sense, recognizes the precise psychological moment to take action. It is true that with experience and empathy you can learn to sense the situation and become more aware of buying cues. The harder you work, the luckier you will get.

To become a good closer, you must begin by building your close upon the broad base of the total interview. First, you must *expect* to make a sale. Then, step by step, as your sales talk progresses, you build up and emphasize reasons for your prospects to buy. Use trial or test closes at strategic places in your presentation. These periodic closes get commitments that narrow the range of topics to be discussed, and sometimes they lead directly into the final negotiating phase.

Assumptive Close

Your presentation is designed to sell a series of disturbing, thought-provoking ideas. You ask for agreement on these ideas. This technique is referred to as *clinching*. If you have done a good job with an open-minded prospect, that individual has agreed on most of your selling points and is genuinely interested in investing in your proposal. The only natural thing to do is to close. If you do not, your prospect may feel that you are suggesting an action that most others would not take.

The representative who does not assume the sale and close is waiting for the customer to say, "I'll take it." Expecting your prospect to show more conviction, belief, and initiative than you do is expecting your prospects to close on themselves! It is much easier to get people to do the thing you want them to do if you *assume* they are going to do it.

Assuming the sale in a natural expectant manner shows your conviction in your products. No prospect will be critical of this belief. Thus *closing*, like *selling* itself, is a state of mind. You must have a *closing attitude*. You must assume that you are going to get that order and even visualize how you will feel and act during this moment of truth. You must always ask for the order and get it—or get out of selling.

Purchasing agents are paid to buy, and sooner or later they expect to be asked. They assume that you are there to sell, and it is logical that you should assume that they are there to buy, and preferably from you. We suggested several assumptive closes when we discussed making it easy for the customer to buy. Sometimes merely pointing to the appropriate place on the contract and handing the buyer a pen is enough.

You can reinforce the assumptive close by starting an action, such as writing up an order, that your prospects will actually have to stop if they are not going to buy. For example, ask a series of questions and fill in the answers on the order form. It should be clear to all that you are writing up an order. If your prospects are not ready to buy, they are free to stop you with objections.

The assumptive close is most effective with the Avoider/Abdicator, Achiever/Craftsman, and Power Boss/Commander. It combines verbal, nonverbal, and action language to reinforce your control of your presentation. It forcefully sweeps away all tacit objections in the close. Often, buyers are relieved to have the burden of decision making removed from their shoulders. You have assumed that burden yourself, and it is easier for them to approve a decision that you have made in their best interests than to continue to resist you. You have made it easy for them to buy.

The Alternate Choice

Sometimes called the decision on a minor point or the fatal choice, this closing technique combines implied consent with a choice between two positive decisions. You assume that the customer will buy from you now, and you ask, "Which one do you prefer?" rather than "Do you want it or not?"

Use a fatal choice question whenever you want definite action or agreement. It is well suited to Avoiders/Abdicators, Achievers/Craftsmen, and Power Bosses/Commanders. Offer your clients a choice of agreeing with you one way or agreeing with you another way. For example, you might ask whether they prefer delivery at the beginning of the month or the middle, or you might offer a choice of models, colors, sizes, accessories, payment plans, or quantities required.

Direct Imperative

If the business of buyers is to buy, why shouldn't we come right out and ask them to do it? The often-overlooked direct imperative method of simply asking for the order may very well be your most effective close. The odds are certainly in your favor, as the more often you ask, the more often you will receive. Typical examples are as follows:

"May I have your order now?"

"Why don't we get started on the program now?"

"Are you ready to buy?"

"Let's start off with six gross of these."

The direct imperative is such an obvious close that some representatives either overlook it, fear it, or just plain forget it. However, it is a good method to use with Affiliators/Pleasers and Power Bosses/Commanders. Many times your customers are merely waiting to be asked. They certainly are not going to ask you to let them buy!

If you ask a direct question and receive a "no" answer, you should ask "Why?" or "Why not?," with a smile, of course. Their responses will now reveal their true objections and show where your closing efforts should best be directed. It is a matter not of rejection, but merely of redirection.

Remember, no one can be *forced* to buy anything through persuasion. People buy what they want from people whom they like. It is your job to make your buying suggestions so logical and compelling that your prospects will want to buy. Get them emotionally involved by appealing to their psychological buying motives and then ask for the order and get it. Sometimes you can even demand it!

Continuous Yes

The idea behind this closing method is to keep asking a series of leading questions that will produce "yes" answers from your prospective clients until the very end of your sales talk. The theory is that they will become so accustomed to responding positively to your little questions and comments that they will be conditioned to answer "yes" to the big buying question.

When asking these continuous questions, you should smile affably and nod your head affirmatively. Whenever you speak and act positively toward others, they usually respond in a similar manner. That is precisely what you want in this closing situation. It is difficult to say "no" while one's head is bobbing up and down in an affirmative way. It is a violation of conditioned voice and gesture reflex response patterns.

Pause and ask your listeners what they think of each closing point as soon as you make it. At the conclusion, you might say, "Now that you've seen the program, how do you like it? Pretty great, huh?"

This positive technique can be combined with the assumptive close and alternate choice methods:

> "If I understand your situation correctly on this printing job, the main factors to be considered are quality, speed of production, and cost. Right?"
>
> "Yes."
>
> "And since we cannot possibly have all three at once without paying a fantastic premium, you indicated that speed of production was most important. Right?"
>
> "Yes."
>
> "You also agreed that our prices and quality were at least equal to the competition."
>
> "Yes."
>
> "In that case, would delivery within six working days be soon enough for you?"
>
> "Yes."

The continuous yes close is a good one to use with Avoiders/Abdicators and Affiliators/Pleasers.

Barrier Close

Best used with Avoiders/Abdicators, Affiliators/Pleasers, and Power Bosses/Commanders, the barrier approach to selling (Chapter 15) is actually little more than a glorified closing technique. It consists of a number of leading questions and is designed to block or eliminate objections in the close. You establish barriers in your prospects' minds, so that their response options are narrowed down to either acceptance of your proposal or a complete reversal of their stated positions.

For best results, you should combine this method with the assumptive close and a few continuous yesses. For example, this five-point close creates strong barriers:

• *Point 1.* "Well, folks, does the program seem complete? Have we done a good job?"
"Yes, it seems complete."

(You are really asking them if you have done a good job of presenting the materials for their consideration.)

• *Point 2.* "If parents can afford it, should children have it?"
"Yes!"

(They are thinking about *other* parents and *other* children.)

• *Point 3.* "Fine. If this were something that you *knew* you could afford, would you want your children to have it?"
"Yes, if we could afford it."

(Although admitting that they want to buy the program, they also have qualified their positive answer. Now they are ready to say "No" to the next question, which they think will be a buying request.)

• *Point 4.* "Have you ever been contacted by one of our representatives before?"
"No! Absolutely not."

(Now that they have expressed themselves, they feel better, and their minds will reopen. This process is sometimes called "ventilating.")

• *Point 5.* "Good. Because my instructions are . . . [showing the appropriate page in your sales manual and reading aloud] 'you are to cover your assigned territory on schedule and must not call back a second time.' So since this is a one-time offer, we need your immediate acceptance or rejection. Now, how long have you folks lived here?"

(You start writing up the order. They can stop you if they do not want to buy.)

The barrier close is a forceful closing technique that paints a prospect into a psychological corner from which you hope there is no escape.

Now or Never Close

The idea behind this method is to create a psychological sense of urgency for buying action now (see Figure 17.4). The main appeal is directed at

Available one day only.

ORIENTAL RUGS—30% to 50% off

New and antique rugs from Persia, Turkey, Pakistan, China,

and India.

Limited quantities—super savings!

Monday, August 3, 1981

The Rug Gallery
495 BROADWAY, NEW YORK

Figure 17.4   Now or never close.

the buying motive of fear—fear of loss if one does not act immediately. In real estate selling, the last lot or home on a popular tract is used. In life insurance sales, a prospect's own birthdate becomes the focal point, as premium rates increase with age.

Sometimes called the standing-room-only (SRO) close, this powerful technique must be used advisedly as some personality types will react violently to it. It is best used with the Power Boss/Commander, Affiliator/Pleaser, or Achiever/Craftsman. If you were to say "now or never" to some people, it would always be "never," and if you asked them for a yes or no decision, it would always be no. Size up your prospects before you start closing. Your awareness and customer empathy will enable you to select the most appropriate closing technique.

The Premium Close

Sometimes offering a premium or special inducement to buy now will help undecided prospects make up their minds. This premium close is suited to Achievers/Craftsmen, Manipulators/Gamesmen, and Power Bosses/Commanders. The premium close is designed to eliminate hesitation in the close and forestall customer callbacks. However, if you fail to obtain the order on the first attempt and then give the special buying inducement during a subsequent visit and closing, your clientele will quickly learn that they could have had the premium whether or not they had purchased when originally requested. When used inappropriately, this fine closing technique degenerates to the level of a cheap trick. Your source credibility will soon disappear.

Sample Order Close

Sometimes the only way to get started with a new account is to settle for a sample order or the position of a secondary source of supply. It enables the Avoider/Abdicator, the Achiever/Craftsman, and the Manipulator/Gamesman to try out part of your line to see if it meets their needs.

Secondary suppliers sometimes become primary sources of supply, but this half-a-loaf technique encourages weak selling. Sometimes pushing harder would have obtained the whole loaf of bread. Sample orders seldom get a fair chance to prove themselves.

Never settle for less than your full potential or the purchasing capabilities of your customers. If they have large buying budgets, you should get your fair share of their business. In industrial selling, however, the sample order is usually the only possible route to follow with a new customer.

Reasons for Buying Now	Reasons for Not Buying Now
Need ⎫ Use ⎬ Value ⎭	Price
Features ⎫ Advantages ⎪ Benefits ⎬ Buying motives ⎭	Competition
Speed of delivery ⎫ Order processing ⎪ Inventory control ⎬ (No stock-outs) ⎪ Distribution system ⎭	Time

If the reasons for buying now far outweigh the reasons for not buying now, a purchase order should be forthcoming. Once this summary close is completed, you should ask for the order and get it.

Figure 17.5   Benjamin Franklin or T-account close.

Summary Strategy

Summarizing and drawing conclusions wherever possible during your sales talk reinforces the benefits of your proposal. The summary strategy restates these major selling points and important ideas to the prospect in capsule form at the end of your sales interview. Probably the best known application of the "nutshell" principle is the Benjamin Franklin or T-Account Close (Figure 17.5), in which you take a piece of paper and draw a line down the middle of it and state

> "Let's make a list of all the reasons why you should buy our product and place them on the left-hand side of the sheet of paper. Now, let's also list all the reasons why you should *not* buy our product now, and place them on the right side."

If you have done a good job of presenting your product to a well-qualified prospect, the reasons in the left-hand column, should far outweigh those in the right. Your Achiever/Craftsman, Avoider/Abdicator, or Manipulator/Gamesman prospect can see from this highly visual technique that there are far more advantages than disadvantages in investing in your proposal now.

Whenever possible, let your prospects do the summarizing themselves. Put them into action. You should dictate the reasons and have prospects write them down. Soon the facts will speak for themselves, or you will simply point them out and then ask for the order. In either case your buyer has a clear perception of the benefits of your offer.

For You Alone Close

Particularly useful with Manipulators/Gamesmen and Power Bosses/ Commanders, this closing technique involves an offer to make a change in the product, price, credit or delivery terms in exchange for a commitment to buy. Once agreement is obtained, you start working for your customers in helping to get them what they want from your company.

Direct questions and comments will enable you to close the order.

"If you give me your purchase order now, I'll try to get these changes approved by my company's management. I'm sure that a bona fide purchase order will go a long way toward convincing them of your sincere interest in doing business with us. . . . Don't worry, I'll do a real selling job for you, so that we can get exactly what you want. Remember, I may work for them, but I'm on your side as well. Your interests are my own best interests. We are in this together, you know. We really depend on each other."

"In other words, if we can build that special unit according to these revised specifications, you will give me your order now? Fine, what purchase order number should we use?"

"If we could provide that extra feature, would you take it? Fine. Let me have your order now, so that I can get it for you."

For you alone implies a special deal for the prospective buyer and is a direct appeal to pride and ego needs. If your offer is indeed special or uniquely designed to relate to a specific buyer or problem-solving situation, then it can be a powerful closing device. If you "say it to all the guys," then you are asking for trouble in the long run.

The Take Away

This emotional close is a form of reverse psychology, effective with Avoiders/Abdicators and Power Bosses/Commanders. Fear of loss is a powerful motivating force. People are afraid of passing up a bargain or missing out on a sure-fire deal. Sometimes it is sound strategy to dramatize the importance of a benefit by taking it away from your prospects and then giving it back. When they realize that maybe they cannot have it, some people will want your proposal more! Being able to select the right psychological moment for the threat to take it all away is crucial to the success of this emotional close.

The take away fits well into the selling of any item that must be custom-designed in some respect, such as color, size, or special shape or function.

"Well, it certainly seems like the ideal thing for you, but you'll have to let me check with the factory—you don't mind if I use your phone? There's just a possibility that they can't do it. But let's find out before we get all worried."

The Doorknob Close

This tactical maneuver for use with Manipulators/Gamesmen and Power Bosses/Commanders is a trap designed to unmask the hidden objection. It is most effective late in a sales interview when you have tried every possible closing device and still have failed to make the sale. You sense that there is still an order to be had from your prospect at this time. A high level of interest and desire exists, but something apparently is blocking the client's resolve to buy.

Admit defeat and start packing up your sales kit. Your prospect will immediately relax because he or she has won and you have lost the great sales debate. Slowly rise and start leaving the room. As you stand at the threshold with your hand on the doorknob, suddenly stop short and pause reflectively as if recalling something painful. Then turn toward your would-be customer and plaintively ask "Before I go, will you do me one favor? I realize that I blew this order, but to help me improve as a salesperson, will you please tell me where I failed with you today? Why didn't I get your business?"

At this point, you usually will receive a truthful response. The prospect, who seems to have won, is no longer defensive. The real objection can now be safely stated. Once it is brought out and you are sure that it is indeed the real reason for their buying hesitation, slap your forehead and exclaim "Oh, is *that* all!? Well, perhaps I didn't make myself clear before. . . ." Promptly retrace your steps, reopen your kit, and start selling against that objection.

You may recognize this method as one used by the television detective Columbo. He always had just one more question as he stood at the door—and it was the one that broke the case.

Emotional Close

Presenting is rational, but closing is usually emotional. Buyers rarely want to *think*, they emotionally enmesh with what they *feel*. These individualized feelings are emotional activators as well as barriers to communication.

The emotional closing techniques appeal to love, fear, pride, emulation, greed (profit), and need (utility). Here you can apply your understanding of buying behavior to closing more orders.

Verbal proof stories about benefits gained or lost by others in similar circumstances can dramatize the urgency for acting now. For example, you might conclude by saying

> "Ten years from now, nobody will ever remember what kind of car you drove, what kind of house you lived in, or the type of furniture you owned. But they will sure know how your children turned out. Buy them those books now; their education can't wait. It is far better to be able to say 'I'm glad I did' rather than 'Gee, I wish I had.' Don't make the same mistake Larry Loser did. Let's get you started on this program now, so you won't have to worry about *that* any longer."

In most cases your prospects are not even aware of that situation until you bring it to their attention. Fear of missed opportunities, injury, or financial setback will arouse their emotions to a decisive point. Remember what our Bible salesperson said about having to make his prospects cry and then laugh before they would buy. Sometimes you have to be a dramatic actor to get the job done! This is the utmost in mood selling.

This powerful technique, however, should be considered only as a last resort. When all else fails, try to play on the emotions of an Affiliator/Pleaser or a Power Boss/Commander, but do it with caution. This close is a form of extreme high-pressure selling, and it can have severe repercussions.

Build-up Close

The build-up close is intended to build up or create value in a prospect's mind so that the price pill will be less bitter by contrast. The separate values of components of the product, service, or program are noted and summarized. The actual selling price will always be substantially less than the total perceived value of a proposal. "You get this feature (which is a $100 value), this feature (worth $200), and this feature ($150), all for only $300."

The Puppy Dog Close

This closing technique is particularly effective at the retail level with Affiliators/Pleasers and Avoiders/Abdicators. For example, have you ever walked into a pet shop just to look around and had an alert sales clerk observe you admiring a cute little puppy dog? Assuming your interest in the animal, this salesperson probably would say, "Why don't you take him home for a few days and see how you like the little rascal?"

If you follow the vendor's advice, you will eventually become so attached to the little rascal that you will keep him permanently. Very few puppies are ever returned after the trial period is over. This is the method behind the madness of this closing technique. Thus when the appropriate closing situation arises with a hesitant prospect, you might smile and suggest:

> "Why don't you take one home and try it? If you don't like the merchandise, please feel free to return it. Otherwise we'll just charge it to your account. OK?"

The 10-day free trial is the selling psychology behind the Book or Record of the Month clubs that sell by mail on an approval basis. Once a prospect is "hooked" on the product, returns are few and far between.

The Long Wait

One of the most effective closes, although it can be an emotional strain on both you and the customer, is to indicate that you now have done your job of presentation; it is up to the prospect to buy. Then maintain complete silence until the customer speaks. The rule of the Long Wait is that the person who speaks first loses. If the customer speaks first, you have sold a product or service; if you speak first, the customer has sold you an objection. This very forceful technique is suited to Power Bosses/Commanders and Avoiders/Abdicators.

HOW TO HANDLE "NO"

As we have mentioned, if your customer does not voice an objection, but simply says "No," you should respond with "Why?" or "What did you like best about it?" This tactic should bring out an objection or some kind of opening for continued communication.

At retail, a "no" from a customer may mean that this person simply does not like you. Perhaps you resemble someone whom the customer has always disliked, or perhaps it is that elusive thing called "chemistry." At any rate, you never will be able to sell to someone who dislikes you. You should learn to recognize negative personal signals from a customer and turn over the sale to another salesperson.

Buyers may make negative nonverbal signs such as crossing their arms and frowning while talking to you or giving no reaction at all to your sales talk. They may object vehemently to something you have said or take exception if you inadvertently misquote a price or miss a product feature that they do not like. Any overt argument or dispute is a good sign that you should turn it over (TIO) to another salesperson.

To TIO effectively, you must lay the groundwork ahead of time with your peers. Under a team selling arrangement, it should be agreed that commissions on such sales will be divided between the salespeople involved on a prearranged basis.

Do not hang on to a customer out of pride when you see that you cannot make the sale. Turn it over. Half a commission is better than none. Introduce your colleague to your customer as the expert who really knows this particular product or service as a specialty:

> "Mr. Prospect, before you leave, I'd like you to meet our manager, Ms. Lopressure. She really knows a lot more about this particular model than I do. She'll make sure you know the whole story."

Be sure that in the process of turning over the customer, you acquaint your colleague with what you have told the customer.

> "I've been telling Mr. Prospect about the need for making a special order as soon as possible if he wants to receive it by April—so he already knows about that."

Thus you keep your colleague from irritating the customer further by repeating what you have said or by contradicting it.

STEPPING UP THE RETAIL SALE

Most veteran retailers will tell you that a close is not really a close until you have done it all—stepped up, traded up, built up, and finally rung up the sale. Increasing the amount, number, or variety of items bought is variously called suggestion, add-on, or tie-in selling. You may suggest coordinated items to accompany one that a customer is considering, and the package may then prove more appealing than the original item. A tie and shirt that complement a jacket are examples. You may suggest a larger quantity of an item already decided upon.

> "These soaps will be going up in price next month—why not buy a box now, instead of one cake?"

> "Why have to run down here for a new roll of twine every week? You should take advantage of this larger bolt size. And it's cheaper this way, too."

"Will there be anything else?" is *not* suggestive selling. The suggested related items should be specific and logical: high-speed film for a camera already decided upon; a color-coordinated blouse with a suit; a suede brush with a pair of suede shoes.

To succeed with suggestion selling, you must commit yourself to your customer's buying problem. You can derive a lot of personal satisfaction from making customers' shopping expeditions more successful than they would have thought possible. This kind of selling makes the work day much more interesting and challenging than one spent saying "Sorry, we don't carry those."

Larry Ferguson recalls a story about Senator Barry Goldwater that contains an object lesson for every retail salesperson.

> When he was active in the family department store business, the senator was always on the lookout for good sales personnel. Many times, when he was away from home, he would need a shirt or tie, socks, or other accessories.
>
> If he asked for a shirt and the clerk asked if that was all he wanted, he would say "yes," and that was the end of the transaction. However, if the clerk suggested cufflinks for the French cuffs, he would buy them—and a tie, handkerchief, socks, underwear, maybe even a suit. Then he would hire the clerk to work at Goldwater's in Phoenix![1]

IS THE PRESSURE ON YOU?

Many beginning salespeople—and some experienced ones—feel that they are under great pressure during the close. Actually that is not so—the pressure is on the buyer. This pressure is a matter of perception: if you *feel* that the pressure is on them and not on you, then it is so.

During the pennant race in 1978, the Dodgers and Giants were tied for first place and were playing a crucial three-game series in San Francisco. Dodger Billy North was up to bat late in the game, the score was tied, the bases were loaded, and the count was three and two with two outs. Asked if he didn't feel the pressure when he was up to bat, North replied, "No, the pressure was on the pitcher." Sure enough, the pitcher could not come in with the pitch and walked him, forcing in the winning run. The Dodgers went on to win the game and ultimately the pennant.

Another tale of pressure also originates in baseball. Pitcher Tommy John had an innovative operation to transfer a tendon to his pitching arm from his other arm, and had made a remarkable comeback after being absent from the game for a year. At the age of 37, he signed a lucrative free agent contract with the Yankees. Everyone thought that he was too old to pitch anymore, particularly with that rehabilitated arm. When he was asked if he didn't feel extra pressure now when he pitched, he replied that he didn't look at it that way. "After all, my arm is only four years old," he said. That year (1979), Tommy John won 21 games for the Yankees and then 20 in 1980.

Thus selling is an *attitude*, a state of mind in which you perceive yourself to be a winner or loser. It is all tied to a person's self-image.

BUTTONING UP THE SALE

When prospects have time to review their buying decisions—after the sales interview, they sometimes cancel the order or return the merchandise. They suddenly become affiliated with that rare occupational disease called *buyer's remorse* and lose confidence in you and your proposal. Therefore, you must try to "button up" or confirm the sale before the interview ends.

What to Do

There are several steps you should take in the correct sequence.

CONGRATULATE YOUR CUSTOMER

After the buying decision, never thank your customer immediately. To do so implies that the buyer has done you a favor by taking questionable merchandise off your hands. Instead of thanking customers (which you should do later on as part of customer maintenance), congratulate them on their wise decisions. It is *you* who have helped *them.*

REASSURE THE BUYER

Buyers may be afraid of rushing into wrong choices or not getting their money's worth. Move smoothly from congratulations to reassurance that they have done the right thing. Avoiders and Affiliators need their reassurance.

RESELL THE PRODUCT OR SERVICE

Summarize the benefits the buyer will gain or the losses avoided through the purchase. Recapitulate and reinforce buying reasons. Achievers and Manipulators appreciate this summation.

OBTAIN FURTHER COMMITMENT

You can help to pin down a shaky order if you get agreement on delivery dates, obtain cash in full payment with the order, or secure a large down payment or a cosigner. Avoiders/Abdicators will be relieved.

LEAVE PRODUCT LITERATURE

Provide the buyer with whatever brochures, instruction manuals, and so on that you can. They will reinforce the benefits of the product when the buyer consults them after you have gone, and help the customer to "sell" the purchase to his or her peers or boss.

DON'T HANG AROUND

Once you have made the proper congratulating, reassuring, and reselling remarks and provided the buyer with literature, terminate the interview politely but quickly, say goodbye, and leave.

TWO QUESTIONS

After you have left, or after the customer has left your store, answer two questions for yourself:

What did I obtain?

What do I do next? Follow up? Call again?

Make a note of your answers. Over a period of time, you will learn from them.

Why We Do These Things

The steps of congratulation, reassurance, reselling, and leaving literature are designed to protect the sale from buyer's remorse. Avoiders/Abdicators and Affiliators/Pleasers are particularly prone to this ailment. Getting money as a further commitment has a slightly different function.

COGNITIVE DISSONANCE AND BUYER'S REMORSE

Sometimes a buyer's enthusiasm for a product or service just purchased begins to cool immediately. Most people find decision making difficult to begin with and need constant reassurance that they have not made mistakes in buying. Friends or associates may criticize their choices and imply that they are "ripped off" by fast-talking salespeople. Now buyer's remorse occurs, and they want to cancel their orders.

Why should mature adults suddenly want to change their minds after going through the buying process? Leon Festinger's theory of cognitive dissonance[2] provides insight into this conflicting buyer behavior. Cognitive dissonance means recognition of conflict, or disharmony. The basic assumption in this theory is that people try to maintain consonance, or consistency, between what they know or believe and what they do, or between two different attitudes. Thus they try to avoid situations, people, or communications that are dissonant or inconsistent with their opinions or beliefs. In other words, when dissonance exists, an individual tries to reduce this disequilibrium by changing behavior. If behavior cannot be changed, then opinion will change.

"I've bought that horrible suit and now I'm stuck with it—so I might as well wear it and try to enjoy it."

The purchase of a new car sometimes produces a different kind of buyer trauma.

"Did I buy the best model?"

"Did I get the best deal?"

"What will my friends and relatives think?"

These typical buyer concerns can be easily influenced by peer-group attitudes. For example, if you purchase a blue Ford and all your friends in the neighborhood own red Chevrolets, you are likely to experience dissonance on your way home from the car dealer. Unless you can change your purchasing decision (cancel your blue Ford order), you will try to change your opinion and those of your friends regarding the superiority of your new car. Most likely you will try to remember the main selling features that the new car salesperson stressed, and you will read as much product literature as possible so as to be able to justify your purchase to your red Chevy friends. That is why many new car advertisements are read more carefully *after* a customer's purchase than before. The information contained in those communications tends to reduce dissonance.

The special significance of Festinger's theory of selling is that customers look for reassurance that they have indeed exercised good judgment and made the best deal possible for themselves or their companies. This is the precise psychological reason why you should congratulate your new buyers rather than thank them for their orders at the time of purchase. You can always write them thank-you letters later, but they need reassurance now.

They will be quite receptive to verbal or written communications that will help reduce dissonance or buyer uncertainty and will be correspondingly resistant to those messages that might increase it. Therefore, in addition to your personal reassurances, you should provide some of your firm's product literature or advertising material with your prospect before you depart. (Note that the hang-tags on new garments serve this function and should not be removed.) A review of this literature will provide your new customers with enough information to justify their buying decisions to their bosses, spouses, or friends, whoever the potential sale-killer might be. Thus you can use the theory of cognitive dissonance to help eliminate buyer's remorse.

PAYMENT AS A COMMITMENT

Getting money for a product or service that requires cash with the order buttons up the sale. Payment of even part of the cost of the purchase enables the buyer to take mental possession of the merchandise and view it as personal property. Cancellation is much less likely after this point. This is the idea behind layaway sales.

Do not be afraid to ask for money. Handle it in a nonchalant, almost indifferent manner. If you treat collecting money as a matter of course, so will the buyer. "By the way, will that be cash or charge?"

PROMPT DEPARTURE

Why should you leave so quickly? Some salespeople are so relieved to get an order that they refuse to leave. They feel that the struggle is over and they can relax and be "friends" with their customers.

Not only does familiarity breed contempt; it also induces premature buyer's remorse. Sales representatives can never know too much, but they certainly can talk too much. Often they have been known to talk themselves right out of orders. Do you remember the Samson Syndrome?

The buyer is a busy person who has other matters to attend to. If you hang around and force the customer's attention to remain on you, a new thought pattern may emerge:

> "Why did I allow myself to be rushed into buying now, when it is obvious that I really didn't have to? That purchase could have been put off until next month when I know that I'll have a bigger buying budget. . . . My salesperson is acting pretty nonchalant about the order too. Apparently there's no big hurry to enter my order . . . maybe my business isn't appreciated!"

> "Hmm . . . I wonder why she's spending so much time hanging around here. Doesn't she have something better to do with her time? Either she's got some ulterior motive or she doesn't have any other appointments today. Perhaps I'm her only customer, after all. Well, I'm certainly not going to be the only sucker. . . . I want out! I'm going to cancel my order!"

ETHICS

How do you reconcile concern for the purchase order with concern for your own self-respect? Do you have to surrender the latter to get the former? Some people will tell you that to succeed in selling, you must sacrifice everything for the almighty commission check. You must emphatically reject that specious philosophy. As a professional salesperson, you offer two values to your clients: your expertise and your reputation. Compromising one impairs the other. As Shakespeare observed, your reputation is your immortal part. Sell your product, but not yourself.

The issues that arise in a competitive marketplace sometimes are difficult to sort out on the basis of right and wrong. You will face over and over again situations that are not ethically black or white, but shades of gray. Each time, it will be your responsibility to decide what your personal ethical code will permit you to do. In addition to managing and developing your territory, you must manage and develop yourself.

Buyer Games

Immature or insecure purchasing agents sometimes will try to ensnarl you in rigged games during the close. Because of their needs to dominate or gain recognition, some Power Bosses/Commanders or Manipulators/Gamesmen will try to rig outcomes to their own benefits. They may threaten not to buy or to "pull" their business from your firm unless certain concessions are made. These concessions may range from better payoffs to sexual procurement or favors.

Who is really selling whom? These buyers are trying to close you while you close them. As with the simultaneous sale concept, only one sale really will be made. If you "buy" the proposal of unusual concessions, you have lost in the long run, because the demands for concessions will only increase.

Here are some typical demands made by game-playing buyers:

No new order now unless present unsold inventory is accepted back for return for credit.

No more business unless an extra discount is provided.

Small orders only unless extended credit terms are offered.

Exclusivity or no deal—you cannot sell local competitors.

Demands of gifts, weekend trips, vacations, outright payoffs.

Reciprocity—exchange of business between firms.

Procurement—buyer's needs extend beyond what your product can satisfy.

Extended courtship—personal needs for attention, dominance, recognition, etc., cause buyers to lead salespeople on with promises of eventual orders that never come.

Although many of these payoffs are illegal or immoral, their introduction into the close can severely test your character. You must *automatically* refuse to participate in such games, without even appearing to consider them seriously. If you deny the payoff or refuse to play, the manipulation game quickly collapses.

For Whom Are You Working?

Even if a buyer is not trying to manipulate you, you may find yourself confronting a lot of role conflict and ambiguity. You occupy a boundary position in your firm, and you must try to satisfy the expectations of both the people in your own firm and the customers outside.

Customers concerned about achieving their own objectives in a transaction may not understand your firm's policies and constraints and may expect behavior from you that would conflict with your company's demands. Again, in confronting such conflicts, you must assume the burden of deciding what is the appropriate behavior. There is nothing your sales manager can do to alleviate this problem. The burden is clearly on you. The bottom line is that your customers pay your paycheck in the long run. Therefore, you should treat them as the profit centers that they, in fact, are.

Reciprocity

One of the most intractable problems you face as an industrial sales representative is reciprocity. This sometimes illegal arrangement amounts to the exchange of purchases by two firms: your prospect will buy from you only if your firm will buy an equivalent value from the prospect firm. This concept is as old as business itself. It simply involves doing business with one's friends, and it is most prevalent in homogeneous products such as steel and coal, where the name of the supplier makes no difference in the quality of the product and very little in price.

It is very difficult to break in as a new supplier where your prospect already has a reciprocal arrangement and the purchasing agent is under orders to retain it. Do the best you can, and then let the chip's fall where they may.

Expense Accounts and Buyer Gifts

The control of the expense account and the question of buyer gifts are difficult areas for the beginning salesperson. In general, a lunch, dinner, or gift that you give to a buyer should be a recognition of an established business relationship, not a bribe that precedes any orders. The gift is a reward for business placed, not business chased.

Look carefully at your expense record to see who is benefiting from your (actually your company's) generosity. We all have a tendency to call more often on those buyers whom we regard as friendly acquaintances, while leaving off those who might give us orders but are sure to give us a hard time. Are you putting your expense money where the business is?

A fat expense account eventually must be justified by proportionately fat sales, and your customer pays the expense tab in the end. Sooner or later, you must produce more business than your salary and expense account cost your company and your customer, or you will lose your job. Don't become a defanged ex-fat-cat.

> When Sharon tried to charge a new hat to her expense account, claiming that she was "dressing for success" for her northeastern fashion buyers, her sales manager objected and deducted its cost from her expense check. Her next expense report contained the following footnote: "See if you can find the hat now!"

Never commit the fraud of padding your expense account. No matter how justified doing so may appear to be, in plain terms it is simply stealing. If you cannot make a living on your salary or commission earnings, you should change jobs.

The business lunch is an institution that both buyers and sellers use to establish their personal relationship, extend mutual trust, and generate new ideas rather than to write actual orders. A dinner provided by you is a larger gesture than is a lunch. A gift may range from a calendar or novelty with your company name on it, given free to present or prospective customers, to such things as clothing or travel. The larger gifts are given only when a valuable business relationship has already been established. In general, you create good will by remembering clients with small gifts on holidays, birthdays, and family celebrations such as weddings or bar mitzvahs.

> Harry, a food-service equipment manufacturer, had a sense of humor that nearly made a travesty of the time-honored industry custom of giving large gifts at Christmas. He sent out greetings to each consultant with whom he had dealt, enclosing a picture of a Rolls Royce with the following statement: "Season's greetings! You deserve the very best. Your new model is on the way."
>
> Some of his customers, feeling that the old boy had finally gotten around to showing his deserved appreciation in a tangible form, were understandably chagrined when toy model Rolls Royce kits eventually arrived. Luckily, most of them had senses of humor also.

HOW TO BE A SUCCESSFUL CLOSER

To convince present and potential customers of the value of your firm's products, you must first assume in your mind that each of them is going to have it. This closing attitude is axiomatic to successful selling. Your confidence that your customers *are* going to own your product will have a positive impact on them.

How do you feel about asking people to invest in your company's product? Are you sufficiently sold on it to buy it yourself? Nobody will ever be critical of your being sold on your own products. On the contrary, no one will want to buy something to which you yourself are not committed.

Henry Aaron once said that he swung for a home run every time he was up at bat. You should have the same attitude toward closing.

Practice

We already discussed the need for practice at every opportunity. Let us emphasize again that practice before a live, critical audience or a videotape recorder will improve your techniques. The continual practice of many actual sales presentations will make you a professional.

Analyze Your Efforts

After each call, ask yourself three questions:

> What did I obtain?
> What must I do next?
> How could I have improved this interview?

How Many Will Buy?

With each sales presentation, you will become a better closer, but even as a veteran you will come upon those times when a whole string of interviews produces no sale. Handling this repeated rejection of your closing efforts is probably the single most difficult psychological obstacle in selling. It is the reason why so many people leave the field.

When you do not get an order despite your best efforts, remind yourself that sales is merely a numbers game, and you do not expect to close more than a certain percentage of your customers. Alfred J. Sloan, who built General Motors Corporation into one of the largest business enterprises in the world, admitted in his memoirs (*My Years with General Motors*) that he was right only once in every three decisions. George Brett, who is an all-star third baseman with the Kansas City Royals, gets one hit out of every three official times at bat, and is "out" twice as many times as he is "safe" on base. In other words, you do not have to be right, "score," or close an order every time in order to be a success in selling.

You cannot sell "them all" and you do not have to sell everyone in order to make a good living in this profession. There is plenty of room for everyone in the field. Just remember that the more customer contacts you make, the more presentations can be made, and the more presentations that you make, the greater your chances for closing orders shall be. With experience your closing rate will improve arithmetically while your earnings will increase geometrically.

Notes

1. Larry Ferguson, "Retail Sales Could Begin to Climb if Salespersons Did More Selling," *The Phoenix Gazette*, July 4, 1975.
2. Leon Festinger, "Cognitive Dissonance," *Scientific American*, October 1962.

Chapter 18
After the Sale

In their never-ending search for new customers, some salespeople neglect a common business courtesy—the maintenance of close contacts with men and women who bought in the past. Yet working with established customers is an important part of professional selling. In some industries this is called not customer relations, but sales maintenance. Good relations with past clientele are essential since they frequently become repeat customers. These people also are your primary source for referrals, the best of all possible leads.

SALES MAINTENANCE

Maintaining your present list of customers is actually more important than scrambling for new ones. You do have to chase rainbows, of course, but you should also safeguard the pot of gold you already have. Your objective should be to make a customer, not a sale. Sometimes, you have to forego one to keep the other, but the choice should always be clear. Job satisfaction is in helping customers get what they want; job security is in seeing that they do.

Where sales maintenance is concerned, you should ask yourself this question: "What is the most cost effective level of service I can offer my customers that will sustain their business over the long run?" Your aim is to help guide your customers toward success so that they will, in turn, become even better customers. At the same time, you want to maintain your own strong position by continuing to serve them better than your competitors. You must decide on the level of service that will accomplish both ends.

Building a Relationship

Working with customers after the sale results in several valuable selling tools:

1. It eliminates your competition through superior service. (Avoider/Abdicator customers, especially, love excellent service.)
2. It supplies you with selling points, verbal proof stories, and testimonials—effective with Affiliators/Pleasers and Achievers/Craftsmen.
3. It broadens your customer base through referrals—works well with Power Bosses/Commanders and Manipulators/Gamesmen.
4. The time you spend on your customers' premises gives you a good opportunity to see whether or not your product actually lives up to their expectations or your claims.
5. Attention to their postsale needs builds up your reputation for honesty and dependability—your source credibility is enhanced.

In industrial sales, good clientele relations also involve the customers of *your* customers. For the type of service you provide your customers is only one link in a long chain of transactions, each affected by the quality of those that preceded it.

As a salesperson, then, your long-run success will be determined by how well you help your clients work successfully with their clients. This approach is the essence of consultative selling. It focuses on profit improvement for both your key accounts and *their* key accounts. This professional approach will enable you to enmesh your products and services into their long-term business plans.

The mechanical aspects of customer relations should be part of your regular planning efforts. Many sales executives keep card files on their customers in which each client has a 3- by 5-inch card that notes not only the necessary name, address, telephone, and previous purchasing history data, but also spouse's and children's names, birthdays, and other information that can help to keep up the relationship on a personal level. You should refer to such records before calling on customers.

Retail salespeople seldom are encouraged by their stores to maintain such files, but if you are selling at retail, you should develop one. Organize it by A, B, and C accounts as described in Chapter 9. Unlike the representative who calls on clients, the retail salesperson is faced with slow days and bad-weather days on which few customers appear. On such a day, telephone calls to your A account customers about new merchandise that might interest them will help to generate visits by them or even charge-and-send business where appropriate.

The *tickler* file is another widely used device that is a prompter for customer relations. Organized sequentially by date, it enables you to file reminders under the dates on which those matters should be attended to. As the dates rotate automatically toward the front of the file, items such as client birthdays or promised follow-up calls are brought to your attention for prompt action. Such a file eliminates the need to keep trivia in your head and at the same time raises your reputation for reliability.

If you have many customers and see individual ones rarely, direct mail is a helpful way to keep up your relationship. Tips on forthcoming developments in your company or industry will be appreciated by your customer even if they arrive in bulk-rate form rather than as personal notes. One garment representative whose territory is enormous sees each small customer only twice a year, but he routinely sends flyers much more often that note those styles that are doing well and will be carried over into the next line. Needless to say, his extra commissions have more than paid for the expense of such mailings.

Turn Your Customers into PR People for You

Another excellent promotional device that you should use if it is appropriate to your industry is the customer case history article. Find a satisfied customer who is publicity minded and get permission to draft a news article about how the client company benefited by using one of your products or services. If possible, the story should involve an imaginative or special use of your product, but even an everyday application will do. The important point is that the results or benefits achieved be measurable and understandable to the reader.

Focus the article on your customer and have it carry the by-line of an appropriate customer official. Describe the problem that your customer faced and how it was analyzed and resolved. Mention your own company as naturally and gently as possible in the body of the article, not at the beginning or end. Thus you achieve implied endorsement. Everyone wins: editors love legitimate success stories, as opposed to PR puff jobs; you obtain leads and your client benefits from publicity; and you reinforce your relationship with an important customer. Affiliators/ Pleasers love this concept.

Complaints Are Opportunities

When your customer turns on you with a vociferous and perhaps threatening complaint, what is your reaction? The normal human reaction is defensive: we shout back and maintain our positions, right or wrong, out of fear that a defeat will reflect badly on us. We may feel that if we can choke off a customer complaint at the earliest stage, it may never reach our boss. If we can prove to the customer that the complaint is groundless, the suspicion that we are at fault will be removed.

This behavior is neither realistic nor productive. Complaints are a natural phenomenon of business, and they do not reflect upon one's selling ability or integrity. Properly handled, complaints are not tragedies, but opportunities. John W. Gardner once said that we are all continually faced with a series of great opportunities brilliantly disguised as insoluble problems, and thus it is with customer relations.

EMPATHY

When you receive a complaint, first try to empathize with the customer. Although in a small number of cases, customers may complain to get unwarranted concessions or to grind personal axes of which you know nothing, most customers simply view complaints subjectively according to their own situations. They can experience tremendous difficulties as a result of small supplier or service errors.

A single faulty part can stop a whole assembly line. A late delivery can shut down an entire shift. Think of the cost to your customer of wasted time, money, manpower, and materials! A slip of the pen by your order-processing clerk can send a size 6 wedding dress to a size 16 bride. Can you imagine the emotional storm that your client, the retailer, must endure as a result, not to mention the loss of reputation? Is it any wonder that a client in any of these cases is not exactly cordial when calling to complain?

Try to recognize the fear behind the bluster, especially in the case of Power Boss/Commander or Avoider/Abdicator customers. The fear that you will not care, that you will not help, submerges the Adult in your customer and brings forth the scolding Parent or the screaming Child. In such a pressured situation you can easily pick out the Achiever/Craftsman and the Manipulator/Gamesman, who still will try to use their Adults to get satisfactory resolutions to their problems. Try to establish Adult-Adult communication with all your customers during complaints. Do not, however, be surprised when you cannot call up the Adult in a panicking neurotic customer. Some people simply have very small Adults. Do not allow them to make you defensive by "hooking" your own Parent or Child. Remember that the most disastrous and damaging complaint is the one that your customer never makes to you, but details to others. Girard's Law of 250 states:

Everyone knows 250 people in his or her life important enough to invite to the wedding and to the funeral—250! . . . But the figures prove that 250 is the average. This means that if I see 50 people in a week, and only two of them are unhappy with the way I treat them, at the end of the year there will be about 5000 people influenced by just those two a week. I've been selling cars for 14 years. So if I turned off just two people a week out of all that I see, there would be 70,000, a whole stadium full, who know one thing for sure: Don't buy a car from Joe Girard!

It doesn't take a math genius to know that Girard's Law of 250 is the most important thing you can learn from me.[1]

ADJUSTMENTS

Do you put yourself in a bad light by accepting complaints? You do so only if you misrepresented your product or service in the beginning. Accepting a customer's complaint without an argument does not mean agreeing with that individual on the facts under dispute. It simply means not contesting the issue, neither denying nor agreeing that there is any fault. You merely communicate that if possible, your company wants to make your customer satisfied and that you take seriously your obligation to serve your customer. It implies tactfully to the customer that the concession is not a confession and certainly does not set a precedent for the future. In the case of a game being played by the customer's Child or Parent, this *nolo contendere* solution is simply a refusal to be "hooked."

Before you decide whether to accept a complaint, consider the consequences of rejecting it. Rejection of a large-scale buyer's claim representing only a small fraction of annual business is foolish, whether the client is right or wrong in an absolute sense. Ask yourself this question: *Is it worthwhile to let this customer be right?* Long-term profitability is the key to this decision.

The following eight steps will help you to handle most customer problems in a mutually acceptable way.

1. Listen carefully. Before reacting, be certain that you understand the precise nature of the complaint. When in doubt, have the customer clarify the problem so that you can take the appropriate action.
2. Make notes. By doing so, you create a natural situation for asking customers many questions that might offend them in any other than a record-taking situation. They see you writing, and they pour out the details that may clarify the matter. As they talk, they may even talk themselves out of their anger, either because the talking is a relief or because the facts help them to realize that their complaint is weak. Since they have to talk slowly as you write, customers think seriously about their statements, be-

cause they realize you are taking them seriously. They quiet down—no one can scold at a slow pace.

3. Act swiftly. Time may be the most important element in rectifying a complaint. Sometimes every minute of delay hurts the customer and runs up the claim. Rectify the harm done as quickly as you can, without waiting to finish an investigation of cause or responsibility. If you can do nothing more, you can acknowledge receipt of the complaint (and give the customer a copy of your notes), promise to investigate and report by a certain date, and keep the promise by reporting something specific.

4. Legal responsibility. If your customers can enforce their claims on you as a legal responsibility, do not wait for them to go to court. If the law is on your side, you may want or have to use its protection; but being legally secure is a poor consolation for losing a customer.

5. Make complaints easy for the customer. The object of this policy is not to encourage complaining but to avoid the most dangerous kind of complaint, the one never asserted, the one you never get a chance to rectify. If your customers wish to complain, it is best for you and for them that they should complain to you and not to the world.

6. Prevent future complaints. Always regard a complaint as a specific symptom of a generalized problem. When you have dealt with the individual complaint, apply what you have learned to the overall relation between your company and other customers or clients. They might indicate a pattern of problems in a particular area which needs correction. Try to prevent them from having the same complaint in the future.

7. Justified complaints. Apologize, remedy them cordially and without delay, and take care that they do not arise again. You should give assurance that there will be no recurrence, and you should offer to pay for direct and indirect costs connected with the error.[2]

8. Follow through. Be sure the appropriate action has been promptly taken, then follow up with a letter that covers all details, including an apology for any inconvenience to the customer. Try to analyze the situation to prevent its recurrence. How well did you succeed in this case? How could you improve your approach to complaints?

REFERRALS AND TESTIMONIALS

A referral, as we mentioned in Chapter 10, is merely a lead given to you by a satisfied customer. A testimonial is a written or oral statement by a satisfied customer supporting the merits of your product or service. Both appeal strongly to the emulation motive in the prospective buyer, particularly the Affiliator/Pleaser. The third party's endorsement tends to verify what you say and support your source credibility, especially in the eyes of Avoiders/Abdicators and Achievers/Craftsmen.

Asking for Leads

The best time to ask a new customer for a referral is during the close, when everyone is feeling good. The customer has just made a buying decision and feels proud of it. Tension is reduced, and mutual congratulations are in order. Now is the time to ask

> "Tell me, Mr./Ms. Customer, can you think of the names of six people just like yourself who would have the same appreciation of this fine product as you do, and who might be interested in purchasing it also?"

> "Having invested in our program, you are in a position to appreciate the tremendous value of planning your affairs. I wonder if you could think of any other business people who are as financially successful as you are and who might have a need for this planning service. For example, who is your best competitor? If you had to pick one individual who was really going to rise to the top, who would that be?"

Two common referral methods are the letter of introduction written by your satisfied client and the business card with the recommended person's name and your customer's signature on it. Sometimes the referring client will even call and make an appointment for you while you wait or actually escort you into the new prospect's office and make a formal introduction.

Follow up all your referrals while they are hot. Busy people forget casual referrals or letters unless they are followed up right away. Do not delay your contact and run the risk of being forgotten.

Whether the new prospect buys or not, it is your obligation to report back to the first customer on the interview and its outcome. If you do not, your oversight may never be mentioned, but you are unlikely to get more leads from the same person. If you sell the new prospect, the customer will share in your feeling of success; if you do not get a sale, the customer may feel somewhat responsible and provide you with a better lead.

Why Do Buyers Give You Leads?

What psychological forces push buyers of your product or service to turn around and sell the same thing to their acquaintances? Remember Festinger's theory of cognitive dissonance (Chapter 17): a person who has made a decision will seek evidence that the choice made was the correct one. New buyers become avid readers of the selling party's advertising materials in an effort to reduce cognitive dissonance. Your buyer needs reassurance and reinforcement both during the close and after the sale.

Buyers begin to act as salespeople, trying to justify their purchasing decisions by getting the endorsements of friends,[3] associates, and sometimes even complete (but interested) strangers. Thus you may have dozens or even hundreds of highly motivated salespeople working for you right in your own territory. These unwitting salespeople should be supplied with sales aids at the crucial time following their purchases when the need to sell is at its height. Give your new customers whatever brochures, spec sheets, and samples you can. They will use these to enhance their own "sales presentations" to their friends.

In many fields, a small gift or finder's fee is given to anyone who provides a lead that results in a sale. This practice is called hiring "bird dogs" to get leads, and it is very effective in such businesses as real estate. It certainly could be used in fields where it is not now common.

GETTING THE DORMANT CUSTOMER BACK

In the area of sales maintenance, we should not forget the customer who, for one reason or another, stopped buying. Calling upon these accounts gives you an opportunity to turn problems into lucrative sales.

Try writing a letter to your dormant accounts in which you ask them to explain why they no longer buy.

Dear Mr./Ms. Oldbuyer:

We miss you! Our sales records show that you're no longer buying from us. To tell you the truth, I'm a bit puzzled. Our prices are competitive and since our products rate high, I can't figure out what went wrong. That's why I'm writing this letter. Frankly, it would be nice to have you as a customer again.

But we need your help. Would you mind checking the following boxes and returning your reply in the enclosed postpaid envelope?

Yes   No

☐   ☐   Have you changed to a production system that does not require our products? If so, can you give me a brief outline of the changes?

☐   ☐   Did you find that one of our competitors sells a product better suited to your needs?

☐	☐	Do you feel our ads have misled you in any way? If so, how?
☐	☐	Did a competitor offer you a better price?
☐	☐	Were our deliveries late?
☐	☐	Were our products arriving damaged?
☐	☐	Were our products poor in quality?
☐	☐	Did you find our credit terms out of line with those of our competitors?

Thank you for your attention to these requests. I look forward to serving you again.

Sincerely,

A. Salesperson

A personalized letter more suited to dormant retail customers might resemble this one, suggested by Alan W. Farrant:[4]

Mr. Dennis Forrest
7450 Blank Street
Any City, Your State

Dear Dennis:

This letter is written to you for one reason only. We want you back as a customer!

We want you to again contact us and pick out the items you need and say "charge it," just like you used to do. You'll find our stock complete and prices right.

Steady customers are the lifeblood of our business. Those like yourself, Dennis, are the best type to have. Please drop in soon—even if it's just to say hello.

Cordially,

Alan W. Farrant

Be sure to let other salespeople who might greet these returning customers know to whom such letters have been sent. Mr. Farrant's experience suggests that 3 out of 20 former clients thus addressed will return and become regular customers. In the case of a nonretail client on whom you make a follow-up call, you may be faced with insults and verbal abuse for past sins. You must be prepared to listen patiently until the customer calms down. You will learn how to avoid such customer dropouts in the future, and you will be able to reactivate some of these old accounts.

A good technique for flushing out problems *before* they become serious is to ask your clients, "Has everything been going all right? If not, I would like to hear about it." This can produce an amazing outflow. More often, the irritant is something minor that can be resolved easily once it has surfaced.

You may also be able to get referrals through dormant accounts, as our stockbroker friend did through Mr. Big (Chapter 10).

TIME FOR SALES MAINTENANCE

How much of your precious and limited time should you devote to the various activities we have been describing? Recall that in Chapter 9 the appropriate breakdown of your time was suggested to be 75 percent for active accounts and 25 percent for inactive and new accounts. Thus maintaining your relations with regular customers falls into the active account category, while your attempts to get further referrals from old accounts or to reactivate dormant ones fall into the inactive and new-account category.

Less technically, you should take a look at the "down time" that occurs unexpectedly when an appointment is cancelled or an interview turns out to be very short. Are you using this time well? It is similar to the time during which a retail salesperson is forced to wait for customers to appear. This time can be put to good sales maintenance use.

Notes

1. Joe Girard and Stanley H. Brown, *How to Sell Anything to Anybody* (New York: Simon & Schuster, 1977), pp. 58–59. Copyright © 1977 by Joe Girard and Stanley H. Brown. Reprinted by permission of Simon & Schuster, a Division of Gulf & Western Corporation.
2. Heinz Goldmann, *How to Win Customers* (New York: Hawthorn, 1957), pp. 239–241.
3. John R. Stuteville, "The Buyer as a Salesman," *Journal of Marketing*, vol. 32, no. 3, July 1968, pp. 14–18.
4. Alan W. Farrant, "Invite Old Customers Back," *Recreational Vehicle Retailer*, January 1976, p. 61.

Part IV
ADVANCED TECHNIQUES

Chapter 19
Selling to Groups

Group selling is all around us. Some examples that come readily to mind are teaching, political campaigning, and religious evangelism. Group selling, too, is the skill we use any time we enter an established social group such as a club, the co-workers on a new job, or our new spouse's parents. We're accustomed to selling ourselves to these groups. As professional salespeople, though, we may frequently be assigned the difficult task of selling a product or service to a divergent body of men and women.

WHO HAS CONTROL?

In such a situation where you find yourself alone and facing a variety of other people with different needs, wants, personalities, and facial expressions, you may easily feel outnumbered and intimidated. However, in order to succeed in selling to them you must take command and maintain control. In order to do this, you have to understand the group and how its members interact with one another.

STEPS TO THE SALE: INDUSTRIAL GROUPS

The basic steps in a sale to an industrial group are similar to those in any other sale. They start out before the sales interview with precall homework.

Be Prepared

As with a sale to an individual, be sure you understand the prospect firm's industry and customer needs as well as the buying problem that you are to help to solve. Enter near the top of the sales pyramid.

In addition, you must know as much as possible about the group members and their buying habits. Develop informal lines of communication with each committee member if you can, and try to meet each one before the big interview. Joseph W. Thompson has summarized the questions you should answer for yourself in doing precall research about the group.

How important is each participant in the decision-making process? In other words, what is the pecking order?

What is the extent of each group member's knowledge concerning the product or service involved? How many functional experts are present?

How does each executive reach a decision? What behavioral patterns are involved?

What is each person's involvement with the decision-making process? Who is the group leader, and who influences group opinion?

What are each participant's feelings about the other group members involved in the purchasing decision? Which individuals can be manipulated successfully? Is control a factor?

What is the overall climate that prevails in the purchasing firm? Are there politically sensitive areas?[1]

In many cases, outsiders have a large influence on what is purchased and on the behavior of group members. Some groups are so loosely organized that it is difficult to determine committee membership. In almost every committee, however, the concepts of reference-group theory operate. A *reference group,* in sociological terms, is any grouping of people who influence an individual's attitudes, opinions, and values. A reference group's standards of behavior serve as guides for the individual. Peer pressure checks any nonconformist activity.

In group selling, you enter a situation in which peer pressure is exerted by the group as a whole on each individual member. This situation can work to your advantage if you learn how to communicate with the de facto group leader or opinion leader in the group. Your precall research should determine who this leader is; then make your presentation to him or her.

Set Up the Group

Once you have correctly identified the particular group of influential executives within a target prospect company, you must develop a strategy for making contact and then present your product or service for their consideration on an individual basis *before* the group meeting. The first step is to "sell the appointment"—to set up the group for a sales meeting. For example, this approach is used to sell seminar services:

> "Well, Mr./Ms. Vice-President, it is certainly very possible that some of your department heads and associates may think of people who could really benefit from this program—people that haven't even occurred to you. When will you be talking to your department heads? . . . In cases like this, we are usually invited to meet for a few minutes with the group and answer their questions. You know, *their* questions are just as important to them as yours have been to you . . . and this way they'll be able to give you an informed opinion which will mean more to you. It will take 10 to 15 minutes—no more. What time is the meeting scheduled for?"

> Cy, an electronics engineering consultant, knew how to handle a tough government buying committee, after a previous setback. He obtained a list from the federal government of the committee members who would be reviewing his proposal. Outside of the usual attorney, accountant, financial and staff support people, there was only one functional expert in his area of expertise. He made an appointment with this individual and discussed his concerns satisfactorily. The group meeting was then a mere formality. He got the order.

Group Presentation Guidelines

When you make your actual presentation, take command and set the stage for your performance. Position yourself so that everyone can see and hear you clearly. Do not be afraid to move people and furniture to achieve this goal.

Your opening comments should be brief and to the point. These busy executives are taking precious time from other work to listen to you. Do not waste time with asides or irrelevant comments. You should set the pace by asking questions that will focus the whole group's attention on the problem to be solved and its possible solution. After the initial exchange of comments and opinions, you should follow up with other questions that will encourage everyone's participation. Without their involvement, you will be deprived of a most valuable source of feedback. Try to obtain everyone's viewpoint.

Sometimes other members of the group might be encouraged to answer an objection or buying reservation raised by one group member. The ultimate effect of this technique is that you get the members of the group to sell each other.

Thus the keys to gaining acceptance of your proposal can be found in advance preparation, subtle group control, a positive attitude, persistence, and sensitivity to the group's needs and aspirations. Your selling strategy should always focus on problem identification and solution as you endeavor to achieve group buying interaction.

STEPS TO THE SALE: CONSUMER PRODUCTS

Although group selling occurs in an official or quasiofficial form in industry, it also is recognizable in large purchases at retail. Where a purchase affects several family members or other group members, the retail salesperson faces a committee whose buying relationships are complicated by interpersonal and family relationships. In such consumer sales as cars, encyclopedias, and houses, you might make your presentation to a husband and wife without having a chance for the preinterview research that would tell you about the dominance of one or the other or the buying habits of the pair. As sex roles change in our society, marketing studies are showing that one can no longer assume that the housewife is the purchasing agent for the home. Who, for example, is the decision maker when a prospect couple turns out not to be married or when three young men or women are making an investment jointly?

These situations require retail salespeople to learn to think on their feet. You must be able to ask questions that will reveal the real buying decision maker and then proceed to sell that person (the opinion leader) without offending the others. If you remain in one product area long enough, general patterns will emerge. For example, it is understood by experienced bridal gown salespeople that of the entire bridal party, the group member most likely to create dissension is the bride's older, unmarried sister, if there is one. The psychological basis of this behavior usually is not hard to understand, and the veteran salesperson must develop proven methods for coping with similar situations.

One should not, however, let such patterns lead one to make assumptions about how customers are going to behave before they open their mouths. Your job is to observe and react, not to eliminate customers who do not fit the mold.

In general, group sales to consumers resemble those to industrial committees, except that you have little chance for precall research and your buyers usually have less knowledge to start with and more time for discussion. In both cases your job is to identify the decision maker and decision influences, and then focus your persuasive efforts on them.

Note

1. Joseph W. Thompson, *Selling: A Managerial and Behavioral Science Analysis,* 2nd ed. (New York: McGraw-Hill, 1973), p. 563.

Part V
LOOKING AHEAD

Chapter 20
What Is Your Future?

The French have a saying, "The more things change, the more they remain the same." It is certainly true that our society is fast paced, and rapid change is routine. In sales, however, some concepts remain the same despite social and economic change. The professional salesperson is the driving force of our economy in good times and bad.

SELLING YOURSELF TO AN EMPLOYER

It will always be true that you should choose to represent the best product or service you can find, and the way to get the job of representing that product or service is unchanging. Securing that good job for yourself is really just like any other sale except that the product/service is *you*. First, you must decide what your service is and where you want to sell it. What do you have to offer? What benefits would hiring (buying) you bring to an employer, or what losses would be avoided? You are an individual, different from any other. Those characteristics that make you unique will be regarded by some employers as valuable. Like the rookie stranded in an unknown territory, however, you have to find these prospects and sell them.

First decide that you will choose to represent a produce or service of only the highest quality. The sterling of tableware, the Cadillac of automobiles, the best of any product category will be something you can believe in, own yourself, and sell better than any other because it will give you source credibility. You might, however, be "turned on" by an underdog company or a new product innovation.

Once you have decided on a field and a geographical area, research the employer/buyers within it thoroughly to determine what problems they have that hiring you would solve. Perhaps they have trouble finding a salesperson willing to travel a very large and rural area—and you would enjoy doing that. Perhaps they have a need for people with a science background who can speak Spanish.

Your presentation to employer/buyers during your interviews should emphasize your ability to solve these problems. Do not forget to close! Ask for the job. If the employer stalls or says no, ask why.

WOMEN AND MINORITIES IN SALES

Title VII of the 1964 Civil Rights Act prohibits sex and other types of discrimination in hiring, promotions, and compensation. Until recently, outside of retail sales, women and minorities have been grossly underrepresented in sales occupations. Women have been concentrated in low-paying industries and have been paid less than male counterparts in equivalent positions. Racial minorities have faced similar problems, although the salary gap in this case has improved faster than has that between women and men.

Sex Stereotyping in Selling

Unconsciously, sales managers often make selection decisions and evaluations using traditional male/female concepts. Even though most sales executives might think they make decisions and evaluations that are not sexually biased, just the opposite is probably the case. A recent survey of 1500 Harvard Business Review subscribers suggests that even the best-intentioned managers often fall back on timeworn ideas of proper roles for men and women, both in the home and on the job.

According to Rosen and Jerdee in *The Harvard Business Review,* Feminists often complain that even the most sophisticated and sympathetic male managers cannot easily shed deeply ingrained attitudes about the proper roles of women in business. They argue that these attitudes creep into a variety of decisions in which a person's sex is not an obvious issue. Most often these are not straightforward decisions to give favored treatment to a man over a woman, but rather decisions that result in specific ways of treating women, without any thought as to how men would be treated in identical circumstances. For example, a sales manager might hesitate to assign a female to a widely dispersed sales territory with a significant amount of overnight travel, while as a matter of course he would assign a similarly situated male.

> These subtle forms of differential treatment could have an important cumulative impact on the self-image and career progress of the disfranchised female salesperson. Concerned career women are often frustrated by the reluctance of some organizations to train and develop female employees. Any such reluctance would tend to put women at a disadvantage in competing with men for choice job assignments and promotions. How many women hold sales manager jobs today?[1]

Therefore, women must assert themselves and communicate their objectives and aspirations to management so they will not be overlooked when desirable opportunities or job openings occur.

The Rosen and Jerdee survey findings reflect two general patterns of sex discrimination prevalent in most American companies:

1. There is greater organizational concern for the careers of men than there is for those of women.
2. There is a degree of skepticism about women's abilities to balance work and family demands.

Beneath these patterns of discrimination there is an underlying assumption that women are expected to change in order to satisfy the organizational expectations. Many managers feel that women must become more assertive and independent before they can succeed in business, particularly in selling. Although these observations are quite valid in many cases, these managers do not see the organization as having any obligation to alter its attitudes toward women.

Neither, apparently, are organizations about to change their expectations of men. Perhaps because it is expected that the job will eventually "win out" over the family, a man is given time and opportunity to resolve home-career conflicts on the job. This in itself says a great deal about how organizations might conceive of a man's relationship with his family—second place. Only when there are clear-cut rules and qualifications will both women and men stand a chance of breaking out of the stereotyped roles written for them.

Four Handicaps

Both minorities and women starting out in sales face the same four handicaps. They and their companies must be prepared to expend more than the usual initial efforts to overcome them.

1. The terms *sales representative* and *female, Black, Chicano,* and so on are still antithetical to many people. These newcomers often

must work harder and longer to gain the acceptance, trust, and cooperation of customers, peers, and employers.

2. Because they are usually their company's first minority salespeople, they are constantly under scrutiny. Knowing that their bosses and other company personnel are watching their every move, they may become inhibited, afraid to make mistakes or to ask questions for fear of appearing stupid.

3. They usually are not privy to the informal network of information and advice that white salespeople share with peers, competitors, and buyers. Ethnic minorities of foreign origin also experience obstacles in communication (verbal and nonverbal) and cultural shock in addition to social bias. Small talk regarding sports, sex, politics, or business can be both awkward and embarrassing. It should be pointed out, however, that women have begun to establish their own networks. Some enlightened companies foster this development. One CPA firm has a formalized buddy system for women at lower job levels and a mentor system for upper-level women.

4. Blacks and other racial minorities traditionally have been confronted with pigmentation prejudices, lack of educational opportunities, and cultural deprivation. Some progress toward debunking the standard myths about minority shortcomings on the job, particularly concerning black salespeople, has been made during the past decade.

Opportunities Increase

The modern business world is entering a period of rapid change. Old prejudices and taboos are beginning to break down under governmental and competitive pressures. An increasing number of lucrative sales positions are now opening up to women and other minority groups that were inaccessible just a few short years ago. New publications for such minority and female business people have appeared, while older business publications now regularly recognize their existence as a special problem.

A Women's Natural Advantages

Women may have advantages in sales because of their people-oriented education. From early youth women surpass males in two of the most important skills required for selling: the ability to "read" people and verbal communications. They receive immediate prospect attention and obtain a great deal of positive interest. What they do with this important initial advantage is, of course, up to the individual sales representative. You always encourage the response in people that you communicate either verbally or nonverbally in the presentation of yourself to others.

Women have the initial advantage of being articulate, and often their appearance brings out less customer defensiveness than does that of men. They command immediate attention, but trouble may start after this initial step. Early programming of the Parent in the first five to seven years may keep women "in their place," making them less able to deal with aggressive customers.

Some women seem to have more trouble with unwanted extracurricular attention from male colleagues, bosses, and customers than do others. Although nearly every female sales representative faces such a situation at some point, you can minimize it by avoiding mixed signals such as business talk combined with provocative dress. Present a consistently businesslike image, including body language. Videotaped practice sessions can help here, as can John T. Molloy's book, *The Woman's Dress for Success Book.*

Opportunities for Spanish-Speaking Representatives

The Hispanic market is the fastest growing one in the United States. Already the second largest minority group, the Latin community may soon become the largest minority market as well. As more Hispanic customers appear, more Hispanic sales representatives will be hired to sell to them. Some progress is being made in this employment area, but a lot more work remains to be done.

If you are a minority salesperson, there can be a temptation to use the "minority approach" to obtain sales or even interviews. In effect, it says, "I'm more minority than my competitors. I deserve a break. Give me an order," or "After three centuries of slavery, you owe it to me."

This is merely another form of begging for business. Do not do it; it merely confirms the position of the bigoted buyer who thinks, "I've got to let this clown in, or the government will be down on my case—but I don't have to buy."

> Luis, a successful sales manager, advises his integrated sales force to sell the product, not their race. "Do not play the minority game. You are not Manuel the Chicano—you are Manuel, period! Forget that you are a minority. The minority approach leads absolutely nowhere."

> Dave, a black pharmaceutical sales representative in reactionary Orange County, California, quickly discourages all discussion, jokes, or inquiries related to his race. "I'll make you a deal, Doctor," he says. "I'll talk only about my product if you promise to listen to what I say rather than concern yourself with who I am and where I came from."

This is sound advice for all salespeople, regardless of background, sex, or race. Sell your product on its merits and yourself on the quality of your service. The combination is unbeatable.

Overcoming Obstacles

Perhaps the key to success for aspiring women and minority salespeople is to develop a positive mental attitude, an open mind, and a high level of self-motivation. Learn as much as you can about your product, selling techniques, your customers, and yourself. It takes the dedicated effort of both the individual and the company to make this selling success become a reality. The individual commits time and talent; the company, training and support.

In the business of selling, every salesperson must be great just to survive! If you are a female or minority representative, this saying is even more true for you, but the way to success is beginning to open up to you.

THE LAST RENEGADE

The salesperson, operating at the leading edge of his or her company, may be the last renegade in our society. Why choose such a term? Webster's definition of a renegade as "an individual who rejects . . . conventional behavior" can be applied to the professional salesperson, who is not bound by the usual business conventions or job rituals. Rather than spending your life at a boring desk job with fixed hours and dull and repetitious work, you are an independent and semiautonomous individual at the fringe of the establishment. What other occupation offers so much personal freedom, mobility, and varied experience? Next to outright company ownership, there are few other opportunities for developing and implementing the entrepreneurial spirit in our modern economic system.

Opportunity and How You Can Increase It

Successful salespeople can find many opportunities for advancement today. The value of a sales background may be seen in the increasing trend to select company presidents who started their careers by selling.

The sales management network, including branch sales manager, regional sales manager, product sales manager, general sales manager, director of marketing, and vice-president of sales and marketing, also offers opportunities for personal growth and earnings potential. If you aspire to a sales management position, however, you should be aware of the instability and dependency factors of the job as well as its limited earnings potential. The best qualified salespeople find that their volume of sales and income show a steady growth as their time and experience on the job increase. For this reason, many good salespeople prefer to remain in a direct selling position, particularly on a straight commission basis. Some salespeople earn more than their companies' presidents do! Which career path will you choose? Only you can make this important decision. Perhaps the information contained in this volume, along with your own personal experiences, will enable you to make an intelligent choice.

As in other vocations, college education enhances opportunities for advancement. A recent survey showed that approximately 18 percent of all men and 2 percent of all women in sales held college degrees. If you are planning a career in sales management, you would be well advised not only to complete college, but to continue your education both personally and professionally to develop your administrative and conceptual abilities. You should maintain active membership in sales and marketing associations and participate in your own industry-sponsored functions and activities. Continue your education through university extension programs and seminars. Read all the available books on selling and current sales publications. Stretch your capacity for growth.

The Depression-Proof Occupation

If you choose to remain in sales, you need never be unemployed. The role of the truly professional sales representative is crucial in both good and bad economic times.

In good times, selling efforts contribute to the high level of business. Customers are able to buy many different kinds of products and services; thus, it takes a good salesperson to establish a specific product high on their list of priorities. In times of economic recession, the professional salesperson creates greatly needed economic activity by stimulating buying.

A good salesperson is rarely out of a job. What other occupation can offer such long-term security and peace of mind?

MASTER OF YOUR OWN FATE

In a society that increasingly fosters conformity, mediocrity, and group activity, the professional salespeople are independent business executives who make things happen by their own individual efforts. As long as individual enterprise flourishes and a dynamic economy continues, personal selling will play a significant functional role. We are the last of the renegades who helped build this great nation. Without us, all economic activity would immediately cease. Why not join the vanishing Americans and select the vocation where you, too, can become the master of your own fate?

Napoleon Hill once said that whatever the human mind can conceive and believe in, it can achieve. Selling is 5 percent ability and 95 percent attitude. What is *your* attitude? Do you really want to be a success in selling? It is really up to you. If you do, and you follow the guidelines presented in this book, you too can increase your selling potential.

Good luck and good selling!

Note

1. Benson Rosen and Thomas H. Jerdee, "Sex Stereotyping in the Executive Suite," *Harvard Business Review,* vol. 52, no. 2, March-April 1974, pp. 45–58. Copyright © 1974 by the President and Fellows of Harvard College; all rights reserved.

Index

82 83 84 9 8 7 6 5 4 3